SIGNS

"This most hopeful work is a peek behind the scenes of the universe; reading it is like receiving a private message from God. Its essence is this: While one's body is temporary, one's love lives forever. What a thought!"

— MARK EPSTEIN, M.D., author of *Advice Not Given: A Guide to Getting Over Yourself*

"Our collective understanding of the nature of reality is undergoing a massive shift that is progressively revealing the interaction between the human spirit and the universe at large. *Signs* offers a tremendously liberating and empowering resource for those willing to take charge of such knowing and awareness. Hardships and difficulties become the engines of our personal growth. Laura Lynne Jackson, a scientifically validated psychic medium, shares her sage observations, which allow any true seeker to participate in the expression of their highest dreams and aspirations. This book is a rare treasure."

— EBEN ALEXANDER, M.D., author of *Proof of Heaven*, *The Map of Heaven*, and *Living in a Mindful Universe*

"This stirring guide . . . asserts that anyone can learn to understand messages that are sent from the "Other Side." . . . For readers struggling with loss who believe it's possible to communicate with the deceased, this book will console and empower them to look beyond their suffering." — *Publishers Weekly*

"A DIY handbook for recognizing and decoding the arcane in everyday life." —*Women's Wear Daily*

PRAISE FOR

THE LIGHT BETWEEN US

"This book will help countless people to heal grief, to let go of the fear of death and dying, and to better understand the spiritual realm. I read *The Light Between Us* with great joy, savoring the wonderful stories and messages of hope. It is a book filled with wisdom and love, exploring the deep bonds that keep us eternally connected to our soulmates. It is a book I highly recommend to all." —BRIAN L. WEISS, M.D., author of *Many Lives, Many Masters*

"Having personally witnessed the reality of Laura Lynne Jackson's mediumship abilities, I was elated to find that she was sharing her story through this marvelous book. Her personal story is beautifully wrought, weaving together the extreme challenge of scientific proof of mediumship with the profound healing aspects of love and the overwhelming evidence for the eternity of our souls and their connections. As the world (including the scientific community) awakens to the far grander capabilities of the human spirit and the deep mysteries of consciousness as fundamental in the universe, this book will serve as a brilliant milestone marking our passage toward comprehending the deeper truths of our existence." —EBEN ALEXANDER, M.D., author of *Proof of Heaven* and *The Map of Heaven*

"Compelling, riveting, and a spiritual game-changer . . . For those suffering a terrible loss, you will find peace and comfort in her story. For those who question the afterlife, you will become a believer."

—LAURA SCHROFF, co-author of *An Invisible Thread*

"Straightforward, unassuming, and profoundly generous . . . The remarkable thing about this book is Jackson's ability to turn her extraordinary gifts into a gift for us all. Brave, honest, and beautiful, this book is a treasure."

—MARK EPSTEIN, M.D., author of
Going to Pieces Without Falling Apart

"One of the most insightful and inspiring books about mediumship I have ever read . . . Destined to become a classic."

—GARY E. SCHWARTZ, author of *The Afterlife Experiments* and *The Sacred Promise*

BY LAURA LYNNE JACKSON

Signs

The Light Between Us

SIGNS

SIGNS

The
SECRET LANGUAGE
of the UNIVERSE

LAURA LYNNE JACKSON

THE DIAL PRESS · NEW YORK

2020 Dial Press Trade Paperback Edition

Copyright © 2019 by Laura Lynne Jackson LLC

Published in the United States by The Dial Press, an imprint of Random House,
a division of Penguin Random House LLC, New York.

THE DIAL PRESS is a registered trademark and the colophon
is a trademark of Penguin Random House LLC.

Originally published in hardcover in the United States
by Spiegel & Grau, an imprint of Random House, a division
of Penguin Random House LLC, in 2019.

Grateful acknowledgment is made to Liveright Publishing Corporation for
permission to reprint an excerpt from "i carry your heart with me (i carry it in my
heart)" from Complete Poems: 1904–1962 by E. E. Cummings, edited by George J.
Firmage, copyright © 1952, 1980, 1991 by the Trustees for the E. E. Cummings
Trust. Used by permission of Liveright Publishing Corporation.

LIBRARY OF CONGRESS CATALOGING-IN-PUBLICATION DATA
Names: Jackson, Laura Lynne, author.
Title: Signs: the secret language of the universe / Laura Lynne Jackson.
Description: First edition. | New York: Spiegel & Grau, [2019]
Identifiers: LCCN 2019007306 | ISBN 9780399591617 |
ISBN 9780399591600 (ebook)
Subjects: LCSH: Spiritualism. | Omens.
Classification: LCC BF1261.2 .J33 2019 | DDC 133.9—dc23
LC record available at lccn.loc.gov/2019007306

Printed in the United States of America on acid-free paper

randomhousebooks.com

19

Book design by Jo Anne Metsch
Interior images: © iStockphoto.com/Katrina Sisperova (Title page),
© iStockphoto.com/Nastasic (Part One), © iStockphoto.com/nicoolay (Part Two),
© iStockphoto.com/domin_domin (Part Three),
© iStockphoto.com/Epine_art (Part Four)

To
Mr. D,
Ray Chambers,
and Jennifer Rudolph Walsh,
*light workers who inspire me and whose kindness
and love lift me on my journey.
I am forever grateful for your light and to the Universe
for bringing me the blessing of your friendship.*

*And to Garrett, Ashley, Hayden, and Juliet,
my North Stars, lights of my life, you hold my heart always.*

*And to my amazing mother, Linda Osvald,
my greatest teacher, fearless light leader, and source of limitless
love—all I am is because of what you have taught me of love.*

*And to you, the reader—
may you know what a gift you are to this world.
You are more important and more loved than your heart can
fathom . . . and the universe is always trying to show you that. . . .*

And above all, watch with glittering eyes the whole world around you because the greatest secrets are hidden in the most unlikely places. Those who don't believe in magic will never find it.

— ROALD DAHL

CONTENTS

PART THREE
NAVIGATING THE DARK

PART FOUR
STAYING IN THE LIGHT

INTRODUCTION

Marie sat in the hospital waiting room. She found it hard to breathe. She tried not to look at the clock on the wall, but she couldn't help it. She looked up and five minutes had passed. She looked again and another five minutes were gone. It felt like two hours, not ten minutes. Time was crawling. Nothing felt real. The waiting, the not knowing, were almost unbearable.

Just a bit earlier, Marie's husband of thirty-five years, Pete, had been wheeled into the OR for emergency heart surgery. The surgeons told her they were hopeful, but Marie knew there were no guarantees. She felt scared and lost, and most of all she felt alone.

God, if you're there, she thought, *please watch over Pete. Please send a legion of angels to watch over him.*

And then she thought of the son she and Pete had lost in infancy years ago. The boy's name was Kerry. It had been nearly three decades since Kerry had crossed, but Marie still felt a deep connection to him. She liked to talk to him in her mind.

Kerry, Marie thought, *if you are there, please send me a sign. Send*

me a sign that your father is going to be okay. Please, Kerry, I am so
scared. It would help me so much to know that you are around, and
that you are watching over your father.

Thirty minutes later, a nurse stepped into the waiting room. She
saw Marie sitting nervously in her chair and approached her. The
nurse asked if she could get anything for Marie. Maybe something
from the cafeteria?

"I would love a coffee," Marie said. "A little milk, no sugar, but I
insist on paying." She took a five-dollar bill from her wallet, handed
it to the nurse, and said, "Thank you so much."

A few minutes later, the nurse was back with the coffee. She gave
Marie the cup and the change from the five-dollar bill. Then she
touched her lightly on the shoulder.

"Hang in there," she told Marie. "I know the wait can be so hard.
God has a plan. None of us are ever alone."

Marie looked down at her hands, moved by the nurse's compas-
sion.

There, in the top-left-hand corner of one of the dollar bills the
nurse had given her, was a name, written in capital letters in black
marker.

KERRY

Marie stared at it, blinking back tears. She felt a great wave of relief wash over her. Relief and love. She knew at that moment that
Kerry was there with her, telling her his father would be okay.

Suddenly Marie felt like she could breathe again. She thanked
Kerry for sending her such a powerful message, and she tucked the
dollar bill in a safe and special place in her wallet.

Two hours later, the surgeons came into the waiting room and
told Marie the operation had been a success. Marie smiled.

She knew. She had already gotten the message.

———

My name is Laura Lynne Jackson and I am a psychic medium. I help connect people to the Other Side. And the first thing I want to tell you is this:

You don't need a psychic medium to connect with the Other Side.

Don't get me wrong—I know the things I do can be enormously helpful to anyone who is open to them. The messages I'm able to convey from the Other Side can bring us the deepest happiness and invest our lives with a heightened purpose and clarity. They can set us on our highest life paths, the ones we were destined for.

I can connect people to loved ones who've passed and to a common wellspring of energy—a great big tapestry of love and light—that fuels our lives in a way nothing else can.

All of these things are beautiful blessings, and when I'm able to share them with someone, it brings me incomparable joy.

But the truth is, you don't need me to share in these blessings. You don't need me to tap into this incredible power. You don't need a psychic medium to recognize and access the signs that I think of as the secret language of the universe—a form of communication that is all around us every day, available to us all.

It's my hope that this book will teach you to how to tune in to this language and help you see light where before there was darkness, and meaning in places where before there was confusion. This knowledge can lead you to shift paths, push you toward love, help you find joy, and maybe even save your life.

I want you to understand that this book has found its way into your hands for a reason. That you are reading these words right now is not an accident. It is an invitation from the universe. In whatever way this book and these words have found their way to you, please know it wasn't a random event.

You are *meant* to be reading these words.

The central principle of this book is that the universe brings the people, information, and events we most need into our paths. Powerful guiding forces exist that steer us toward happier and more authentic lives.

Another truth that I have come to know: Each of us has a Team of Light—a group of unseen helpers who work together to guide us to our highest path. This team is made up of our loved ones who have crossed, our spirit guides (also commonly known as guardian angels), a higher angelic realm, and God energy, which is based in the strongest force there is or ever will be: love.

If you open your mind and heart to the secret language your Team of Light uses, the very way you live your life will change. Your relationship with the world and with the universe will be different: better, brighter, more powerful.

When we learn to recognize and trust the many ways in which the universe communicates with us, we experience what I call a Great Shift. This change in perspective leads us to heightened engagement, connectivity, vibrancy, and passion. It makes it easier for us to grasp the true meaning of our existence. And it makes the journey so much more beautiful and meaningful.

Once you learn to see these signs and messages, you will never be able to *unsee* them. They will forever have the power to infuse your past, present, and future with new and profound meaning, and in this way transform your life.

Here's another truth: The universe has been conspiring to help us since before our souls' arrival on this earth. Our teams have long been in place. Our job is simply to remain open to receiving these messages of love and guidance. When we do, we will know the most powerful truth of all—that the universe is constantly loving and supporting and guiding us, even on our darkest days.

And now this book is in your hands. It is there for a reason. This book is your invitation from the universe to connect with your Team of Light and discover your truest, bravest, and brightest self.

Before we begin, I'd like to give you a little background about myself. I am a wife and a mother of three children. For nearly twenty years, I worked as a high school English teacher on Long Island, in New York. I studied Shakespeare at Oxford and was accepted into two top law schools, but decided to follow my passion for teaching instead. At the same time, I slowly came to accept my abilities as a psychic medium—someone who gathers information about people and events through means other than their five senses, and who can also communicate with people who have passed from this earth.

My abilities as a psychic include clairvoyance (getting visual information without the use of my eyes), clairaudience (perceiving sounds through means other than my ears), claircognizance (knowing something that is unknowable), and clairsentience (feeling things through nonhuman means).

I am also a medium, which means that I use these gifts as tools to communicate with people who have passed from this earth. I impart this information through a reading, during which time I become a conduit between the Other Side and the person I am reading for (who is known as the sitter). I become a messenger, an instrument—a way for energy and information to flow from one side to the other.

At first, I was troubled by my abilities—even skeptical of them—so I sought to have them verified. I applied to be tested so that I could volunteer as a medium for the Forever Family Foundation, a nonprofit organization aimed at helping those in grief, particularly parents who have lost children. The Forever Family Foundation is very protective of the people who come to them for support, who are at their most vulnerable, so their screening process is quite rigorous. I passed their tests and have been volunteering for the foundation as a medium since 2005. In 2011, I submitted to an eight-step, quintuple-blind screening administered by scientists at the Windbridge Research Center in Arizona. I became one of only a small group of Certified Research Mediums around the country. I've been working with scientists ever since, exploring the mystery of our interconnectedness and of how consciousness survives bodily death.

I told the story of how I eventually came to embrace my abilities in my first book, *The Light Between Us*. That book featured stories of people who, with my help, discovered the many ways they are connected to the Other Side—the vast tapestry of light and love and energy that exists just beyond our five senses. But a great part of that book was about me, and about my story. While I will share some stories of personal connections I have witnessed and experienced in these pages, this book is different.

This book is about *you*.

It's about the path that awaits you.

It's about connecting you to a very simple but powerful idea—that the universe is *always* sending you signs and messages in order to communicate with you and steer you to a higher life path. It's about how many miraculous and beautiful truths go unseen in our lives, and how, with a subtle yet meaningful shift in our perception, we can begin to see them.

A NOTE ON TERMS

Before you begin to read the stories in this book, I wanted to clarify the meaning of some of the terms I use.

A **sign** is a message sent to you by the universe.

The **universe** is the term I use when I refer to God energy—the all-encompassing force of love that connects us all and that we are all a part of. The universe also includes the angelic realm, spirit guides, and our loved ones who have crossed to the Other Side.

The **Other Side,** simply put, is where our loved ones go when they pass, and where our spirit guides reside while they watch over us. It is the heaven many people speak of. The Other Side is our true home. It is the place we will all one day return to. It is a place ruled by love and only love.

Signs are a method of communication from the Other Side. Signs can come from different sources—our departed loved ones, our spirit guides, and God energy. These are all part of the universal Team of Light that each of us has working for us every single day.

At first, the Other Side will use what I call **default signs** to communicate with us: objects, animals, or events that jolt us into seeing a meaning that might otherwise escape us. Default signs might be coins, birds, butterflies, deer, numbers, and electrical disturbances, such as empty cellphone messages, among other things. You find a dime standing on its edge in the dryer just as you are thinking of and missing someone (this very thing happened to me). A butterfly lands on your arm for an instant on your birthday. A car drives past with a license plate that has the birthdate of a loved one who has crossed, who was just on your mind. You get blank cellphone messages on the anniversary of a loved one's crossing.

Another default sign is what we might call a meaningful coincidence, or **synchronicity**. Synchronicity shows our innate and active connection to one another and to the world around us. You think of someone, and all of a sudden they are right in front of you. You hum your favorite song, and suddenly it starts playing on the car radio. You're doing a crossword puzzle, and the very answer you're looking for appears on the TV news. All of these things can happen without us asking for them or expecting them.

Distinct from default signs are signs that we specifically request— objects, images, words or phrases, however unusual or obscure. This is the secret language we can co-create with the Other Side.

I have co-created this language in a variety of ways. With my spirit guides, I usually ask for oranges. With my loved ones who have crossed, I ask for armadillos, aardvarks, and anteaters, which I chose because they're sufficiently rare and are hard to miss. With my father, who only recently crossed, one of the signs we share is Elvis Presley. This book will show you how to create your own language with the Other Side, so that when your signs come, you will not only recognize them but also feel the extraordinary power they bring!

You might wonder, how can we trust that a sign is truly a sign and not just a happy but random coincidence?

The Swiss psychoanalyst Carl Jung coined the term *synchronicity* to describe a seemingly meaningful coincidence. Jung was fascinated with the idea that the events in our lives are not random, but rather express the reality that we are all part of a deeper order—a unifying, universal force he called the *unus mundus*, Latin for "one world."

Over the years there has been a great deal of study and debate about the meaning of coincidences. Some scientists, like Dr. Kirby Surprise, a psychologist, have studied what he calls **synchronistic events** (SE) and concluded that they have no meaning beyond that which we give them.

But other scientists, researchers, and philosophers aren't so sure. Dr. Bernard D. Beitman, a professor of psychiatry at the University of Virginia, has even sought to establish a new, transdisciplinary field called Coincidence Studies to examine the truth behind synchronistic events. Simply concluding that coincidences are random assumes that coincidences are inherently meaningless or insignificant. Dr. Beitman has said, "Without supporting evidence, this assumption is hardly scientific."

As we go through our lives, we decide for ourselves what these synchronistic events — these magical coincidences — mean to us. Are they random? Or are they signs? It comes down to personal belief.

Glennon Doyle, a writer and light worker whose work inspires me, has said, "Faith is believing in the unseen order of things."

I know what I believe. I have spent my life working to understand my abilities, and I've read for hundreds and hundreds of people. I have seen enough and learned enough to conclude that signs are a very real occurrence. My faith in this language of connection is steadfast.

I can't point to a definitive scientific study that categorically proves this is true. But I can show you the evidence that has persuaded me — the remarkable, powerful stories of people who have opened their hearts and their minds to a new way of looking at the world, and who have undergone a Great Shift that has transformed their lives. I have watched people move to a higher and more vibrant life path — and in turn share their beautiful light with the world around them. I have witnessed people connect to their Teams of Light on the Other Side, so that they finally understood the beautiful truth of the universe.

We are all leaves on different branches of the same tree.

We are never alone.

Each of our lives matters greatly.

We are forever connected to one another, and to the light and love and energy of the universe.

Earth is a school where we are all learning a collective lesson in love. We are spiritual beings here to learn about connectivity and kindness. When we trust in the reality of signs, we begin to learn this lesson more rapidly and in the most beautiful and fulfilling way. We actually begin to *see* the connectivity. We begin to understand that being alive on earth right now, in this moment, is a great gift—and that our choices affect not only our own lives, but also the great tapestry of light and energy that is our world.

That is why I have written this book. It is in your hands now because I believe we are meant to take this journey together to a more mindful, attentive, and meaningful way of living. We are meant to shine our truest light fully and bravely in this world.

DEATH IS NOTHING AT ALL

Death is nothing at all.
It does not count.
I have only slipped away into the next room.
Nothing has happened.

Everything remains exactly as it was.
I am I, and you are you,
and the old life that we lived so fondly together is untouched,
*   unchanged.*
Whatever we were to each other, that we are still.

Call me by the old familiar name.
Speak of me in the easy way which you always used.
Put no difference into your tone.
Wear no forced air of solemnity or sorrow.

Laugh as we always laughed at the little jokes that we enjoyed
*   together.*
Play, smile, think of me, pray for me.
Let my name be ever the household word that it always was.
Let it be spoken without an effort, without the ghost of a shadow
*   upon it.*

Life means all that it ever meant.
It is the same as it ever was.
There is absolute and unbroken continuity.
What is this death but a negligible accident?

Why should I be out of mind because I am out of sight?
I am but waiting for you, for an interval,
somewhere very near,
just round the corner.

All is well.
Nothing is hurt; nothing is lost.
One brief moment and all will be as it was before.
How we shall laugh at the trouble of parting when we meet again!

— HENRY SCOTT-HOLLAND

PART ONE

ALWAYS
WITH US

"I realized for the first time in my life: there is nothing but mystery in the world, how it hides behind the fabric of our poor, browbeat days, shining brightly, and we don't even know it."

—SUE MONK KIDD

TAKE A WALK OUTSIDE AND LOOK AT THE WORLD around you. At the trees and houses, the sky and clouds, the cars and street signs and people passing by. When we slow down our lives for a moment and truly take in the beauty and spectacle of the world around us—when we become more mindful—we can better appreciate just how blessed we are.

But what if, when we take a long, mindful look at everything around us, we're not actually seeing everything? What if we're only seeing part of what's really there? What if we are missing an entire layer of reality?

And what if, by simply opening our hearts and our minds to a new vocabulary of seeing and understanding, we begin to see a much bigger picture? What if the world suddenly becomes a magnificent tapestry of connections and signs and light and love, all woven into the ordinary fabric of life that we're so used to?

The stories that follow are about people who did just that—people who opened their hearts and minds and discovered a beautiful new way of seeing the world around them.

Once they began to see these things, they could never unsee them. They were forever changed. And that turned out to be a wonderful thing.

A wonderful thing that can happen for you, too.

1

—

ORANGES

HAVE you ever had one of those moments when you're about to do something important, and you're way out of your comfort zone, and there's a lot at stake, and the pressure is on, and of all the positive things you could be thinking, what you're actually thinking is: *What on earth am I doing here?*

I've lived through those moments. More often than I'd like to admit. Not long after *The Light Between Us* was published, I was asked to give a speech at a big corporate event in California. I understood immediately that the universe was calling on me to share the Other Side's message, and I felt completely humbled and honored.

I'd have to get up onstage in front of six hundred of Hollywood's movers and shakers and tell them something that would move and challenge and inspire them. What's more, I was sharing the stage with seasoned, powerhouse speakers, including a former U.S. president! I'd never been called upon to deliver a speech like this before. And since the universe had chosen me for this task, I also felt pressure to convey its message powerfully. I didn't want to let the Other Side down.

Strangely, I didn't feel terrified. I was nervous, sure, but I was also excited. I *wanted* to get on that stage. I *wanted* to honor the message sent to me by the Other Side. And so I went out there and delivered my speech, and only afterward, as I was walking offstage, did it occur to me to wonder: *Did I fully honor the Other Side's message the way I was supposed to? Did I do a good enough job?*

I knew the Other Side had steered me onto this path, but still I longed for some kind of affirmation. As I sat backstage, I directed my thoughts to the Other Side and asked for a sign that I had honored their message.

I asked the universe to send me a single orange.

That's what I asked for—an orange.

If the universe somehow put an orange in my path, I'd know I was exactly where I needed to be, doing what I needed to do. I'd know that I had delivered their message fully.

After the lecture portion of the event concluded, all the speakers and attendees were ushered outside, into a big open space where lunch was being served. I turned a corner and saw big wooden tables leading into the main dining area. They were there for decorative reasons, to establish a mood, and normally they'd be covered with fresh flowers or plants or some other lovely arrangements.

But not that day.

That day, they were covered with oranges. And not just a few. *Thousands and thousands of oranges.*

I mean, they were everywhere. Piled up in the entranceway, stacked up next to the serving stations, on every single table. It was dazzling. Of course, one's rational mind might say, *Yeah, but long before you asked for that sign, someone decided to use oranges as a decorative theme.*

But that's not how I received the oranges. To me, the oranges were a beautiful affirmation. My prayer to the Other Side has always been, "Use me however I can best be of service as a vehicle of love and healing in this world. And please just guide me along the way." And that's what these thousands of oranges were—a sign. The universe was telling me, "You're a member of this team, and you did your part. You honored your role. Thank you."

When I saw the oranges, I gasped, and then I smiled, and then I started to cry. You see, I asked for one single orange, and the universe sent me thousands of them! *That* is how loved and supported and cared for we are.

The oranges reinforced four truths for me:

We are all constantly being watched over by a Team of Light;
We are loved;
We are all connected and invested in one another's journeys;
When you ask for signs from the Universe, the Universe speaks
    back.

The oranges, to me, were a startlingly clear exchange—I asked, and the universe answered. And yet this call-and-response isn't always easy to see. The clutter and doubt, the fear and noise that come with everyday living can obscure our ability to perceive things that aren't so obvious.

The stories that follow are about people who weren't at all sure about what they were seeing. Some of them didn't even believe in the possibility of communicating with the Other Side, but the experiences related here forever changed their beliefs and their worldview. Everyone's journey is different. Some people are more skeptical than others and need more affirmations. Some feel the love and support right away and quickly learn how to tap into the mystical power of signs and use them to bring change and meaning to their lives.

What's true in all the stories is that the signs themselves are often simple or ordinary things. They are things that exist in everyday life, and things we normally might not look at twice. A simple orange, for instance. But in choosing an ordinary object or phrase or song or number as our sign, we create a means of connection.

The signs are there. The affirmations are there. The *love* is there. All we need to do is learn how to receive it.

2

CEREAL IN THE CAR

Back in 2015, I was asked to speak at an event hosted by my publisher, Penguin Random House. A car was sent to my home on Long Island to pick me up and bring me into Manhattan. During the drive, I was quiet. I was thinking about the talk and the things I wanted to share with those in attendance. I should tell you that I have two modes: normal mode and reading mode. When I am open to the Other Side, I am really open. But when I am in normal mode, I'm shut tight. I've found that if I'm open too much and do too many readings, it can be physically and emotionally exhausting for me. I can get worn down.

What's more, reading someone's energy without his or her permission is invasive—kind of like peeking at someone's underwear; it's just not right. So on the drive into the city, being in normal mode, I shut off that part of myself that is open to the Other Side.

And *still* . . . someone pushed through.

Someone connected to the driver.

I didn't say anything at first; in fact, it was the driver, a pleasant middle-aged man named Maximo, who spoke first.

"If I may ask, what is your book about?" he said politely.

I told him who I was and what was in my book.

"Oh, well," Maximo said, "that will be a good book for me to read."

That was all it took. That was all the permission the Other Side needed. Now whoever was pushing through came *crashing* through.

I paused, trying to decide if I should share what I was getting. But since Maximo had opened the conversation, I felt it would be okay.

"You have a son on the Other Side, don't you?" I asked him, though the connection was so clear it was more of a statement than a question.

"Yes, I do," Maximo said. "My stepson. His name is Rodrigo."

That wasn't the name I was hearing.

"Hmmmm," I said. "The name that I'm hearing is a *V* name. It actually sounds like the word *version*."

"Oh my God," said Maximo. "Virgil. We called him Virgil."

Then Virgil showed me something that seemed completely random.

"Why is he giving me a bowl of cereal?" I asked the driver. "Why does he want me to talk to you about cereal?"

Maximo took a deep breath.

"He was known for eating cereal," he said with a laugh. "Breakfast, lunch, dinner, every day. I was worried he wasn't getting enough nutrients. He just loved eating cereal."

Then Maximo said he thought he'd recently received a sign from Virgil.

"You know, we had a conversation once, out of the blue, about what signs we would send each other if one of us died," he explained. "And his sign was Ninja Turtles. He adored the Ninja Turtles."

Maximo told me how he had forgotten that conversation by the time Virgil crossed in his early twenties. But then one day, Maximo's young daughter came home and announced her new obsession.

"She is crazy about the Ninja Turtles," Maximo told me. "Suddenly she has to have everything with a Ninja Turtle. It came out of nowhere. I knew that was Virgil coming around, and that he was watching over her. I knew it was a sign for me, too."

Virgil then showed me one more thing—an older man with a name that began with M. He showed me that the man was his grandfather, and that they were together on the Other Side. I shared this with Maximo.

"Oh my God," Maximo said. "Virgil came to me in a dream, and I saw him with my father, who was also Maximo. They were together."

At that moment I realized that every message Virgil conveyed to me was a message that Maximo had *already received.*

"You don't need me," I told him. "You're already communicating with your son. He came through just to validate your experiences. But you are already connecting with him all the time."

My whole conversation with Maximo affirmed what he already knew—that his son was still with him, deeply wishing to connect. Maximo already knew that Virgil was reaching out to him through his dreams, through his daughter, and in other ways. The signs, the language, even Maximo's acceptance of the connection were all already there. If he had any doubts about the veracity of this form of communication, they were chased away by Virgil, who validated them through me.

Chances are, you and I are not going to end up in the same car together. We might, but, you know, it's not something we can count on happening. So let me take this opportunity, right here, right now, to give you what Virgil gave Maximo through me—validation:

You *are* receiving signs. The universe, God energy, your loved ones on the Other Side, and your spirit guides are sending them to you, reaching out and trying to connect with you. It is happening. It is happening a *lot.* And deep down, you already know it is.

———

Okay, you're thinking, *but how does it happen?* How does a sign manifest? What is the engine that drives these signs and makes them possible? What is their battery, their power source?

We are.

When we shed our bodies, we all become part of the same universal life force—a massive swirl of light and love and energy. In other words, our energy—our light and our love, our consciousness—does not end when we physically die. It endures, and it links with the light energy of everyone else in the history of existence, connecting into one great, universal life force. This is the energy behind the powerful cords of light that connect us to the Other Side—and the energy behind the signs the Other Side sends us.

The energy is us. The battery is light and love. The power source is the eternal universe itself.

And the result is a force that can send us an orange—or a thousand oranges—just when we really need it.

3

TEAMS OF LIGHT

We all have a Team of Light on the Other Side. These teams send us signs. And these signs come from three distinct forces:

1. We receive signs from God energy, which is what I mean when I say signs from the universe. This is the highest and most powerful source of love, and we are each directly connected to it, and also to one another through it.
2. We receive signs from our spirit guides/the angelic realm.
3. We receive signs from our loved ones who have crossed.

While we may be most familiar with the idea of God energy and the universe interacting with us, you may be wondering who—or what—our spirit guides are.

My experience has taught me that we all have teachers, mentors, and protectors on the Other Side whose purpose is to watch over us and guide us toward our best and highest life path. Some call them guardian angels. I call them spirit guides. These guides are not any-one we knew during this lifetime, such as friends or relatives who have crossed—although these friends and relatives certainly help guide us, too. Spirit guides enter into what I call soul contracts to play a role in our lives before we are born.

Our relationship with them is uncomplicated. They are simply there to help us, and that's it. They ask nothing in return. They have no other mission. They are a part of the vast, loving energy of the universe, and they have been specifically assigned to us. They are connected with the purest, highest form of the love and energy that constitute the universe, which encompasses both this side and the Other Side. They are tasked with, and devoted to, making sure every-thing that happens in our lives is geared toward our soul's develop-ment.

As I noted earlier, spirit guides together with God energy and our loved ones who have crossed make up our Team of Light on the Other Side.

If the concept of spirit guides sounds a little strange to you, you should know that it's not a new concept—it's been around since the dawn of humanity. Different cultures have different names for them, but they have always been a part of the tapestry of human existence.

In Christianity, they are called angels, or guardian angels, and they play a prominent role in the Bible.

In Hinduism, they are called devas or devis, and they are consid-ered heavenly beings that cannot be seen by the human eye, but can be detected by those who have opened their "divine eye" and been awakened.

In Islam, a belief in angels who are made out of light and function as Allah's messengers is one of the six pillars of the faith.

The ancient Greeks, too, believed in angels. In fact, the word *angel* comes from the Greek word ἄγγελος, or *angelos*, which means "messenger."

Can we know who our spirit guides are? Yes. One of my spirit guides came through to me in a flash vision while I was taking a shower, and I was able to hear her name and feel a connection to her.

But that doesn't always happen. I think we need to be in a highly receptive and open state of consciousness—much more than we normally are in our busy, chaotic lives—in order for that kind of interaction to happen.

But we don't need to know who our spirit guides are, because they know who *we* are. Ultimately, it will always require a measure of trust for us to fully and entirely accept and appreciate our spirit guides—even if, like me, you know her name. What's important is that you know you can call on them at any time to help you (yes, even to find a parking spot!).

I have been open to the Other Side for so much of my life, and I have seen the impact spirit guides have had on the lives of hundreds and hundreds of people. My experience has helped me appreciate the intense devotion and power of our Teams of Light on the Other Side.

We are connected to God energy. We are connected to the angelic realm and to our spirit guides on the Other Side. And we are connected to our loved ones who have crossed. Together, these forces of love make up our Teams of Light.

And our Teams of Light send us signs and messages all the time.

People will come up to me at events and share their stories of connection, because they know I am a "safe place"—I won't scoff or laugh; I will honor their stories. In fact, this doesn't only happen when I am at an event—one of my doctors recently confided something to me in the middle of an exam.

Dr. G had been my doctor for years—he even delivered one of my daughters—but he never knew I was a psychic medium. When he heard I was writing a book, he asked me what it was about, and that's how he learned what I do. He paused, got a bit pensive, then almost reluctantly shared the story of something "strange" that happened to him.

He told me that a number of years earlier, he'd been out fishing on a boat in Florida when, all of a sudden, he felt an overwhelming rush of energy pass through his body. A torrent of electricity that swished right through him. When it happened, he immediately felt his father's energy and presence. He felt a deep sense of love for his father rushing through him, right there in the middle of the water. None of it made sense to him.

His first thought was, *Am I crazy or was that my father coming to say goodbye to me?* His father had been ill, but no one felt his passing was imminent. Then he looked at his watch and noted the time. He tried to call his mother, but he couldn't get a signal out on the water. About an hour and a half later, he reached the shore and called his mother again.

Before he could say anything, she gently told him that his father had just passed.

He asked her what time, exactly, it had happened. He learned that it was the very moment he felt the swoosh of electricity on the boat.

"I never told anyone that story," he said. "Not a soul. I didn't think anyone would believe it really happened, and I struggled to accept it myself. But it was so powerful that it happened at the exact time my father passed. I think it was my father saying goodbye."

"Believe it," I told him. "It was real. What a beautiful goodbye your father gave you."

I encouraged him to share the story with others, starting with his mother. It was a gift that was *meant* to be shared.

Sometimes when we get signs from the Other Side, we dismiss them or let our logical minds talk us out of them. We don't mention them to anyone because we're afraid they'll think we're crazy.

But deep down, we recognize that they are real. These are stories to share and honor and celebrate. Once you accept these stories as your truth, your life transforms.

4

I CARRY YOUR HEART

JUST before a little boy named Caleb turned six, he asked his mother a strange question.

"Mommy," he said, "how much life do I have left?"

His mother, Eliza, took a deep breath. She knew her son had a kind of obsession with turning six. She knew he didn't *want* to turn six. Something about it frightened him—he'd spoken about it before. Eliza pulled up the right sleeve of her blouse and stuck out the length of her arm.

"This is your life," she told Caleb, pointing to her whole arm. Then she pointed to a spot near her shoulder. "And this is where you are right now," she said. "Your life is just beginning."

Caleb asked her what happened to people when they died.

Eliza told him that people had different beliefs about this. She chose to believe that the people who pass away come back in a different form.

"How would you like to come back?" she asked Caleb. "Would you come back as Salami?" Salami was the family cat.

Caleb thought about it for a moment.

"I wouldn't want to come back as a cat," he finally said, "because then I'd have to lick my own bum."

Eliza and Caleb made a deal: When she came back, she would return as his mother, and when he came back, he'd come back as her son.

"We shook hands on it," Eliza says. "It was like a contract."

"Caleb, oh, well, he's just a really special kid," Eliza says when describing her son. "Early on he stuck really close to us, he was very shy and a little anxious, and he was either on his father's shoulder or in my arms all the time, cuddling, very affectionate, very physical, very sweet and loving. Around other people he could be quiet and reserved, but around us he talked a mile a minute. He was so full of ideas. He was *bursting* with ideas. And he could tell stories, made-up stories, really elaborate, and he built little worlds with his blocks, with any building material, and he'd build these big fire stations and movie theaters with seats and moving parts, and he always had an explanation for everything he built—for why the helicopter had to come down in case the bridge might break, and so this is where the helicopter lands, and all of that. He just loved telling stories and building things. A really amazing boy."

When he was five years old, Caleb was just learning how to write. But he had a big story he wanted to tell, so his parents bought a little notebook with a canvas cover, and they sat with him as he dictated the entire story to them. It was called *Llama and the Dominina*, and it unfolded over many days and nights. It was about the family cat, Salami, and Caleb's rubber bathroom animals going on a camping trip together. Eliza and Tim recorded the story just as Caleb told it. Every word was his.

By the end, they had filled all ninety pages of the notebook.

When Caleb was six and a half, his parents took him to the dentist. He had an extra tooth among his adult teeth, and it had to be removed. When the dentist told them he would need to drill through the bone in Caleb's palate to remove the tooth, Tim and Eliza chose to sedate him for the surgery. The dentist put Caleb under general anesthesia—but something went wrong.

All of a sudden Caleb's heart stopped beating.

"The dentist finally realized what was happening, but then he failed at all the basic lifesaving techniques—CPR, intubation," says Eliza. "They resuscitated Caleb, but he experienced organ failure."

Caleb spent the next two days in the hospital. His heart repeatedly gave out, and doctors repeatedly revived him. Other organs were failing, too, including his lungs. "He failed every neurological test," Eliza says. "By the morning of the third day, the doctors were saying we had to let him go."

That's when Eliza called me. We had a mutual friend who urged her to talk to me. Finally she called me from the hospital. As soon as I got on the phone with her, I saw Caleb, and I saw where he was.

"He is already on the Other Side," I said. "I am trying to walk him back into his body, but I'm being stopped. Is his body on ice?"

In fact, the doctors had surrounded Caleb with ice, to try to lower his temperature. During the call, I tried to coax Caleb to come back, but nothing was working.

"What can I do for you, Caleb?" I asked him. "What do you need me to do?"

For a moment, I thought Caleb might come back. In his hospital room, Eliza noticed that Caleb's pupils, which had begun to appear uneven, had suddenly evened out. It was a moment of hope—a tiny indication that Caleb might be trying to come back. But it didn't last. Caleb slipped away.

"It became very clear that Caleb wasn't going to make it," Eliza says. "Not much later, we lost him."

The loss was devastating. The only thing that allowed Eliza to keep going was the need to take care of her daughter and her family. I told Eliza she could call me whenever she wanted, but I didn't hear from her for a while. I hoped she might reach out when she was ready. "I was stuck in black mud," Eliza later told me. "I felt like I wanted to die. All I could think about was Caleb's world going black. Was he trapped somewhere? Did it all just end? Where is he? I went through weeks of this intense, desperate sadness and depression. I was searching for Caleb in all this blackness, and I just couldn't find him."

What Eliza didn't realize was that Caleb was searching for her, too.

He was coming through. He was trying to send his mother a message. I had our mutual friend forward Eliza a text from me. I wrote, "Caleb is not gone. Souls go on. They continue to grow on the Other Side. Caleb crossed surrounded by love, and he was not alone, and he is okay and he loves you and he's trying to send you messages."

When Eliza read my text, she stopped cold.

"It was like, in the midst of all that blackness, a light suddenly came on," Eliza says.

We spoke soon after. Eliza explained that she already suspected that Caleb was sending her messages, but she couldn't bring herself to believe they were real. For instance, Caleb had always been very interested in specific numerical sequences, particularly 1111—four ones in a row. Whenever he came upon a clock that read 11:11, he made his parents take a picture of it. Two weeks after Caleb passed, Eliza met a friend in the park. After talking for a while, the friend left to buy lunch. She texted Eliza a photo of her lunch receipt: $11.11. The next day, that same friend went to a new restaurant. She sent Eliza another photo, this time of the restaurant's address number—1111.

"Everything was coming up 1111," Eliza says. "And then I was having these very vivid dreams of Caleb riding on Tim's shoulders—so, so vivid. It felt like Caleb was really happy, like that's what he was trying to tell me. But I didn't know what to believe."

Our reading was powerful. Caleb came through so forcefully. All of the energy and passion that had marked his life on earth was still there, only amplified. He was brimming with love and excitement.

"He wants me to explain to you what it feels like on the Other Side," I told Eliza. "He says it feels like the most love you can ever possibly feel, multiplied by eight billion percent."

There was so much more—a steady stream of impressions and ideas.

"Mommy, Daddy, it is amazing here," Caleb said. "It's like outer space, but better. I can be everywhere at once. I can be both dark and light. You wouldn't believe how incredible it is.

"I am home now," Caleb told his mother. "And it's your home, too, you just don't remember it."

Caleb's message was very specific. He wanted his parents to know that their job had been to give him unconditional love, and that they'd done their job beautifully and completely. He said his time on earth was supposed to be brief, and that he was never meant to suffer, which he didn't. He kept saying how dying was like falling asleep and waking up in the best dream ever. Most of all, he wanted his parents to know that he was okay—and that they would be okay, too, because they hadn't lost him after all. He was still with them, and he always would be.

"After the reading, some of the grief and the terror went away, because I truly believed Caleb was in this beautiful place," Eliza says. "The loss was still devastating beyond words, but I now understood that we were all part of this profound karmic thing that happened— this plan for us and for Caleb. The realization that we are all con- nected, and that because we are, we can never really die. What happened was supposed to happen, and it happened with no pain or suffering, and that made it possible for me to let go of the anger."

Yet Eliza was, by her own admission, "still hesitant." Still not ready to fully trust in her lasting connection with Caleb. And Caleb knew this. He knew he needed to do more.

So Caleb decided to send more signs.

They came through in my reading with Eliza. Specific signs designed to convince his parents that he was still here. At his memorial service,

Caleb's parents released six hundred balloons. Eliza never mentioned this detail, but during the reading Caleb had me tell Eliza that he got all the balloons—and that he was going to send them back to her as signs.

"He says he even got the red balloon," I told Eliza. "Was there a red balloon?"

Eliza didn't understand. The balloons were all different colors, so why would Caleb mention just a red one? And then it hit her—the memory of a younger Caleb getting a red balloon from a salesman at a car dealership, and letting it slip out of his hand, and crying as he watched it float away, and weeping for hours because he'd lost it.

"I have it back now," Caleb said.

In the days and weeks after the reading, Caleb sent back his balloons. Eliza and Tim were sitting on their backyard deck one evening, thinking of Caleb and crying together, when a balloon slowly floated past.

"It's Caleb," Tim said.

A few days later, on a weekend drive, Tim and Eliza took a detour on a street they'd never driven on before. When they turned a corner, they saw an enormous mural painted on the side of a building— a mural depicting giant, colorful balloons. The next week, another balloon floated into their yard, hovered for a long while, then slowly floated away.

"No matter where we go, we see bunches of balloons or single balloons floating right by us," Eliza says. "They are everywhere."

I also told Eliza that Caleb was sending her a poem.

I couldn't make out what poem it was, but it was clear that it was a poem. Eliza said that in the weeks after Caleb passed, they'd received many gifts from friends and family, but a book of poems, or even a single poem, wasn't among them. A few days after the reading, Caleb came through to me again and asked me to send his mother a bracelet for Mother's Day, which was coming up. He wanted a line from a certain poem inscribed on the bracelet.

The line was, "I carry your heart with me."

I got the bracelet and mailed it to Eliza, with a card explaining what had happened. "You may have already received this poem from Caleb," I wrote. "He said he already sent it to you." Eliza thought long and hard, but still couldn't figure out how Caleb had sent the poem.

Then it dawned on her.

Eliza ran to a bookshelf in the hallway of her house. She scanned the shelves and then pulled out a book. It had been a gift from a friend in the days after Caleb crossed. The book was an illustrated children's book featuring a well-known poem by E. E. Cummings, called "I Carry Your Heart with Me."

> *i carry your heart with me(i carry it in*
> *my heart)i am never without it(anywhere*
> *i go you go, my dear;and whatever is done*
> *by only me is your doing,my darling)*
>
>   *i fear*
> *no fate(for you are my fate,my sweet)i want*
> *no world(for beautiful you are my world,my true)*
> *and it's you are whatever a moon has always meant*
> *and whatever a sun will always sing is you*
>
> *here is the deepest secret nobody knows*
> *(here is the root of the root and the bud of the bud*
> *and the sky of the sky of a tree called life;which grows*
> *higher than soul can hope or mind can hide)*
> *and this is the wonder that's keeping the stars apart*
>
> *i carry your heart(i carry it in my heart)*

There was one more sign Caleb was determined to send.

Caleb had a very specific message for his father, Tim, who during the reading was lying next to Eliza on Caleb's bed, listening in.

"Caleb is saying, 'Daddy, you have something in your pocket or in your wallet that is really significant,'" I told them. Tim was in his pajamas at the time and didn't have his wallet, but he was wearing a necklace and asked if that was what Caleb meant.

"It's not a necklace," I conveyed. "It's like a little piece of art. And Caleb wants you to know that he is as close to you as that little piece of art in Daddy's wallet."

But Tim knew what was in his wallet, and there was no piece of artwork in it. He was so sure it wasn't there, he didn't even bother to look.

It was only later that day that Tim sat down and emptied out his wallet, just to double-check.

And in it, he found what looked like a small receipt. It was a tiny piece of folded-up paper. Tim carefully unfolded it, and gasped.

It was a drawing of three yellow flowers next to a tree, by Caleb.

I told them that three yellow flowers and a tree would be another sign that Caleb would send them.

The next morning, Eliza sat in her dining room and stared out the window. There were trees and yellow flowers everywhere, so how was she supposed to know which ones were sent by Caleb?

A small sticker on one of the three picture windows in her kitchen caught her eye, and she got up to remove it. Caleb had put dozens of stickers of flowers and butterflies and leaves on the windows; over time some had fallen off and some had been scraped off. Nearly all of the stickers were gone. In fact, there were just three stickers left.

Suddenly Eliza froze in her tracks. She stepped back to look at the last three stickers.

Each one was of a yellow flower.

Eliza sat back in her chair. She called Tim over from the living room, and she showed him the three yellow flowers.

"That's pretty close," Eliza said. "All that's missing is the tree."

Tim laughed. Then he sat down next to Eliza and pointed.

"Look *through* the window," he said.

And there in their front yard, framed perfectly by the windows and the three yellow flower stickers, was a big, beautiful, arching green tree.

———

The signs have continued. On a recent camping trip, Caleb's three-year-old sister Jenna innocently handed her mother a tiny bouquet of flowers she'd just picked—exactly three yellow daffodils.

"Why are you giving me these?" Eliza asked.

"I don't know," Jenna said. "Something just told me to give them to you."

And balloons—*always* balloons. And consecutive numbers, too. "Just yesterday, the range on my electric car said 111 miles," Eliza said. "I thought, *Gee, that's neat,* but I let my logical mind kind of talk me out of it being a sign from Caleb. The very next day, after driving somewhere completely different, I came home and plugged in the car and the range was 111 miles again. The signs just keep coming, and if I ever have a doubt, something incredible will happen that just smacks me in the face."

Tim, who has always been the more skeptical of the two, decided to ask Caleb for a secret sign on his own. He didn't tell another soul about it. The morning after he asked for the sign, Eliza told him to go outside and bring in the family cats.

"Why?" Tim asked.

"Because I smell skunk."

Tim sat back down on the bed.

"What's wrong?" Eliza asked.

"The skunk," he said. "I can smell it, too. I asked Caleb to send me a skunk. And now, here it is—a skunk."

Caleb had told me one other thing during my reading with Eliza—he said that his parents were going to fight for a law that would bear his name.

Today Caleb's Law—which requires dentists to have an anesthesiologist present during all surgeries, rather than administer the anesthesia themselves—is on its way to being enacted in Caleb's home state.

"The dental lobby is powerful, so it's been a hard fight," said Eliza. "But Caleb is fighting right alongside us. The first time Tim's sister, who is a doctor, sent an email to our local congressman about the bill, the email went out at exactly 11:11 A.M."

Despite all the signs and messages from Caleb, there are times when his loved ones still feel the pain of his loss from this earth. Some nights, Eliza and Tim will sit together and read from *Llama and the Dominina*, so that Caleb's voice—so full of love and passion and excitement and ideas—can come alive in their home once more.

"I miss him every single second of every day," Eliza says. "But there is also a lot of joy in knowing that he is still here with us. When my friends ask about Caleb, they always ask, 'How is he?,' as if he's still around."

. . . even out of unspeakable grief,
beautiful things take wing.

—A. R. TORRES, "The Lessons of Loss"

5

—

DRAGONFLIES AND DEER

THEY called themselves the Four C's—Carla and Chris and their two young sons, Calder and Caleb. They were a team, always together, always laughing, always having fun. "Calder's joy in life is joking around," says Carla, who married Chris in 2003 and started a TV production company with him. "Caleb is such a joker. Calder and Caleb shared a room and they loved cracking each other up."

Their happiness was like a dream, beautiful and perfect—until, inconceivably, the dream came to an end.

When Calder was just seven years old, he was electrocuted by a faulty light in a swimming pool, and crossed.

It was unthinkable, impossible—why did all the laughter have to stop? Carla and Chris searched for answers, searched for solace, but nothing seemed to help.

Yet in the days and weeks following her son's passing, Carla could not shake the feeling that Calder was still, somehow, present.

"I had this feeling that he was sending me messages," Carla told me. "But it didn't make any sense, so I felt like the real explanation had to be that I was going crazy."

One afternoon, Carla was driving her car when a tiny baby dragonfly flew around her head and landed next to the driver's-side window. She had no idea how or when it got into the car. She kept driving, and the dragonfly didn't move. She stopped at a red light, rolled down the window, but the dragonfly didn't budge. "When I finally got to my destination, I got out of the car and the baby dragonfly got out with me, flew around me for a while, and then just flew away."

And in that moment, Carla had a thought.

"I wondered, *Was that Calder?*" she says. "The pain was still very raw, and I realized I'd been crying the whole drive, and then I stood there and tried to figure out what had just happened. It *felt* like Calder was trying to send me a message, but I just couldn't quite grasp that it was real."

For the rest of that summer, Carla saw dragonflies everywhere. On the doorknob. On a wall. In the bathroom. "I was in a swimming pool and my sister-in-law said, 'Do you know a dragonfly has been sitting on your head for a while?'" Carla says. "And all these kids were around me and splashing the water and making all this noise, but the dragonfly just sat there on my head. It didn't want to leave."

But how could a dragonfly possibly be a message from anyone?

Carla found her way to me through a mutual friend, and she came to my house on Long Island for our reading. I made sure that my mother took our dog Roscoe to her house so he wouldn't interrupt the reading, but I let our cat roam free. Then Carla and I sat down at the kitchen table. Moments later, Calder pushed his way through. He showed me something that led me to ask Carla a question.

"Do you happen to be allergic to cats?"

Yes, Carla said, she was.

"Okay. Well, I have a cat that always sits with me here in the kitchen, and Calder is telling me, 'You shouldn't have sent the dog away, you should have sent the cat away,' and now he's going to keep the cat out of the kitchen for you."

Sure enough, our cat—who always sits with anyone who comes into the kitchen—was nowhere to be found during the reading.

Calder continued to come through in the most remarkable way—so full of energy and excitement and love.

Typically, when I connect with someone on the Other Side, I ask them to send me their name as validation. However, I don't always get the full name. I might get a strong sound or the image of a single letter. In Carla's case, I picked up on a big C, referring to someone on the Other Side. Then I picked up that there was another C, and another one, and another, all of them here on earth—four C's in all. I told Carla about the four C's, and she told me what they meant—her and Chris, and their sons Caleb and Calder. The core, the unit, the team.

Then something amazing happened in the reading.

Calder showed me that his family was about to go on a trip, and Carla confirmed that this was true. Calder then showed me the exact way he intended to send a message to Carla during the trip, so she'd know he was there with them the whole time. It's very unusual for someone who has crossed to be so specific about the sign they are planning to send, but Calder was very clear.

"Calder is going to send you a deer," I said. "I see it very clearly. And he wants you to know that you will have a direct encounter with the deer. Carla, he is saying that this is for you, so you will know that he is with you and around you the whole time. He wants to send you a direct message, so the encounter between you and the deer will be a direct one."

Calder had one other important message to share with his mother.

"He is sending you messages all the time, and he sees that you are getting them, but that you're immediately questioning them," I said. "Calder is telling you, 'Stop doing that. Stop questioning.'"

After the reading, Carla kept the message about the deer to herself. She didn't quite know what to make of it. A direct encounter? What did that mean?

A few weeks before the family left for England, Chris and Carla decided to go to the Florida Keys for the weekend. On the long drive down, Carla fell asleep. She was startled awake by Chris saying, "Oh wow."

"What is it?" Carla asked.

"We just passed them," he said. "On the side of the road. I've never seen them before!"

"What was it? What did you see?"

"Four key deer," Chris said.

Key deer are a rare and endangered subspecies of deer that live only in the Florida Keys. They are smaller than regular deer and very elusive. Chris had been to the Keys many times, but he'd never seen a key deer. And now, suddenly, there were four of them at the side of the road.

"Can you believe it?" Chris said. "Four key deer!"

Carla's reaction surprised him. She started to cry, tears streaming down her cheeks, devastated that she'd missed the message intended for her.

"I was devastated," she said. "I didn't see them. Chris woke me up a second too late. I told him why I was upset, because Laura had said how the deer message was supposed to be for me. Chris offered to turn the car around and look for the key deer, but I thought, *Okay, don't be so picky.* What are the chances of seeing not one but four key deer on the road? We were the four C's, and there were four deer. So I let it go, and we had the most wonderful weekend. But inside, I was still devastated."

They left Key West on Sunday morning and started the long drive home. Just minutes into the drive, Chris pulled the car over at a bar called the No Name Pub. He told Carla he needed to use the bathroom, and went inside.

Chris hadn't been totally truthful, though. He did go to the bathroom, but not for the obvious reasons. Chris had heard about the bar and one of its traditions: Patrons would write someone's name on a dollar bill and tape it to the wall or the ceiling, to honor them. With a Sharpie, Chris wrote CALDER on a bill and taped it to a choice spot on the wall. He left the bar and headed toward the car, but was stopped cold in his tracks. He couldn't believe what he was seeing.

While Chris was in the bar, Carla stayed in the car with Caleb. She stared straight out the front window, lost in thought. She was thinking about Calder. A light rain was falling, and the parking lot was empty except for a few other cars and some picnic tables. A movement caught her eye and she turned toward the edge of the parking lot.

There, emerging from a small row of bushes, was a deer.

Carla gasped. She slowly and carefully got out of the car, careful not to frighten the deer away. But he didn't seem scared. He looked straight at Carla and then—incredibly—began slowly walking toward her. That was the moment that Chris came out of the bar.

"Don't move," Carla told him. "Just take a picture."

The deer came within ten feet of her, close enough for Carla to look into his clear, beautiful eyes. Then he crept two feet closer. And then closer still. Carla held her breath and didn't move. The deer came even closer.

Finally, only two feet separated Carla and the deer. Slowly, she extended her hand, palm up. The deer stepped forward and gently put his nose in her hand. He stayed there for several moments, allowing Carla to cradle his face. Then the deer tilted his head and looked up at Carla. Their eyes locked. After what seemed like the longest time, the deer turned around and walked away. Carla, Chris, and Caleb remained motionless, watching him head back toward the bushes—where he turned around, gave them one last look, and then disappeared into the foliage, out of sight.

Carla stood there in something like shock. Other than cats or dogs, she had never been that close to an animal before, much less a wild animal. As the deer approached her, she felt nervous, but when he laid his head in her hand, she felt only sweetness and joy.

"What just happened?" she asked Chris. "Was that real?"

"It was real," Chris said. "Very real."

Carla took stock of her emotions. She thought she might cry, but she didn't. "There was nothing sad about what happened at all," she says. "At that moment, all I felt and all Chris felt was awe. Sheer awe."

Standing there in the parking lot, Chris was the first to speak.

"Well, if that wasn't a message from Calder," he said, "I don't know what is."

Back in the car, Carla cried. "It wasn't out of sadness or grief or anything like that," she says. "It was more out of relief. Relief that I hadn't missed my big moment with Calder. I was so upset about not having seen the four key deer. I tried not to show it, but the whole weekend I was just so upset. But then Calder—Calder was never going to let me miss that moment."

After that, deer became one of the signs that Calder uses to let his parents know he is still around, still with them, still part of the family.

"We see them everywhere, but in kind of unusual ways," Carla says. "One time, we took Caleb to the water park and on the big waterslide. As we stood in line to go down the slide, I started thinking of Calder, because going down the slide with his brother was always one of his favorite things to do. And just then I looked up, and the man standing in front of us in line was wearing a muscle T-shirt that showed a big tattoo on his biceps. It was a tattoo of a big, beautiful deer."

In that instant, Carla says, "I knew Calder was right there on the slide with Caleb and me."

For Carla, receiving that remarkable sign—and accepting it as a communication from Calder—changed her life.

"It gave me strength, and it opened my heart and my mind to getting signs from Calder," she says. "It convinced me that Calder really is always with us. Losing a young child so suddenly, I can't even explain how hard that is. And I really feel like getting that message from Calder helped me get through it. It was such a blessing. The Four C's are still together, and we always will be."

6

—

BUDDIES ON
THE OTHER SIDE

ONE more remarkable thing happened in my reading with Carla.

Very early in the reading, when Calder came through, before I knew his brother's name, he was very insistent in bringing forward another boy who had recently crossed. He gave me a lot of information about this boy—his name, how he died, how he was doing now—and I shared it all with Carla.

"He's bringing me a boy on the Other Side named Caleb," I told her. "This is a boy who went to the dentist and got anesthesia and crossed over. Calder is telling me that he and Caleb are together and working as a team on the Other Side." I knew immediately who Caleb was: Calder had brought Eliza and Tim's son to me.

Carla and Eliza were strangers, but their sons no longer were. Their sons, who had crossed at different times and in different ways, were buddies on the Other Side. Carla didn't quite know what to make of this. Then Calder came through with more information.

"Wait a minute, is there also a boy named Caleb here?" I asked.

Yes, Carla said. Calder's younger brother was named Caleb.

"That's what Calder is saying," I went on. "He is laughing about it and he is saying that he has a Caleb here and another Caleb there."

For Carla, it was a beautiful validation not only that her son was still with her, but that her grief and sorrow were not hers alone. The Calder-Caleb friendship was an affirmation that we are *all* connected to one another, and *all* meant to help one another to heal and grow here on earth. And that those on the Other Side work together to facilitate it.

Calder told his mom that he and his new buddy Caleb had a plan: They wanted their moms to meet.

After the reading, Carla reached out to Caleb's mother, Eliza, and the two did indeed become good friends. They had something in common that not many other people could relate to—both having a young son cross. In fact, Calder and Caleb had crossed within months of each other. Carla and Eliza were able to share their feelings and help each other cope with their grief. In a way, Eliza was one of the very few people who could provide this kind of solace to Carla—and Calder saw this and came through, steering her straight into his mother's path. And of course, Caleb did the very same thing for his mother, Eliza.

Think about that! These two boys who crossed got together on the Other Side and led their mothers to each other, as a way to help them heal. What a powerful demonstration of the continuing presence and guidance of our loved ones who cross!. And what a powerful testament to the interconnectedness of our paths here on earth.

In fact, I have seen this happen quite a lot—souls teaming up on the Other Side to engineer important events here on earth. They work together in what I call expanded Teams of Light, and they push us to forge and appreciate our connections to other people who can enrich our lives and help us grow.

Calder was able to engineer his mother's connection to Eliza through me, but as I've said, you don't need a psychic medium to receive and act on these signs and messages. Most likely, you are already receiving them, because our Teams of Light are relentless when it comes to getting our attention.

But as I noted above, the clutter and chaos of our busy lives often overwhelm these signs and messages. We don't see them, or we see them but they don't register, or we dismiss them. That's why it's so important for us to be on the lookout for them—to be in a heightened state of alertness to the loving connections that are available to us here on earth. We need to be open to the people being steered into our paths, because those people may have been sent to help us heal and grow.

Later on in this book, we'll talk about how to achieve that state of heightened awareness. But for now, I hope the interconnected stories of Caleb and Calder impress upon you the awesome power of our workers on the Other Side, and how they deliver life-affirming and life-changing messages to us all.

7

HEARTS AND PLAYING CARDS

NANCY Miller was walking through a tiny fishing village in the remote countryside of Vietnam as part of a tour group when she spotted something unusual on the ground. In the middle of nothing but hills and lakes and dense forests, with no villagers in sight, several playing cards were scattered in a small area on a dirt path. Nancy asked her guide why the cards might be there and whether they had any cultural significance.

"No, no significance at all," the guide said. "Don't know what they're doing there. Makes no sense to me."

And then, for some reason, Nancy thought about her mother, also named Nancy.

"This thought just popped in my head," she says now. "I thought, *You know, if my mother was a playing card, she would be the Queen of Hearts, because of what a loving person she was.*"

The group kept walking, and Nancy forgot all about the playing cards.

———

Nancy's parents were junior high school sweethearts who married in their early twenties. They stayed married for sixty-four years. They had four children—Nancy and her three younger sisters, Linda, Kim, and Meg—and seven grandchildren. They were an exceptionally close family.

"Family was *everything* to my mother," Nancy says. "The most important thing in her life was having all of us around her. She loved to cook for us and decorate for the holidays and go on family vacations. And when she went on vacations without us, all she did was shop for something she could bring back for each one of us. We all had a very deep connection with her."

A few years ago, Nancy's mother's health began to decline. Wheelchair-bound, she had to be attended to by her husband, Kenny, and by hospital aides, in her home on Long Island. Nancy, who lives in New York City, called every day to check in.

"The morning my husband and I were supposed to go on vacation to Vietnam, I called and asked my father how she was doing," Nancy remembers. "He said, 'Not great, but don't worry. She'll be fine.' So we got on the plane for the twelve-hour flight to Hong Kong."

During the flight, in the middle of the night, Nancy got up to use the bathroom. When she locked the door behind her, she began to cry. "I had this horrible pain in my shoulder that woke me up, and all of a sudden I just started weeping," she said. "I didn't know why I was so emotional."

When they landed in Hong Kong several hours later, she checked her phone and saw a text message from her sister Meg. "Call me" was all it said.

Meg told her sister that their mother was gone. "She passed right when I got the shoulder pain. My father told me that one of the last things my mother did was call out, 'Kenny, I love you,' while he was in another room."

With a heavy heart, Nancy continued on her tour of Vietnam.

When she got to the fishing village and saw the playing cards in the dirt, she thought about her mother and how much she already missed her.

The next day, the tour group trudged along a dirt path that led to an ancient Buddhist temple about four hours from the fishing village. And there, along the path, was *another* scattered pile of playing cards. *What a weird coincidence*, Nancy thought.

The next day, the group traveled to a remote town several miles away and walked along a path toward a rice museum. And there, just a few feet to the side of the dirt path, was yet another set of scattered playing cards.

"This time, I stopped to take a look at them," Nancy says. "My mother's favorite saying was, 'Third time's a charm.' And this was the third time I'd seen playing cards on the ground."

Nancy took a single step toward the cards and then stopped.

"One of the cards was off by itself," she says. "All of the other cards were facedown. This one card was faceup."

Nancy bent down to pick it up. It was the Queen of Hearts.

The statistical probability of drawing any one specific playing card from a standard deck is fifty-two to one. In other words, there's a less than 2 percent chance of naming a card then picking that card out of a deck. If you're a gambler, those aren't great odds.

But still, it's *possible*. It could happen. Some might say that Nancy spotting the Queen of Hearts in the countryside of Vietnam was just a random coincidence.

"To me, it was clearly my mother sending a message," she says. "And when I saw the card, I said, 'Okay, Mom, I know you're okay. Thank you for letting me know.'" Nancy took a picture of the card, texted it to her sister Meg, and wrote, "You won't believe what happened."

"And Meg just said, 'Okay, I'm going to ask Mom to send *me* a Queen of Hearts, too.'"

Back in New York, Meg stayed alert to any sign of a Queen of Hearts. But a week went by with no sign of the lucky card. Meg had forgotten all about her request when she went to her office early one morning—earlier than she usually arrived. She was sitting at her desk getting ready for the day when she heard someone in another office yell out three words.

The three words were "Queen of Hearts."

Meg jumped up and ran into the office a few doors down. There were two women sitting there, and Meg asked which one had just called out "Queen of Hearts." The woman behind the desk said that it was her.

"Why did you say that?" Meg asked.

"Oh, I was just trying to remember the name of this dress shop for my friend Nancy here, and I couldn't remember it, and finally it just came to me," she said. "It was called Queen of Hearts."

And the friend's name was Nancy, to boot!

After that, other family members wanted to receive *their* signs from Nancy. The Queen of Hearts became their shared language for connecting with her.

"My sister Kim was shopping in an antiques store, which is something my mother loved to do with us," Nancy said. "She was just about to leave the store when she spotted a single playing card on top of a bureau—the Queen of Hearts."

Kim immediately texted Nancy: "I got my heart!" Soon after, Kim's daughter Ali drove to the home of one her work clients and was introduced to a woman with a big, bright tattoo of the Queen of Hearts on her left shoulder.

"I got my heart!" she texted her aunts. Then Nancy's aunt Sue went to see a Broadway show. She sat close to the stage, and while she was waiting for the curtain to rise, Sue noticed a playing card sewn into the bottom corner of the curtain. It was the only thing that was sewn in, and it seemed totally random—and it was the Queen of Hearts. "Got my heart!" she told everyone. It happened over and over. On the way to her mother's memorial celebration, Nancy spot-

ted a powerboat in a backyard along the side of the road. Its name—
Queen of Hearts. Then she saw her sign on a greeting card. Then a
painting. An ad in a magazine. Always, the Queen of Hearts.

"I understand some people will say it's all a coincidence," Nancy
says. "What I would say is, 'That's an awful lot of coincidences, isn't
it?'"

Two months after her mother crossed, Nancy contacted me and
asked me to do a reading for her and her dad and her sister Meg on
Meg's birthday. Originally, I was scheduled to travel to an event that
day, but at the last minute the event got rescheduled, and I was able
to do the reading. In fact, I felt *pulled* to do the reading. When I sat
down with Meg, Nancy, and their father, I told them how strong and
powerful Nancy's mother was on the Other Side.

"She is really making things happen there," I said. "I can't believe
how strong she is."

Although Nancy's mother had only crossed two months earlier,
she was already a seasoned professional at delivering signs and messages. Immediately she conveyed to me what she'd been using to connect with her loved ones on earth.

"I am seeing that she is sending a big heart to all of you," I said.
"Hearts, hearts, hearts."

"When I heard that, I just said, 'Wow,'" Nancy remembers. "We
already knew we were getting hearts from my mother, so when she
confirmed it, it was amazing. Even my father was impressed."

Nancy's father was the skeptic in the bunch. Kenny was an internist and scientifically minded. He wasn't a believer in the family
being able to connect with his wife. Yet the more he heard about his
daughters "getting their hearts," the more intrigued he became.
When Nancy asked him if he wanted to tag along for Meg's reading,
she fully expected him to say no—and was happily surprised when he
agreed. "Whenever we'd tell him about all the Queen of Hearts, he
was like, 'Are you kidding me?'" Nancy says. "Slowly, he was starting
to come around."

What her father needed, Nancy believed, was a sign of his own.

Kenny's eighty-sixth birthday fell on St. Patrick's Day, just a few weeks after his wife had crossed. The entire family gathered to celebrate, with a cake, cards, and gifts. The next morning, Nancy came down to the kitchen and found her father sitting at the table, reading. The kitchen was quiet, except for a faint, musical sound. She tried to figure out where it was coming from, but couldn't quite place it. It sounded like someone singing "Happy Birthday"—almost like one of those greeting cards with a musical chip inside.

"Dad, do you hear that?" she asked.

"Hear what?" he said. Nancy knew her father's hearing wasn't the best, so she let the matter drop. A few minutes later, her husband, Stu, came into the kitchen. "What's that singing?" he asked.

Kim came in and heard it, too, but no one could figure out where it was coming from—nor could Nancy's father hear it.

Finally the group decided to track down the source of the faint, mysterious chorus of "Happy Birthday." They opened every drawer and every cabinet. They opened the stove and the refrigerator. Eventually, someone opened the cabinet beneath the sink.

"All of a sudden the singing got louder," Nancy says. "And my father said, 'Oh, now I can hear it.' And just after he said that, the music stopped."

Nancy and her sister pulled out the trash can and looked through it to find the greeting card. But it wasn't in the trash. It wasn't anywhere else in the cabinet, either. "We went through every envelope in the garbage, every bit of wrapping paper, everything," Nancy says. "Finally we gave up. We never figured out where the music was coming from."

But that doesn't mean they didn't know *why* they heard it.

"As soon as my father finally heard it, it stopped, and that's when I knew," Nancy says. "It was my mother, singing him 'Happy Birthday.' She needed him to hear it, and finally he did. It was her special sign to him."

The family keeps seeing hearts everywhere. The heart-shaped foam in a cup of coffee. The heart-shaped clapper inside an overhead bell. The heart-shaped etching above the entrance to an old church in Barcelona, where Nancy and her husband recently traveled. The heart-shaped helium balloons each of twelve tourists carried past Nancy's outdoor café table.

"At the last minute we decided to stay at this one particular hotel on a trip to Barcelona," Nancy says. "It was the hotel where my mother and father and I had stayed in 2008. And when we got there, I immediately noticed something in the front window." There, impossible to miss, was a collection of colorful metal hearts strung around the name of the hotel. "I asked the concierge, 'What's the significance of all those hearts?' And he said, 'I have no idea, they just arrived yesterday and someone put them up.' So all these hearts arrived just in time for my visit."

For Nancy, all the hearts are part of the beautiful vocabulary her mother uses to remain connected to the family she loves so much. They are their shared secret language.

"I have no doubt that my mother is always with us," Nancy says. "Always *always* there. And when I have a bad day and really miss her and feel like I need her around a little more, I'll say, 'Mom, I need you, send me another sign.' And then I'll see a heart somewhere. I still miss her every single day. But knowing she's still with us is a great source of comfort."

Even her father is now fully on board, and keeps looking for—and acknowledging—signs from the woman he spent his life with.

"My mother's great gift to him was letting him know that dying isn't the end," Nancy says. "He's a believer now. He understands that there is something really, really beautiful waiting for us on the Other Side."

8

HUMMINGBIRDS
AND LIGHT

WHO doesn't love seeing hummingbirds?

To me, they are truly amazing creatures, even if I don't get to see them very often. Hardly ever, now that I think about it. But when I do spot one, I just marvel at it. I wonder how something so tiny can bring so much happiness and joy. The average hummingbird doesn't even weigh an ounce—in fact, it weighs less than one-tenth of an ounce.

But in that tiny package comes a big burst of magic.

Did you know that hummingbirds have been around for forty-two million years? And that a hummingbird's heart beats more than twelve hundred times per minute? That's roughly twenty heartbeats *a second*! A hummingbird's tiny wings can flap as fast as ninety times per second! All that flapping makes the hummingbird the only bird that can hover in the same spot for a long stretch of time. That's why, when we do spot a hummingbird, we often get a pretty good look at it—because hummingbirds love to stop and say hello and hang out for a while.

Maybe that's why hummingbirds play such a prominent symbolic role in so many cultures. Native Americans, for example, see hummingbirds as healers and helpers who bring luck and love to those they visit. The ancient Aztecs believed hummingbirds were commissioned by the gods to carry out tasks that required exceptional lightness, such as delivering blessings from one person to another. "Hummingbirds lead from here to there the thoughts of men," one Aztec saying goes. "If someone intends good to you, the hummingbird takes that desire all the way to you."

In my experience, hummingbirds have played all of those roles — helper, healer, messenger, bringer of love — except with a twist: These special creatures are frequently messengers from the Other Side.

Priya Khokhar was one of four daughters of the man she lovingly called Abba — the Urdu word for "father." Her father, Shahid, had a profound influence on all of his children. "He was just this force to be reckoned with," Priya says of Shahid, who worked as a landscape designer. "A very strong personality, always in charge. He was also extremely creative and supportive. Many fathers in Pakistan want their daughters to be married by twenty-one or twenty-two, but my father never treated us as inferior or unequal. He raised us to think with an open mind and to be our own people. He never said, 'You can't do this.' It was always, "'You can do this and more.'"

After college, Priya moved to the United States to work in the tech industry. Her sister Natasha lived nearby on the West Coast, and the two spoke just about every day. One day, Priya got an unexpected visit from Natasha and her husband, John.

"John looked at me and said, 'Abba was shot,'" Priya recalls. "I had trouble comprehending what that meant."

"Is he okay?" Priya asked.

"No," John said, "he's not."

Shahid had been shot and killed outside his home in Pakistan, in front of his wife.

"Pakistan is a very violent country," Priya explains. "Lots of crime, family feuds, politics, bad blood. Our family had experienced our share of litigation and drama over the years, so my father always carried a gun. But that morning, for the first time in forty years, he walked out of his house without a gun. A man dressed in black just came up to him and shot him."

The sisters were in shock. It didn't seem possible.

"All I wanted to do was fly back to Pakistan so I could see him before the burial," Priya says. "But in the Muslim faith, burials happen quickly, so that wasn't possible. I went home anyway and stayed there for two months. I didn't cry, and I didn't really process it. But when I came back to the U.S., I had a breakdown—I took off from work and didn't get out of bed for a month."

On Shahid's birthday, Priya and her family would get together and toast his memory with a shot of Johnnie Walker Black, one ice cube—their father's favorite drink. "We would also go to Costco to buy flowers—which he loved—and eat one of those one-dollar Costco hot dogs, which he also loved," Priya said. "That was our ritual, and that was how we kept him alive—by remembering and telling stories and laughing."

Still, her father's absence weighed heavily on her, especially after she started dating a co-worker, Dave, and the two eventually decided to get married. "I just had all these moments when I would think, *What would Abba say about this?*" Priya says. "What I wanted was my father's reassurance, just the way he had always given it to me."

I have a connection to Priya—her sister Natasha is married to my brother John. When Priya's mother came to visit, I offered to give her a reading. The morning of the reading, something startled me awake at five A.M. Something *strong*. It was Shahid, who could not wait to be connected with his family. "Your husband has a really powerful personality," I told Priya's mother during our reading a bit later in the day. "He's been harassing me all morning."

In the reading, Shahid was very clear about what he wanted to convey to his family. He wanted them to know that when he crossed he felt no pain, that it was over very quickly, and that, in fact, he had been feeling tired, and—though he was dearly sorry to leave his family—he was in a good place and surrounded by people who loved him. He was *happy*. Shahid's niece had died young, and Shahid was now reunited with her on the Other Side.

Hearing this was a great comfort to his wife. Priya herself, though, was more of a skeptic. "I guess I'm not such a spiritual person," she says. "I didn't have the belief that we could connect with the Other Side."

Priya never asked me for a reading, and I never gave her one, but the family was gracious enough to invite me to her wedding. It was held in the sunken rose garden of a beautiful old mansion in Fremont, California, on the day of an astonishing blood-red moon.

Just before the ceremony began, Priya's mother approached me. She was very happy for Priya, she told me, but she also felt a heaviness because Priya's father wasn't there.

"I miss him so much," she said. "It's just so sad."

Then she lowered her voice and asked me, "Is he here?"

And *boom*—his energy pushed through forcefully on my screen.

I told her that Shahid was definitely present. Not only that, he was telling me he was going to make his presence known during the ceremony. "He is not letting me know how," I said, "but he is so excited because he says he will be putting on a show. But he wants it to be a surprise."

Priya's mother's face filled with excitement. To be honest, I was excited to see what Shahid had planned for us, too. Some of the guests overheard my conversation with Priya's mother, and soon the word was out—Shahid had a wedding surprise in store. We were breathless, waiting for the show to begin.

The ceremony itself took place under a cloudy sky. An imam presided over the service. In his speech, he talked about the Islamic view of the afterlife, and compared it to a cone. If you had made many connections and brought light to many lives, in the afterlife you would be at the top of the cone, where the most light reaches. He spoke of the intense connection between Priya and Dave. He said that they were beams of light that had connected before this life, connected again in this life, and would be together in the afterlife.

Listening to the imam speak, I was struck by how closely his words resonated with the lessons I've learned from the Other Side—what I call the light between us, the brilliant cords of light that connect us. The belief that we are light bodies, traveling through time and space, spanning worlds, eternally connected to one another and to a vast, higher energy force.

As the imam spoke, Priya and Dave stood facing each other, hands clasped together. All of a sudden the clouds shifted in the sky and the sun's rays burst through. "I felt it before I saw it—I felt the heat on my skin," Dave recalled. "I looked up and I saw a single beam of light shining directly on Priya. She was shimmering, while everything else around her was dark."

It was true—the sunbeam landed on Priya and no one else. Photos taken during this part of the ceremony confirm it—everything was dark and shadowed, except for Priya, who was resplendent. "I felt the sun shift, and then I realized it was shining right on me," Priya says. "I didn't attach any significance to it right away. But that was only the first amazing thing that happened."

Just a few moments later, while Priya and Dave were still facing each other, some of the guests began to gasp. At first, I couldn't tell what was happening, but soon I saw it, too.

In the space above where Priya and Dave were standing, maybe just six inches above their heads, a beautiful hummingbird danced and flitted and finally stopped and hovered, floating in the warm air for what seemed like forever.

The hummingbird's arrival at the ceremony, at the precise moment that Priya and Dave were to be married, and the way it lingered there, watching, waiting, blessing the couple—how could that not be a sign?

"I started bawling," Priya recalls. "In that moment, it really hit me—my father is here. I could feel him. He is here with me now.

And for that hummingbird to show up right when it did? You could call it a coincidence. But to me, it wasn't a coincidence. It was my father, telling me, 'I love you. I am here.'"

Since that remarkable day, Priya and Dave—but especially Dave— have seen hummingbirds everywhere. "Not two days go by without me seeing one," says Dave. "The day after the wedding, I noticed a hummingbird fly right up to me, look at me for two or three seconds, then dart away. I can't remember that ever happening before."

In this way, hummingbirds became a sign from Shahid to his daughter and her husband. It is his way of letting them know he is watching over them. "I see them all the time," Dave says. "On trees, bushes, benches, in the walkway behind my apartment, everywhere. They've become a mainstay of my life. People are sick of my stories about them."

"It became this running joke between us," Priya says. "When we saw hummingbirds, we knew it was my father checking out Dave to make sure he approved of him." And Dave isn't the only one who sees them. One day, Dave was walking arm in arm with Priya's mother when a hummingbird shot right in front of them and hovered for several moments.

"That's him," Priya's mother said. "That's Shahid showing us he's with us."

When Dave and Priya were looking for a new home, they went to see a house for sale near Natasha and John. The neighborhood was desirable, but Priya and Dave didn't love the house. Then Dave walked out on the balcony, and a hummingbird flew right in front of his face and hovered there for five seconds.

Count out five seconds. It's a longer time than you'd think. Dave ran inside and told Priya, "This is a sign. We need to buy this house."

They had to switch real estate agents, juggle finances, and basically jump through hoops, but in the end they bought the house, and they are very happy they did.

"We are so close to my sister and her family," Priya says. "My father would have wanted us to be together. Family was the most important thing to him. He always said, 'A family sticks together.' And so he made sure we got that house."

Not long ago, Priya and Dave attended Burning Man, the annual weeklong gathering in a section of the Black Rock Desert in Nevada. They were sitting at their campsite with ten or so friends when the subject of their wedding came up. "We told them about the hummingbird, and how we see hummingbirds everywhere, and someone said how great it would be to see a hummingbird that day.

"But we were in the middle of the desert," Dave says. "There were no trees or bushes. Basically there was no chance we'd see a hummingbird."

The group got on their bikes and rode the short distance to a nearby encampment, the Skinny Kitty Teahouse. "I went up to the counter and asked for some tea, and then I looked up and let out a giant squeal."

The rest of the group came over to see what Priya was squealing about.

"I couldn't believe it," says Dave. "The camp had all this taxidermy stuff all over, and right there at the counter was a little stuffed hummingbird. Everyone was like, 'Wow, this is crazy.' And it *was* crazy. I mean, we found a hummingbird in the middle of a *desert*."

Dave understands some people won't be quite as impressed by all those hummingbird appearances as he is. "I'm used to people sometimes rolling their eyes when I tell them my stories," he says. But he doesn't mind the skepticism. "I can't argue with people who say it's a coincidence. All I know is that to *me*, the hummingbirds mean so much."

"When people tell me they don't believe in that stuff," he says, "I always think, *Okay, but if you're not at least a little open to it, you could be missing out on something really amazing.*"

For Priya, those tiny, fluttering creatures have become a significant part of life. "You may say it's a coincidence, but it's not a coincidence to me," she says. "It's my father letting me know he is with me and watching over me. And that gives me so much comfort.

"What I would say to people who aren't so sure is to stay open to the possibility. Stay open to your loved ones. There is much more at work in the universe than we know."

Death ends a life, not a relationship.

—MITCH ALBOM, *Tuesdays with Morrie*

9

—

GIRAFFES, EIFFEL TOWERS, AND A SONG ABOUT CATS

WHEN Alexander was a boy, he had a strange curiosity about what happens after we die. "It was an odd thing for an eight-year-old kid to be doing while playing basketball—thinking about where we go when we die," he says. "Yet that's what I did. I thought about it a lot. I grew up afraid of death, afraid of losing my parents, and afraid of not being able to play basketball with my dad anymore."

Over the years, this curious obsession stayed with him. He read books about the afterlife and near-death experiences. He never really understood why he was so intensely interested in death and dying, but then, in 2013, it suddenly became clear.

"If you look at the arc of my life, it was like the universe was preparing me from an early age for what happened in 2013," Alexander says. "It was the darkest year of my life."

Alexander grew up with the most loving, supportive parents anyone could wish for. "My mother was my heart," he says. "She was the most extraordinary, selfless person, and she had an incredible zest for life and passion for learning." His father, a very successful business-man, was his mentor and his best friend. "I spoke to him pretty much every day," Alexander says. "He was an enormous part of my life."

Alexander went to college and on to law school, but even then he knew he wanted to follow his father into the world of business. So Alexander, too, became a successful businessman, inspired by his parents at every step. When he got married in early 2013, his mother and father were there to walk him down the aisle.

A few months later, Alexander called his mother to say good night. "We made plans to see each other the next day," he says. "I remember she didn't sound right, but I didn't think it was anything too serious. The next day she had a massive stroke and fell into a coma."

His mother came out of the coma for only a few hours ten days into her hospital stay and then reverted to a minimally conscious state. Five months later, she passed away.

In the months that followed, Alexander and his wife tried to conceive, but were unsuccessful. After a few months, the couple began fertility treatments. On the day they were supposed to drive to the airport to fly to the beach to spend the weekend with Alexander's father, they had to cancel because of the IVF schedule. "I called him and told him I was sorry we couldn't make it, but we were going to try to bring him a grandchild," Alexander says.

That night, the phone rang at ten-thirty. It was his father's assistant calling to tell him that his father had been on a plane, and the plane had crashed. His father was gone.

"My wife and I would have been on that plane," he says. "And now my father was dead."

The news brought him to his knees. "It was devastating," he says. "It destroyed me. It destroyed every fiber of my being. Nothing made sense, and I cried myself to sleep every night. It was an incredible amount of pain."

A close friend connected him to me, hoping a reading would bring him some comfort. The friend withheld all information about Alexander, and in fact only gave me the *wrong* initial of his first name — a test I had to pass to overcome Alexander's skepticism, I suppose.

My reading with Alexander was extraordinary. His loved ones on the Other Side must have known that he would need a lot of affirmation to be convinced that he was connecting with his parents.

His father came through first. He told me how he had crossed to the Other Side and gave me the first names of the other people who had perished on the plane along with him. His father let me know that he had not one funeral, but two. He even gave me the name of one of the political dignitaries who spoke at the funeral.

Still, Alexander needed just a little more affirmation.

Over the next few months we spoke and texted on and off, and in one of our talks, Alexander asked for a very specific sign from his dad.

"We had a song," Alexander says. "It was our song. Maybe five people in the world knew that we shared this song—my wife, my sister, two people who crossed, and me. Not even my best friend knew it. So I asked my father to send Laura the lyrics to that song—it would be a sign that he was with me."

Alexander asked me to contact him again when I had received the lyrics to their song.

Weeks passed, then months, and nothing happened. No song came to me. Alexander's father came through several times, including in readings I was doing with other sitters that I had no idea he'd known—until he showed up in their readings, that is. He always burst right through, as if he had VIP status. My spirit guides—or, I guess, my spirit "bouncers"—clearly couldn't keep him outside the ropes. He'd also come to me at random times on random days. He was such a forceful, beautiful presence, it was like he became a part of my life. I'd tell Alexander when his father had visited me, and he loved hearing about these welcome intrusions, but still, no song.

One evening, after a rough day, Alexander and his wife went out to dinner at a Mexican restaurant. I happened to text him while they were at dinner, because I'd gotten a message of encouragement from his dad that he wanted me to pass on to his son. Alexander read the text and smiled and then handed the phone to his wife.

She read the text and began to cry. "Did you see this?" she said.

"See what?"

When Alexander first read the text, he'd only read the opening lines—it was in fact a long text. The part he could see ended with an arrow, which opened up the rest of the text on his phone. So he only read the top portion of the text and missed the arrow. But his wife had read the whole thing. The text contained the lyrics to "Cat's in the Cradle" by Harry Chapin—the song Alexander and his father shared!

I'd felt Alexander's dad around just as I was falling asleep that night, and I got the song lyrics in my head. I googled the lyrics and copied them into a text to Alexander.

Ever since, the song has become a sign for Alexander of his father's presence. One day, Alexander had an important business meeting—he was connecting with three people he'd never met before at a coffee shop. On the way there, he was anxious. As he slid into the booth, he had the thought that he wished he could have talked to his father before the meeting.

At that very moment "Cat's in the Cradle" came on over the coffee shop speakers. It arrived just when he needed to hear it. Alexander lowered his head as tears filled his eyes. He excused himself and went to the bathroom and cried.

"It was just such a beautiful moment of connection with my father," he says. "It was my father letting me know that I was doing the right thing, doing a great job, and that he was there, watching over me."

Alexander's projection of his need for his father's support, and his dad's instant response—playing that exact song at that exact time—is *precisely* how the secret language of the universe works.

After his mother's crossing, Alexander also created an unusually specific sign for her to use.

"My mother's favorite animal was a giraffe," Alexander says. "She loved giraffes, and we'd always joke about giraffes. And her favorite city in the world was Paris—she spoke fluent French." So what was the sign he asked for? A giraffe and an Eiffel Tower together. Not separately, but together, at the same time.

When Alexander told me about it, I laughed. I remember thinking it was a very particular sign, but I also knew that, when we talk to our loved ones on the Other Side, they listen. And the universe has magical ways of bringing our signs to us.

Not too much later, I went to do a group reading in the house of someone I'd never met. Right before I began the reading, I asked to use the bathroom so I could freshen up. As I entered the bathroom, something on the wall caught my attention—and at that very instant I felt Alexander's mother's energy push into my screen. I looked at the thing that had caught my eye and then leaned in to get a closer look.

Could it be?

Yes, it was.

It was a framed pencil drawing called *Metamorphosis*. On the left side of the drawing, there was a giraffe. As the drawing moved from left to right, the giraffe began to change shape. On the right side of the drawing, the giraffe had been completely transformed . . . *into the Eiffel Tower.*

I took a photo of the drawing and immediately texted it to Alexander. "It was exactly what I asked for," he says. "And since then, I've seen giraffes and Eiffel Towers together on greeting cards in stationery stores, in toy stores, in a gift shop. Sometimes I'll be pulled toward it. Every time, it's a magical feeling."

Just as he had when he was a boy, Alexander spent a long time thinking about what the signs meant, and what they taught him about the afterlife.

"Look, if you live in this physical world, you are always going to have doubts and skepticism about the hereafter," he says. "You will always wonder if we really do continue to exist after we die. I mean, I have had that very question since I was a boy of eight years old. So maybe that's why I asked my parents for so much validation. And sure enough, they sent it to me. They sent it to me over and over and over again.

"For me," Alexander continues, "there simply could not be any other explanation for the song lyrics and for the giraffes and Eiffel Towers except that it was my mother and father, communicating with me and letting me know they were with me."

Not a day goes by that Alexander doesn't miss his parents, because no matter how many signs we get, the sense of physical loss is always there. He feels the heartbreak of their absence, and it is crushing. Some days, Alexander will pull out a pair of his father's shoes that he's kept—they wore the same size—and slip them on and go for a long walk. "I literally walk in his shoes and think of all the questions I want to ask him, and the answers he wants to give me often just form in my head. And so that is one way I communicate with him. By taking a walk in his shoes."

These days Alexander doesn't see giraffes and Eiffel Towers quite as often as he used to, but he still sees them from time to time, and whenever he does, it is special.

"I've learned how to trust in these signs, and I've become a more intuitive person," he says. "I completely understand how skeptics feel, because I used to be one. But there's a lot about life and death that we don't understand, and I am open to all kinds of possibilities now."

The couple has two beautiful young children, a girl named for his mother and a boy named for his father. "I want them to know everything about their grandparents," Alexander says. "Everything that's happened has taught me that we need to get the very most out of the life we get to lead on earth. We have to take full advantage of the time we have here."

His experiences, both good and bad—and all the remarkable signs he's received—have taught him something else, too.

"They have taught me that when we put energy out into the universe, the universe responds," he says. "And they have made me believe that my mother and father are still very much 'alive,' and very much with me every day."

Six weeks after his death my father appeared to
me in a dream . . . It was an unforgettable
experience, and it forced me for the first time
to think about life after death.

—CARL G. JUNG

10

DEFAULT SIGNS, DREAMS, AND INTUITION: TUNING IN TO THE SECRET LANGUAGE

E VEN if we are new to the concept of a secret universal language—even if we're skeptical that such a language exists at all—the Other Side is already using it, and has been using it, to speak to us.

Our Teams of Light want so much to help guide us, and are so excited to see us happy, that they often simply can't wait for us to co-create a language of signs. They choose to send us signs of their own in the hope that we will recognize them and act on them. They are resourceful and relentless, and they will use everything and everyone, and try anything, to get our attention. They will keep on trying until we can't ignore them anymore. Even the biggest skeptic will encounter a sign or an event that he or she can't so easily shrug off. Let me give you an example.

Michael Shermer is a science historian and the founder of The Skeptics Society, a group that investigates what it calls pseudoscientific and paranormal claims. In lectures and debates, Michael has spent nearly three decades publicly challenging the belief that strange and inexplicable events have meaning. He has said that he doesn't believe in God. By any measure, Michael is a skeptic with a capital S.

In June 2014, Michael married a woman named Jennifer. Three months before their wedding, Jennifer shipped boxes of her belongings to Michael's house in California. Many of the boxes contained precious heirlooms that she'd inherited from her beloved grandfather Walter who was the principal father figure in her life, and who crossed when she was sixteen. Unfortunately, many of these items were damaged or lost during the shipping process.

One box, however, arrived intact. It contained Walter's 1978 Philips 070 transistor radio. It hadn't worked in decades, but Michael decided to open it up and try to bring it back to life. He tinkered with it for hours, but the radio was dead, so he put it in the back of a desk drawer in their bedroom and forgot all about it.

Three months later, on the day of their wedding, Jennifer was deeply missing her family back in Germany. She also wished her grandfather were there to give her away.

Jennifer was feeling so upset that she and Michael headed to their bedroom so she could take a quiet moment to gather herself. As they approached, they could hear music playing in the bedroom. Michael later wrote about this incident in an article. "We don't have a music system in there," he wrote, "so we searched for laptops or iPhones and even opened the back door to see if the neighbors were playing music."

Suddenly Jennifer turned to Michael. "That can't be what I think it is, can it?" she asked.

She opened the desk drawer, and the strains of a beautiful, romantic song filled the air. The song was coming from her grandfather's old transistor radio.

"My grandfather is here with us," she told Michael. "I'm not alone."

What was especially interesting to Michael was that the music only started playing *after* Jennifer expressed her loneliness. The radio continued to play music throughout the night, but stopped working the next day. It never made another sound.

"Had this happened to someone else," Michael later wrote, "I might suggest a chance electrical anomaly and the law of large numbers as an explanation—with billions of people having billions of experiences every day, there's bound to be a handful of extremely unlikely events that stand out in their timing and meaning." But even so, he wrote, "the eerie conjunction of these deeply evocative events gave Jennifer the distinct feeling that her grandfather was there and that the music was his gift of approval. I have to admit, it rocked me back on my heels and shook my skepticism to its core."

Michael's followers often ask him if he has ever encountered an event that he simply could not explain in a logical way. After Walter's special wedding gift, Michael wrote, "My answer is yes, now I have."

The Other Side does not wait until we are perfectly open to receiving signs. Our loved ones and spirit guides will send us signs and messages whenever we truly need them, ready or not. Which means that before we devise a language of our own creation, the Other Side will use default signs to try to connect with us.

DEFAULT SIGNS

Here are many of the most common default signs sent by the Other Side:

- Birds and butterflies
- Deer
- Electrical events (often with cellphones)
- Coins appearing in our path
- Rainbows
- Pictures
- Slogans
- Billboards
- Magazines
- License plates

- Street signs
- Music/songs
- Feathers
- Ladybugs
- Numerical sequences

There is a reason the Other Side uses these things as signs: They tend to be easier for us to recognize—and easier for them to manipulate and put in our path.

The conductive force behind any sign is energy. The universe is made of matter, and all matter is essentially condensed energy. The Other Side comprises the light and energy of all our souls put together. Energy, therefore, is the currency that binds us all—the connective tissue of the entire universe. Even Albert Einstein cited the connection between matter and energy, stating, "Mass and energy are both but different manifestations of the same thing—a somewhat unfamiliar conception for the average mind." Our Teams of Light on the Other Side can manipulate energy fields in a way that makes them ideal for sending signs.

I suspect they do this by utilizing the earth's magnetic field. This field is a massive jumble of charged particles that stretches all the way from the earth's interior to the farthest depths of space. Scientific studies have shown that many animals use the earth's magnetic field to orient themselves and to navigate their way in the world. One study in the *Journal of Experimental Biology* referred to this phenomenon as "nature's GPS."

What's more, all living beings generate electromagnetic energy— a form of energy that emits from objects through electrical and magnetic waves. Animals can sense each other's electromagnetic fields, or EMFs. Butterflies send out ultraviolet signals, while many birds have built-in compasses that are guided by the earth's magnetic field. And hunters have long complained about a sixth sense employed by deer, because deer are extremely tuned in to EMFs.

This is why the Other Side often sends us animals and insects as signs, as you've noticed in some of the stories you've already read.

The Other Side will also use strange and unlikely electrical occurrences—cellphones acting weirdly or receiving inexplicable texts and calls, lightbulbs flickering or burning out, and broken transistor radios suddenly playing music, to name a few.

Coins, too—since they consist of metal—have a level of conductivity that seems to make them easy targets for the Other Side. Look for coins appearing in unlikely places or at unlikely times, specifically when you are thinking of someone you love who has crossed, wrestling with an important decision, or having a difficult day. I once found a dime standing on its edge in my dryer—at the exact moment that I was thinking about my father, who had crossed. The Other Side finds a way to grab our attention, so I interpreted that unusual coin behavior as a sign—a hello and a hug from my dad.

Rainbows are another powerful and popular sign. A rainbow is essentially a refraction and dispersion of light energy, and the Other Side *loves* playing around with light energy. The appearance of rainbows, and even double rainbows, at perfectly timed moments is a sign our Teams of Light often choose to send.

But the Other Side is extremely clever and resourceful, so you might get a rainbow sign that has nothing to do with an actual rainbow. For example, if a rainbow is one of your signs, part of the secret language your loved one on the Other Side has chosen to use, then you may spot a rainbow decal on a car, or a rainbow printed on a paper bag, or an inflatable rainbow strung across a parking lot. The same is true of animals—instead of a flesh-and-blood deer, you might stumble across an illustration, or a tattoo, or a photo, at precisely the right moment. That's also where billboards, newspapers, and magazines come into play—they may contain images of the sign intended for you, and they will be shown to you at a time and in a way that makes it clear they are signs.

License plates and street signs also often turn up as signs. I believe this is because, when we drive, our minds shift into a sort of flow state that makes us more open. So it's a good time for the Other Side to reach us! Similarly, our teams also use music to communicate with us—through cellphones, iPads, car radios, stereos, even elevators.

They have a special talent for letting us hear the song we need to hear exactly when we need to hear it.

Numerical sequences are another common default sign. Consecutive numbers, birth dates, street addresses, telephone numbers, numbers that add up to a meaningful total—these can all be considered attempts by the Other Side to get our attention. Once again, these numbers often appear on electronic devices such as clocks, cellphones, and TVs, and sometimes also on license plates. This makes it easier for the Other Side to put meaningful numbers in front of us and alert us to the sign they are sending.

There are many other default signs—feathers, ladybugs, balloons, colors, clouds, pictures arriving in the mail, even people out in your path. Have you ever thought of someone you haven't seen in a long time, and a day later you turn a corner and there they are? The appearance of a default sign at an uncannily opportune moment is often referred to as synchronicity—a "meaningful coincidence," the occurrence of events that seem to have no causal relationship to each other, yet also seem to be meaningfully related.

I noted above that it was Carl Jung who coined the term *synchronicity*; Princeton University Press published his book *Synchronicity* in the mid-twentieth century. Uncanny phenomena have been studied ever since, with various terms used to describe events that defy easy, scientific explanation—such as *CMPEs* (Conjunction of Meaningfully Parallel Events), *simulpathity* (feeling someone else's pain from far away), and *supersynchronicities* (extreme cases of inexplicable connections between events). There is no scientific consensus about any of these events and experiences, but science has not closed the door on the possibility that these phenomena have meaning beyond what can be rationally explained.

I have heard about or experienced thousands of remarkable synchronicities. I have furthermore seen how drawing meaning from these events can change people's lives in very substantive ways. They are too important, too powerful, too *consequential* to simply shrug off or ignore.

So be aware of the many default signs our Teams of Light use to connect to us. Because even if we're not properly paying attention, the Other Side will keep sending them to us until we finally take note.

SIGNS DEFY THE ODDS

One good way to tell if an event or incident is a sign is to consider how unlikely it is. Seeing an elephant in a zoo, for instance, is a lot less surprising than seeing an elephant waltzing down Fifth Avenue. Things that are out of place, or out of season, or otherwise unusual in their timing or appearance are good candidates to be signs.

Our unconscious minds and our bodies will often alert us to these signs before our rational mind perceives them. We may have a physical reaction—a feeling of awe, wonder, or maybe chills running down our spine. We may experience a burst of emotion, a rush of joy, a reflexive smile or laugh.

And when that happens, we need to pause and search for the hidden connections between what just happened, or what we just saw, and the circumstances of our lives in that moment. If a beautiful wild horse runs alongside your car on a country road, maybe that is a message about freedom and self-empowerment. If you're debating whether or not to quit your job and open your own business at that very moment in your life, then maybe *that* is the hidden connection that gives special meaning to the wild horse.

Pay attention to the happenings in life that provoke an involuntary response in you. The Other Side is endlessly inventive and creative, and the members of our Teams of Light are, in a way, big show-offs. They *love* to dazzle us. And if they can knock our socks off, even better. If something happens that strikes you as totally odds-defying, chances are the Other Side has just worked its magic.

CONSIDER THE TIMING

Not every sign needs to be a showstopper. The tiniest, most common, least glamorous thing or being or event can also be a major sign. An ant can be a sign, or a cotton ball, or a button. Sometimes what's exceptional about a sign is not the sign itself, but its *timing*.

Your favorite pick-me-up song plays on the radio just when you're feeling especially down. The number 100 appears on your Starbucks receipt just when you're worrying about flunking a test. The answer to a crossword puzzle clue is randomly spoken by someone on TV just when you're about to give up on it. All of these simple, surprising occurrences can be signs from the Other Side, because their timing makes us feel connected to the world in a way we can't quite explain—as if all we have to do is release our feelings of fear and doubt into the universe, and the universe will respond with playful, wonderful reassurances.

And that, in fact, is exactly what happens! The universe is very responsive to our needs—the Other Side *knows* when we need to receive a sign. A bit later on, when we talk about asking the Other Side for specific signs, you'll see that timing is also important. But for now, even when we don't ask for signs, our Teams of Light know when we need them and will send them to us in small but powerful ways. So if the timing of an occurrence seems uncannily perfect, take note—the Other Side understands that timing is everything.

REPETITIONS

What if an event keeps happening over and over in our lives? What if we keep seeing a certain object or hearing a certain phrase time and time again? Are these just random occurrences, or are they something more?

One of the central truths about signs is that they don't always accomplish what they attempt to the first time around. So it's not uncommon for the Other Side to send us the same sign over and over again. Or it could be that the Other Side simply wants to reinforce the message or the greeting it is sending. Seeing a purple balloon sail past us once isn't much to get excited about. But seeing purple balloons everywhere—in the sky, on greeting cards, in advertisements—is kind of special. The point of a sign may be in the way it keeps repeating— *that* could be the method the Other Side is using to get our attention.

The repetitions could also be suggesting that we examine some unhealthy pattern in our lives that also keeps recurring. One of the primary functions of our Teams of Light is to help us learn the life lessons we need to keep ascending to a higher and better path. And if we don't learn them on our first opportunity, the Other Side will give us additional chances to learn them.

Perhaps we keep entering into toxic relationships, or we allow self-doubt to prevent us from being the brave, light-filled people we're meant to be. Maybe we keep listening to—and surrounding ourselves with—people who knock us down rather than lift us up. Repetitive signs can be directly linked to these issues—the purple balloon, for instance, might be the Other Side urging us to take flight—or they may be repeated prods urging us to examine an unhealthy pattern in our life.

So if something keeps happening to you—if the purple balloon just won't stop following you—pay attention. Your Team of Light is trying to tell you something.

WHAT WE LOVE, WE TAKE

The love we hold in our hearts on this earth does not disappear into nothingness when we cross—it travels with us and becomes a part of the massive, universal life force that is the collection of *all* of our love and light.

In the same way, our passions and our unique individual gifts and personality come with us, too. Someone who is an artist on earth will be an artist on the Other Side. Someone who was an incorrigible jokester here on earth will be the same once they cross. If we adored elephants when we were in our bodies, we will still adore them once our consciousness has transitioned out of our bodies and turned into pure light energy.

What we love, we take.

That is why, when looking for signs, we should be aware that our loved ones will often use the very things they loved or were good at here on earth as a way to connect with us. They do this because they still cherish these things, but also because they know we recognize them as things that were cherished by the soul that passed.

For example, if a loved one's favorite color was yellow, be on the lookout for signs that somehow involve yellow. If a loved one always rode around on a rusty red bike, keep an eye out for rusty red bikes. If a loved one's reaction to a sudden storm was to dance joyously in the rain, don't be surprised if you see an image of someone dancing in the rain on a day you're feeling down and discouraged.

Our loved ones on the Other Side send us signs designed to make us think of them. They do so to remind us that they are still connected to us in very real and powerful ways. The love that bound us here on earth continues to connect us after they've crossed. The interests we shared, the joys we had in common, the memories that make us laugh—these are all part of the ongoing and everlasting connection between us and the Other Side. They are all part of the vibrant cords of light that pass between all of us on earth, as well as between us and the Other Side. And they are tools our Teams of Light use to get our attention and steer us toward our highest path.

So if you see something or feel or hear something that reminds you of a loved one who has crossed, and makes you think of how much they mean to you, be ready to accept it as a friendly hello, a gentle reminder, a cosmic wink—an especially beautiful sign from the Other Side. And then say thank you to them in your mind, as a way to acknowledge to them that you received their message, and also to honor it.

DREAMS

The dream state is yet another way for our loved ones who have crossed to connect with us. It is not uncommon for us to have dreams that feature someone who has crossed. We can easily recognize them in our dreams, and when we wake up we can experience the same intense feelings of love we had for them when they were here. We can also interact through dreams with loved ones in ways that alter or advance our earthly relationships with them. Healing can often take place during dream visitations.

Dream visitations are a very real thing. As I've said, I believe we all have the capacity to experience the nonphysical, spiritual energy of souls that have crossed. But the cacophony of our busy lives overwhelms us and makes it quite difficult for a message to break through. It's like being stuck on a radio frequency that produces nothing but static. We are often hopelessly locked in the brain's frontal lobe, the control panel that handles our language and math skills and our analytical thinking—in short, all our cognitive skills.

Except, that is, when we're sleeping.

When we sleep, our brains go offline. We drift away from consciousness. The noise and the static quiet. Our brains shift in and out of the frontal lobe. We enter into something called slow-wave sleep, and beyond that, REM sleep—the deepest level of sleep, the state in which we dream. Ironically, our brains are nearly as active during REM sleep as they are during waking life, with remarkable bursts of electrical activity. REM is also the level when our bodies and our brains are most divorced from each other—our bodies are essentially paralyzed, leaving our brains to devote all their power to nonphysical experiences.

The brain scientist Jeff Tarrant explained that when I do readings, my brain literally shifts from a state of consciousness to something resembling deep meditation, or even unconsciousness—even though I am awake and alert and aware. That shift is very similar to what happens when we are all deeply asleep.

When we sleep, we can achieve a state where we can more readily experience the spiritual energy of people who are part of our lives, both on earth and on the Other Side. That is why these dreams often seem impossibly vivid, as if they are really happening.

I refer to these dreams as 3-D dreams, and I think of them as glimpses of the unseen reality of existence. The things that happen in these dreams are, in a way, really happening. We can meet with and get messages from our loved ones in dreams, and we can experience new facets of our relationships with them. What happens in these 3-D dreams most definitely matters to us. In a way, it's like getting a download from the universe, with extremely useful information we might otherwise have been too busy or too distracted to receive.

So pay attention to your vivid, 3-D dreams, to these visits from your loved ones, and to the signs and messages the sleeping brain so beautifully conveys. They are all part of our interconnectedness, and honoring them empowers us in a way few other things can.

INTUITIVE PULLS

There's a kind of sign you cannot see or hear but only feel deep inside—an intuitive pull.

We have these feelings all the time. We call them gut feelings or gut instincts, or a sixth sense—a guiding force that exists beyond our rational, logical mind. Turn left, not right. Walk down this street, not that one. Leave this place, the energy feels off. If I stay here, something bad could happen. Go say hello to that person over there because a wonderful connection awaits. We somehow understand things instantly, without consciously reasoning them through.

This is intuition. And those tugs we feel are intuitive pulls.

The energy behind these pulls is connected to a great gift of light, and to what I call God energy. It is the sweeping power of the universe steering us and intervening in our lives. It is our Team of Light on the Other Side strumming the brilliant cords of light that connect us all. And we need to remember that our gut will never steer us wrong. That is why it is so important for us to heed our intuitive pulls. Because when we heed them, we honor them.

And when we honor our endless connection to the God energy of the universe, all of the blessings of existence will flow more easily to us.

Intuitive pulls are the way the Other Side tries to protect us from wrong or harmful decisions on earth. Often these intuitive pulls are actually *counter*intuitive. For instance, we may believe we really want something, but at the same time experience a nagging hesitation. I read for a woman who was very successful in a prominent job and looked forward to advancing even higher in her company. But she also had the persistent feeling that she should leave the job and pursue a new path that excited her. It was completely counterintuitive to what she believed was her best course of action.

So she chose not to heed her intuitive pull and instead stayed at the job. Not much later, her company merged and a new co-worker maneuvered to take her position. She was let go.

It turned out to be a blessing in disguise. When she left the job, she embraced the wonderful, powerful new path she had been pulled to earlier—and her life opened up and transformed in ways she couldn't have imagined. Often, our intuition is one step ahead of us!

In fact, it can sometimes even save lives. I myself recently experienced three instances of this in quick succession.

The first episode was on a mundane Wednesday afternoon. I was out with my kids, running errands. Our destination was Target. As I pulled into the parking lot, I noticed a prime open parking spot close to the entrance. I turned down the aisle to claim the spot, but something made me slow down. I didn't have time to process why—I just stopped the car in front of the spot. "Mom, why are you stopping? What's going on?" my son asked from the backseat. "Aren't you going to park?" At the precise moment my son asked the question, a tiny girl, her black hair in pigtails, darted into the space. My kids gasped. I gasped. The little girl's mother gasped—she was in the spot facing us, struggling with her infant's car seat when her daughter ran away. Quickly, she grabbed the little girl by the hand and led her back to the car. The air around us felt still.

"Mom, what just happened?" my daughter asked. We were all shaken. If I hadn't stopped my car, if I had pulled into the spot at that exact moment, I would have driven straight into the little girl. I said a silent prayer to my Team of Light, thanking them for alerting me through my intuition, thanking them for helping me to avoid a tragedy that would have forever marked both our families.

One week later, I was driving home. As I rounded a corner, I suddenly slowed to a crawl. "Mom, what are you doing? Why are you stopping?" asked my daughter from the backseat.

"I don't know, I just have a feeling," I started to say. And with that, a basketball bounced in front of my car and a boy who looked to be about fourteen ran right after it—right in front of my car—oblivious to the oncoming traffic.

"OMG, Mom!" my daughter said. "That's crazy! It just happened again!"

"Yes," I told her, "that's why it's so important to pay attention to intuitive pulls and honor them. That's the Other Side watching out for us." In a way, I think the Other Side was also using these experiences to teach my children the importance of intuition. Again, I silently thanked my Team of Light.

The last occurrence took place just a few days later. My older daughter, Ashley, and I were in the car, and she sat beside me in the front seat. We were stopped at a traffic light. Ever since Ashley was little, we've played a game at stoplights. She watches for the light to turn green, and when it does, she says "Ping!" in a cute, high-pitched voice—which is my sign to go. On this particular day, the light turned green and Ashley said, "Ping!"—only I didn't go. Something stopped me. I had an instantaneous download that told me to stay put. So Ashley she said it again, louder—"Ping!"—and then, "Mom, why aren't you going?" At that very moment, a huge truck ran the red light and blew past us at fifty miles an hour. We were rattled—if I'd gone, there is no doubt the truck would have slammed into us. Ashley stared at me, openmouthed. We both took deep breaths. "That's why I didn't go," I said. I could feel it. Something inside told me to stay put. And I knew what that something was: my Team of Light.

Intuition is one of the great gifts we have as human beings. But it only works if we heed it. When we begin to look at intuitive pulls as evidence of our connection to a higher source of power, and we begin to honor them in a way that leads us to better decisions, we find our higher paths and attain more fulfilling happiness.

BLOCKED PATHS

There's the famous saying "Be careful what you wish for." The Other Side has taught me a version of this lesson—sometimes it's a blessing *not* to get what you want.

The Other Side tries very, very hard to steer us toward the right decision. Sometimes our Team of Light will even put obstacles in the way of us getting what we *think* we want.

We might, for instance, be constantly thwarted in our efforts to land a certain job, or make a certain move. If we are—if it seems the universe is determined to work against us—we should consider that there is a *reason* why we're not getting what we think we want: It's not actually in our best interest. It won't help us navigate to our best and highest life path.

Think of it as the Other Side staging an intervention. The Other Side wants to help us avoid pursuing something that will not bring us true fulfillment, or something that may lead us down a path of sadness and anger or even danger. If we keep trying to obtain something yet our attempts are blocked from every angle, and we can't figure out why, consider that it might not be the right path for us. Sometimes, surrendering it to the universe and moving on is the most powerful thing we can do—our highest and best path.

Blocked paths are one of the many ways the Other Side intervenes in our lives and tries to steer us in the right direction. This can be true with regard to the people brought into our paths, too. Some people are brought in as blessings, others as lessons—and sometimes, we are a lesson for someone else. Often, once a lesson is completed, the Other Side will shift a particular person away from our path. Understanding that and letting go of these people can be a very powerful tool to help us achieve our best and highest path. It also opens our energy to new and beautiful connections and lessons.

THINK BACKWARD

As hard as our Team of Light may try to hit us over the head with signs, we may not see or receive them. Despite how closely we are connected to the Other Side, there is a necessary difference between our existence on earth (as souls in physical bodies) and what happens to our energy afterward (when we leave our physical bodies behind). They're distinct steps in the journey of our souls. And so the process of communicating isn't always straightforward; it's elliptical. It can be a little like a cosmic Morse code.

And because it is, we are all going to miss a few signs sometimes. They might even be great signs—big, bold, unmistakable. But we'll walk right by them, or we'll be on the phone and not see them, or we'll see them but not really *see* them. That is going to happen. So if you're sitting there thinking, *I never get any signs*, I guarantee you— your Team of Light has been sending them to you. You've just missed them. Our Teams of Light understand this, and that's why they keep sending us signs, over and over, until we finally see them.

But there's a way we can help them out. We can *look backward*.

We can think about events that happened in our lives and look to see a discernible pattern—a cosmic thread of light and connection woven through them. In retrospect, we might be able to make connections we missed the first time around.

Ask yourself, "Did this happen to me before?" Ask, "What sign or moment of connection did I deny or put away on a shelf in my mind?" Ask, "Was there a miraculous occurrence that I maybe casually tossed away?" We can go back in our minds and turn a missed connection into a *made* connection.

Do not stand at my grave and weep
I am not there. I do not sleep.
I am a thousand winds that blow.
I am the diamond glints on snow.
I am the sunlight on ripened grain.
I am the gentle autumn rain.
When you awaken in the morning's hush
I am the swift uplifting rush
Of quiet birds in circled flight.
I am the soft stars that shine at night.
Do not stand at my grave and cry;
I am not there. I did not die.

—MARY ELIZABETH FRYE

PART TWO

CREATING YOUR OWN LANGUAGE

The universe is always speaking to us . . . sending us little messages, causing coincidences and serendipities, reminding us to stop, to look around, to believe in something else, something more.

—NANCY THAYER

IMAGINE YOU'RE IN A BUSY RESTAURANT, AND YOU
see someone you know across the room. You want to get their
attention, so you call out their name. Above the noise, they hear
their name and turn around. You both wave and smile and feel
good about your sweet little moment of connection.

What I'd like you to understand is that connecting with the
Other Side is just as simple as calling out a name in that restaurant.

Our teams on the Other Side are ready and eager for us to
acknowledge this connection. Yes, they send us signs, and
they're very good at it, but they still need us to engage with
them to expand the possibilities of communication by creating
new symbols of meaning—and strengthening the cords of light
between us.

This next section is filled with stories and insights that will
help *you* co-create your own unique and special language with
the Other Side. When you do, two amazing things will happen:
(1) You will find it much easier to receive the signs that can so
significantly affect and elevate your life, and (2) you will bring
tremendous *joy* not only into your own life, but also to your
Team of Light on the Other Side.

11

BRINGING IT HOME

Signs can transform us. Signs can take us from one state of being to another. They can take us from despair to hope, from lost to secure, from stuck to soaring. Think about what an awesome power this is! How many things in this world can be so utterly and positively transforming in such a short time? And all without a prescription!

But that's what signs do—they shine a light on the darkness and give us a new and more empowering way of seeing the world around us.

Signs give us meaning in moments when there seems to be no meaning to be found.

One of the most beautiful ways that signs can transform us has to do with the grief we feel when we lose someone we love. It's very easy for us to get stuck in our grief—to feel overwhelmingly sad and empty and lonely. But our loved ones on the Other Side do not want us to feel that way, so they send us signs that can transform our grief into something quite profound—the feeling that we continue to be, and will always be, connected to those we love, even after they cross to the Other Side.

That's not all. I have seen how individuals who had a hard time communicating with their loved ones here on earth *become much better communicators after they cross*. Which means that our relationships not only continue, but can also *improve*. Think of that! We can find new levels of closeness and contentment with our loved ones after they have crossed. We may even feel their love more purely than we did when they were here.

We can forgive old hurts and heal old wounds.

This is the extraordinary power of signs—and why I say that they have the potential to transform us.

I know this is true, because I experienced it myself not long ago.

A parent's passing is a profound loss, and it is one I experienced in 2016, when my father crossed. The question was, would being a psychic medium, and knowing all I've learned about the Other Side, help me in my own process of grief? I was about to be tested—everything I'd learned was about to be brought home.

My relationship with my father, John, was difficult. I loved him profusely and unconditionally, but he had a lot of issues. He drank too much, and he could become angry and isolated. When I was growing up, he would spend many weekend nights in the basement, playing his guitar. Of his three children, I was the one who'd creep downstairs to see him, drawn to the sounds of his electric guitar. My father loved to put music on and record himself playing and singing along to his favorite songs. That became something we did together. It became our thing. We sang and laughed and sang some more, until my mother would have to come down and fetch me for bed.

As the years went on, my dad drank more and grew more distant. After I moved out and went to college, I'd still call him often and visit when I could. But over time, the calls slowed down. Life got so busy. Days, then weeks, went by without us speaking.

Then one day, out of the blue, I got a very strong download from the Other Side: *Call your father.* That was it, just call him. And in the chaos of every day, I'd be on the go, doing chores and running errands, and forget to call him. I had a sense that there was a reason why the Other Side kept telling me to call my dad, but I pushed the feeling away.

Around that time, one of my father's golfing buddies called my mother.

"There's something wrong with John," he told her. "He doesn't look good."

My mother drove to my father's apartment (my parents were divorced, but remained friends). His friend was right—he looked awful. My mother took him to the doctor, who sent him straight to the hospital. But the doctors there were unable to determine what was wrong with him. They kept him overnight for observation, and I went to visit him the next day.

Walking into his hospital room, I could instantly tell that my father's life energy was off. It was diminishing. He wouldn't be coming out of the hospital. His soul was getting ready to cross. I stayed with my father for many hours, and even though his body was weak, his mind was still sharp. His topics of choice while lying in the hospital bed? French literature and the meaning of life.

As the hours passed, he became less and less coherent.

The doctors ran tests, but they couldn't figure out what was wrong. At this point, my father was no longer conscious or communicating. Even so, one nurse told us she was certain my father would rebound and be released, but that seemed totally wrong to me. My overriding thought, my *knowing*, was, *He's not getting out of this hospital. He is getting ready to cross.* Still, I hoped the nurse was right.

The very day after the nurse made her prediction, my father took a turn for the worse. His vital signs plunged. He was rushed to the intensive care unit and put on a ventilator. I was at home when this happened, taking a shower. As I was getting out of the shower, as often happens, the screen in my mind went on and my father's best friend appeared. I called him Uncle Nick and he had crossed a few years earlier. It was great to see him, and to see that he was positively gleeful. He said he was so happy and excited that he'd get to see my father again. Another of my dad's close friends, Uncle Lee, appeared on my screen, too, and he was just as joyful.

My father's old friends wanted me to know that they would be there to receive him as he crossed.

Just as they started to fade away, I wondered if they could tell me when my dad would be crossing, so I could prepare my family for that time. I asked them, *Wait! Can you tell me when my dad will cross?* A very specific answer came back: *This Thursday*. And then they disappeared. Thursday was four days away.

That same day, I had to appear at an event at a large theater on Long Island that had been scheduled months earlier. Hundreds of people had bought tickets, and I didn't want to disappoint them. Plus, now I knew that my father, who was no longer conscious, wasn't going to cross for four days. The manager of the theater, who knew my father was ill, said, "Are you sure you can do this? I know you want to be there when your father crosses."

"It's okay," I told him. "He is crossing Thursday."

That's how sure I was.

I called my brother and sister, who both live out of state, and told them that they needed to come see our father because he would be crossing on Thursday. That night, right after the show, I went to the hospital, and the nurse told me she felt my father was improving and might even be released soon. I told her I didn't think this was true, but she told me I was wrong.

"He's doing fine," she said. "He's going to recover."

The next day, my father's vital organs began to shut down. Tests came back showing there was no hope.

Because of the Other Side's message, we were all with him in the hospital that Thursday—my brother, my sister, my mother, my father's sister Ann, and me. His body was failing and he could no longer breathe without a respirator. The ammonia levels in his blood were sky-high. He was suffering. We all knew my father wouldn't

want his life to be artificially prolonged, so we made the painful decision to remove him from life support.

We took turns having a private moment with him, so that we could
all say our final words. I told my father how much I loved him and
how much I had always loved him, and how I forgave him for everything there was that might need forgiving, and how I understood how
hard he'd tried to do the right thing for his family. We all told him
that he was loved and that it was okay for him to let go.

But my father didn't let go.

The doctor told us that once the breathing tube was removed, my
father would probably cross within twenty minutes. My first thought
was, *Well, you don't know my dad. He's not going to go that easily.* We
all gathered around his bed, and my mother held his hand. My father's vital signs didn't change *at all*. We sat around his bed for the
next hour, and then two hours, but his condition remained the same.
Finally, we decided to do something to show him how much we
loved him—we sang to him.

My brother pulled out his iPhone and we played all my father's
favorite songs. We sang along to "Sloop John B" by the Beach Boys.
"Folsom Prison Blues" by Johnny Cash. "That'll Be the Day" by
Buddy Holly. Singing and listening to music with my father was one
of the ways we connected with him—maybe even the *best* way. We
all used to sing together as a family on long car rides. And now, once
again, we were singing as a family, and it was so loving and joyful.

We were singing my father home.

"You should play something by Elvis," my mother said. "Your dad
loves Elvis."

Almost in unison, my sister, brother, and I said, "He does?" None
of us could honestly remember my father ever listening to Elvis. So
instead we kept playing songs we remembered that he liked.

About an hour after my mother's Elvis suggestion, I got a text message from my friend Bobbi Allison. Bobbi is also a psychic medium,
and quite often we'll get messages for each other. That's the way it works
when psychic mediums become friends and hang out together—we
wind up in each other's business quite a bit. Bobbi knew my father

was dying, and she knew I was in the hospital with him that night. She also knew that the Other Side had told me he would cross that night. I figured the text would just be Bobbi sending her love.

"I know this is really odd," the text began, "but your father is coming to me. He is getting ready to leave his body, but he's not ready to go quite yet. He keeps giving me a song. I keep hearing this song. He is saying this song is a message to your mother."

It was amazing enough that my father would come through to Bobbi and give her a song precisely when we were all sitting around his bed singing to him. But Bobbi said it was a specific song, and I wanted to know what it was.

"Love Me Tender," she texted back. "The Elvis song."

"Play 'Love Me Tender'!" I nearly yelled at my brother. He put the song on, and I watched my father's face for any reaction.

I saw a single tear form in the corner of his left eye.

None of us children had shared an Elvis song with my father, but that wasn't the point. Elvis's songs were something he shared with my mother. Elvis was *their* thing.

"Mom, this is his message to you," I told my mother.

When the song ended, we were all quietly weeping. We'd witnessed such a powerful moment. Within a minute of the song ending, my father's vital signs began to crash. His heart rate, his breathing—everything—shifted. We laid our hands on him. His heart rate dropped to zero, spiked all the way to one hundred, then stopped altogether. With all of his family around him, touching him and enveloping him in love, my father crossed.

Elvis had been his last hurrah. It had been his final, breathing message of love for my mother—an affirmation that despite all of the hardships, he loved her deeply and always had. My father held on desperately until he could deliver this final message, and with Bobbi's help he did. Then he finally let go.

And in that beautiful moment, my father did something else, too. He established a sign he would use to communicate with us from the Other Side.

His sign would be Elvis.

———

He didn't wait long at all.

The morning after my father crossed, my mother, sister, brother, and I went to the funeral home to make all the necessary arrangements. It was a pretty difficult time for us all. Despite the miracle of my father's last gesture, and all the love we felt, losing him was terribly painful. We all had relationships with him that were unresolved in different ways, and that made the sense of loss even more profound. We all felt a certain sadness and emptiness. Our next task was to pick out flowers, but we decided that we'd all go to lunch first, just so we could catch our breath.

"Where should we go?" my mom asked.

"How about a diner," I suggested.

There were several other restaurants that were closer, but I felt strongly pulled to go to a diner, and to one diner in particular—the Dix Hills Diner. When we arrived, it was packed, as usual. We got the last parking spot in the lot. Inside, we expected to have a long wait for a table. Instead, the hostess came up and said, "We have one booth left, in the back. Would you like it?"

We smiled at our luck and followed the hostess to the one empty booth. We sat down and started talking about all the other things we needed to do. I went back to feeling sad and bereft, and I could tell my mom, brother, and sister did, too. The four of us sat in that booth with a terrible heaviness upon us. We shuffled the silverware and looked absently at menus and kept our heads down and fought off the tears.

And then I heard my sister say, "Oh wow. Look up."

My sister was pointing at the wall right above our booth, where there was a big, framed print called *Heaven's Diner*. It depicted a restaurant with three famous people in it. Marilyn Monroe. James Dean. And Elvis.

Elvis—just when we needed him the most! And in *Heaven's Diner*!

And instantly we were transformed. I could see it in the faces of my family. My father had shown us he was still with us. It was his way of saying, "I'm okay. I am here. Don't be sad for me. I love you all."

But my dad, who hadn't been the best communicator in life, didn't stop there. He wanted to make sure we all knew he was still with us.

One day later, my mother and sister were driving to a liquor store to get wine for the funeral reception. The liquor store happened to be my father's favorite one. Just as they were about to pull into the parking lot, a car screeched out in front of them and cut them off. They both got a good, clean look at the license plate:

Elvis4U

At the very same time my mom and sister were at the liquor store, I was in my kitchen directing my thoughts toward my father and having a little conversation with him. We had all wondered what my dad would need to do, karma-wise, to make up for how hard he'd been on my mother for so many years.

I don't know how you can fix it, I thought. *You'll have to do something dramatic, like make her win the lottery.*

Just then, miles away in the liquor store, my mother was checking out. Her purchases totaled ninety-seven dollars. She handed over a hundred-dollar bill, the cashier punched in $100 in cash, and the register, instead of showing the three dollars in change my mother was owed, showed that she should be given *eight million dollars*!

"Whoa, this has never happened before," the startled cashier said with a smile. "Well, I guess I have to give you eight million dollars now."

Everyone laughed, and when my mother got back to the car she called me to tell me about the Elvis license plate and what had happened with the cashier.

Then I told her about my conversation with Dad.

Maybe he didn't arrange it so my mother won an actual lottery. But, as best he could, he sent her eight million dollars anyway.

And he always had a sense of humor.

The day after the funeral, I had to fly out to California for scheduled work. During the flight, I was miserable. Everything still felt raw and painful. I buckled my seatbelt and sat there in a daze. The monitor on the seatback in front of me was on, and the screen showed a map of the United States. On the right side of the screen, it listed the songs being played on the music station it was tuned to "'50s on the 50."

As I stared at the screen, I noticed that the songs that were playing were all my father's favorites: Buddy Holly. Johnny Cash. Song after song he had loved. I looked around at all the other screens I could see, but none of them were tuned to this station.

I knew the songs were another sign from my father, and I thanked him for sending them to me. One of the last songs to come on was "The Battle of New Orleans" by Johnny Horton. It's an obscure song, but my father and I used to sing it together *all the time* when I was younger. I even remember my father singing to me when I was a toddler. Hearing it again brought back happy memories and filled my heart with love and peace.

"Dad, I'm really impressed," I told my father. "This was quite a display."

The plane started its descent, and just before we landed, the radio station played one last song.

"Don't Be Cruel," by Elvis.

After returning from California, I was back home for just one day before I had to fly out again to Florida, where I was volunteering for the annual conference of the Forever Family Foundation. My friend and fellow medium Joe Perreta was there. He knew my dad had crossed, but nothing more.

"Um, Laura," he said at one point, "I have a message for you from your father, but I don't really understand it. He's not expanding on it. He says just to tell you, to validate, that he was on the plane with you."

I laughed.

"I know he was," I said, and then I told Joe all about the songs.

Things had shifted. I felt an instant contentment, and an instant sense of connection, with my father. In a way, I felt closer to him than I could ever remember feeling when he was here on earth. And that was incredible!

"I hear you, Dad," I told him. "I'm okay. I understand. I know you are with me."

Three weeks later, I drove to the liquor store where my mother and sister had seen the Elvis license plate to pick up a bottle of wine. This time, I didn't see or hear anything that had to do with Elvis. Music played in the store, but it was all more recent songs. As I stood in line to pay, the song "Crazy Little Thing Called Love" by Queen came on.

In a too-loud voice, the cashier turned to his co-worker and blurted out, "Hey, is this song by Elvis?"

"Dude, what?" his friend said. "Why would you ask that? Everyone knows this is Queen."

"Oh yeah," the cashier said. "I knew that. I don't know why I thought it was Elvis."

But I did.

Even when my father couldn't send me an Elvis print or an Elvis license plate or an Elvis song, he found a way for me to hear the name Elvis. It was weird, unlikely, even embarrassing (for the cashier, that is), but it was also incredibly powerful.

Thanks, Dad, I thought.

I realized my father was a better communicator on the Other Side than he ever had been when he was here.

There were other signs beyond Elvis, songs from the 1950s, and eight million dollars.

The day after my father crossed, my mother texted me, asking if I thought my father's issues were all gone now that he was on the Other Side. As I texted back, I started to type "involved."

But my phone autocorrected and wrote the words back to her "I am okay."

Then there were the penguins.

My father loved all animals, and all things *National Geographic*. An hour or so after he crossed, just as I was about to leave the hospital, my friend Nancy D'Erasmo—who is also a psychic medium—texted me telling me my father was showing her penguins for me. She asked if penguins had any special significance, but I couldn't think of any at first. I told her I would remember the message and try to figure out what it meant.

Driving home from the hospital that night, I had a moment of what I call *knowing*.

I felt pulled to go home and look in the top drawer of my dresser. I understood that I had to look for a certain letter that was there—a letter from my dad. I don't know why that thought popped into my head. I didn't even know what the letter was about. All I knew was that I was drawn to that dresser drawer, and I had to look for that letter.

When I got home, I raced to my bedroom and pulled open the drawer. There were, in fact, two letters there. The first one was from 2010. Inside, my father told me how grateful he was to have me in his life, and how I had been a wonderful daughter to him. I sat down on the bed and started to cry. Then I looked at the next letter. I pulled it out of its envelope and gasped.

It was a Mother's Day card, and it showed two penguins—an adult penguin with its baby.

And suddenly I remembered my dad telling me how penguin fathers actively care for and protect their young, how good they are at taking care of their babies. Seeing the card brought it all back to me.

And inside the card, my father told me what a great mother I was, how I always kept my kids safe and warm and surrounded by love. I had saved the cards, and now they were back in my hands on the very night my father crossed.

My father sent me penguins.

It wouldn't be the last time, either.

Nine months after my father passed, I flew to Tokyo to appear on a Japanese TV program. To say that I was out of my comfort zone is an understatement. Although I was thrilled and honored to have been invited to appear on the show, I was a bit worried. I would be trying to deliver messages from the Other Side while wearing an earpiece and having a translator go back and forth with my statements to the sitters. While my prayer to the Other Side has always been, "Use me however I can be best used as a vehicle of love and healing in this world," I guess I never expected to be sent to Japan, jet-lagged and wearing an earpiece to share this message of love and healing through a translator. It felt like there had been some kind of cosmic mix-up.

Just before leaving for the studio, my husband, Garrett, who was traveling with me, assured me that everything would be okay.

"You are here for a reason," he said, "and it's going to be great."

I got to the TV studio, and the producers filled me in on what would happen. I'd be taken to a room that was designed to look like an office in New York. Then I would be beamed into the segment during the Japanese show—as a way of tricking the host and audience into thinking I was being Skyped in from the United States—before I was brought on set to everyone's surprise. I followed the producer to the room where they had set up the fake New York office.

As the producer walked me into the room, I said a little prayer that the Other Side would come through loud and clear, and I asked my Team of Light for support.

In the room, I noticed they had dragged in a generic bookcase as a prop for the office, and they'd put a few knickknacks on the shelves to give it a homey touch.

The knickknacks? They were all *little ceramic penguins*.

Okay, Dad, I said to myself. *I get it. You're here with me. It's going to be okay.*

My whole energy shifted. The show went really well. The Other Side came through loud and clear, and the translations were fluid. The penguins reminded me I wasn't alone. They were just what I needed at just the right time.

But my father wasn't done. Not only was he there to send me signs of support, he made sure to send me a message letting me know that he was proud of me. When I was finished with the show and got into a cab to go back to the hotel, something shiny on the floor of the cab caught my eye. I saw that it was an American dime. I had been randomly finding dimes ever since my father crossed, whenever I was having a hard time with his passing, or making a difficult decision, or just wanting to feel him around me. *Wow, Dad,* I thought. *An American dime on the floor of a cab in Japan! Well done.*

We should always be on the lookout for signs from our loved ones who have crossed. Signs that they are supporting us, being there for us, and loving us, just when we need them most. Could be penguins, could be Elvis, could be dimes—could be anything.

Our loved ones on the Other Side will always find a way to get through.

I could go on and on about all the signs my father keeps sending us.

For example, he loved anything that was made with lard, so we kept seeing things that had to do with, of all things, lard. I spotted someone wearing a T-shirt from a restaurant called The Larder when I was in Los Angeles. My brother, on a plane, saw that he was flying over a town called Manteca—Spanish for "lard"—and when the guy in the next seat got up to use the bathroom, he had a big tattoo on his arm that said, IN LARD WE TRUST.

Whenever one of us gets one of these signs, we text everyone else to let them know. These funny, joyful, loving texts bounce back and forth all the time, and each one brings us closer. I have not the slightest doubt that these signs are my father's way of reaching out to us and letting us know that he loves us and is watching over us. The truth is, after he crossed, it would have been easy to get stuck in my own sadness and miss these signs. But my father was so persistent, and so good at sending them, that I didn't miss them after all. And because I finally opened my heart to receiving them—I was transformed. I was lifted out of my crushing grief. I was able to connect with my father in a new and beautiful way.

Through signs, our loved ones can be much better communicators than they ever were on earth. My father has become the chattiest soul in the universe! In many very real ways, he is more present for me now than he was before. He is more loving. He is more attentive. He is more *responsive*. If I send my love for him out into the universe, he will bounce it right back to me, and more.

And if I ask him for help with something, or to send a sign to let me know that everything is okay, my father will respond in wonderful, magical ways.

My father helped me understand that we need to open our minds and our hearts fully to receiving these powerful messages. It was only when I went through the traumatic process of losing a parent myself that I truly realized how hard it was, and how important these signs could be—if we allowed them to sink in. From the Other Side, he became not only my protector but also my teacher. We were not done with each other. Our relationship continues to grow and evolve.

It wasn't too late for my father and me, because it never is.

It is never too late to heal and grow the relationships you have with your loved ones who have crossed.

12

1379

BRANDON Hugo lived in a small town in northern Iowa—so small, a sign on the border read: POPULATION 95, MORE OR LESS.

He was born on April Fools' Day, which turned out to be a fitting birthday, because Brandon could always make everyone laugh. "He loved practical jokes, but no one ever got mad at him," says his mother, Angela. "He was everyone's best friend, because he was so loving and sensitive and sincere." Brandon had a special magic that drew people to him—he was a good listener who helped you with your problems, a matchmaker who successfully set up several friends, and a peacemaker—the boy who was popular with both the Hicks *and* the Preps.

"He connected people," Angela says. "He bridged gaps. People gravitated to him and he brought them all together."

On the evening of January 31, just two months before Brandon's twenty-first birthday, he and a friend drove five miles out of town to check on a farm scale the friend was interested in buying. On the way back home, they stopped in a tiny bar in the middle of nowhere. "He wasn't old enough to get in, but he got in anyway," his mother says. "He was so responsible, as far as people drinking and driving was concerned, but that night he just decided to have a few drinks."

Brandon and his friends finally left the bar at two A.M. About that time, his mother was startled out of a sound sleep. "I didn't know why," she remembers. "I just had a strange feeling."

A few minutes later, the telephone rang.

Numbers give order to our lives—what time we get up, how much we weigh, our monthly budget. They are among the very first things we learn in life and they are signifiers of the most meaningful things in our day-to-day existence. Birthdays, anniversaries, lucky numbers—we tend to give numbers more meaning than statisticians and mathematicians will tell us they have. We might take note of numbers that *always* seem to come up when we randomly check on the time—6:31, 2:22, 11:47—or we might tend to spot the same sequence of numbers as we go about our lives. We're not alone in this.

St. Augustine of Hippo, around the year A.D. 400, established himself as an early proponent of the power of numbers. "Numbers are the Universal Language offered by the deity to humans as confirmation of the truth," he stated. The way we arrive at that truth, he believed, was by investigating the numbers that appear in our lives and discovering their secret meaning. Through the ages, numerology has suggested that numbers have mystical correlatives in our everyday lives.

In my experience, numbers are one of the most powerful tools used by the Other Side to communicate with us. The key, as St. Augustine of Hippo believed, is being open to the hidden power of numbers, and to their ability to reveal truths we might otherwise not see.

Brandon grew up a good country boy, working on the family farm. He loved getting under the hood and fixing engines, and he had several demolition derby cars in the workshop that he loved taking apart. In high school he was voted the Spring Week King, among many other achievements. He was a sports star, a volunteer fireman, and a mentor to his friend Bert. Bert idolized him and loved him like a brother.

That night at the bar, Brandon drank more than he should have. Bert had plans to look at some organically raised pigs with Brandon the next day, and he was worried that Brandon might be too hungover to keep the appointment. So he and another friend drove to the bar to make sure Brandon was okay.

At two A.M., when the bar closed, a neighbor agreed to drive Brandon and Bert home in his pickup truck. Unfortunately, that neighbor had also had too much to drink. Bert asked for the keys, but the neighbor refused to hand them over—nobody drove his truck but him. It was less than four miles from the bar to Brandon's home, but along the way the neighbor wanted to show them how fast his pickup truck could go. When he drove over a steep hill, he lost control of the vehicle.

He drove the pickup into a ditch, sped another 150 yards, hit a field drive, and rolled end-to-end until it came to a halt on its top. The driver had been thrown from the truck, and did not make it. Bert was badly hurt—broken pelvis, broken ribs, collapsed lungs—but managed to crawl out of the wreckage and call Brandon's mother.

"You have to come here," he told her in between gasps for breath. "The worst thing has happened."

Angela and her husband headed to the scene, not knowing if Brandon had been in the truck or not. When they arrived, there was no sign of their son. Firemen and sheriffs from other towns arrived, and Angela heard one of them say, "There's someone under the truck!" The firemen grabbed wooden posts and used them to lift the truck. Brandon's father went from fireman to fireman, asking, "Is it Brandon?"

It was Brandon, and he had crossed.

The crash itself hadn't damaged Brandon that much—he only had two broken ribs. But he'd been thrown backward and gotten stuck in the cab window, and with the weight of the truck on top of him, he suffocated.

More than five hundred people showed up for his visitation at the funeral home, and the next day seven hundred people packed the church for his funeral—the largest funeral ever held in the town. "Everyone was in tears," Angela says. "Grown men, people I didn't even know, they walked in crying. It was the hardest thing in the world to have to say goodbye to Brandon."

Bert was devastated. After the crash, he somehow made it all the way up to the top of a hill in a cornfield, something the first responders said seemed impossible, given his injuries. Bert believed that Brandon had helped him up the hill—and, in his grief, he began to believe that Brandon could still be alive. "He started leaving all these messages on Brandon's phone, about how he was going to find him," Angela says. Brandon's girlfriend, Lanae, knew his cellphone security code and listened to the voicemails. She grew concerned and told Brandon's parents about them.

Then Bert decided he wanted to erase the messages he'd left for Brandon so no one else could hear them. But he couldn't get into Brandon's phone without the security code—and no one knew the code except for Lanae. A week after the crash, Bert called Lanae and told her he knew the code.

"How do you know it?" she asked him.

"Well, I tried everything," Bert said. "His football number, basketball number, license plate, but nothing worked. Then I had a dream. Brandon and I were driving in a demolition car being chased by cops. It was like I was outside the car, looking at us driving. And then I noticed the number on the license plate, and when I woke up I knew it was the code."

"What was the number?" Lanae asked.

"1379."

She gasped.

1379 *was* Brandon's passcode.

Brandon's mother, Angela, had always believed in God and Jesus and the afterlife, and she, too, had had dreams that she believed were signs from above. So when she heard about Bert's dream, she didn't discount it.

The day after Bert had his dream, Angela took Brandon's teenage sister Lys to see a counselor. "We all needed guidance for how to cope with this loss and how to move on," Angela says. Afterward, they drove to Target to do some shopping.

Afterward, in the parking lot, Lys pointed at the ground.

"Mom, look!" she said.

There was a small, rectangular piece of hard white plastic, with four numbers on it printed in red: 1379.

"How in the world could it be possible?" Angela says. "Of all the parking lots in the world, we park in one where we find a piece of a sign with the exact numbers that Bert saw in his dream fourteen hours earlier? Four numbers that were Brandon's cellphone code? It was incredible."

On the ride home, the song "I Believe" by Diamond Rio played on the radio. Brandon loved Diamond Rio and had attended many of their concerts. "When 'I Believe' came on, that's when we knew that Brandon was still with us," Angela says.

Angela and I met a few months after Brandon crossed. She and her second husband, Martin, signed up for a grief retreat sponsored by the Forever Family Foundation. The first night, I addressed a group of around sixty participants about what I do and how I do it. More intimate gatherings of ten or so people, where I could really zero in on messages from the Other Side, were scheduled for the next night.

But that first night, soon after I started talking, someone pushed through. Actually, two souls pushed through. They were insistent. I was immediately drawn to where Angela was sitting with Martin. I looked at Angela and told her that her mother was very eager to talk with her.

But at the same time, I told her, "A young male is trying to push through, and he is saying he wants to be first. He is telling your mother, 'Sorry, it's my turn now.'"

Brandon told me to tell his mother that his favorite color was green, and that he still wanted her to paint his room green, as she'd promised to—even though he knew she wanted a different color. He also asked why Martin had the big Christmas tree, while he had the smaller one. "That was true," Angela says. "We had two Christmas trees in the family room, a big twelve-footer that Martin put up, and another small one on a cabinet. The smaller one was Brandon's tree. I'd bought it for him when he was little."

Then Brandon conveyed to me that he liked the tattoo.

"I didn't have any visible tattoos and neither did Martin," Angela says. "But then Martin got up and rolled up his sleeve, and showed me the tattoo he'd just gotten. He'd had the number 1379 tattooed on his arm in honor of Brandon. So Brandon was telling him he liked it and he approved."

"Hold on," I told Martin. "Brandon is also saying that you're thinking of getting another tattoo, this time on your butt?"

Martin turned red.

"We were joking about it just last night," he explained. "I told Angela I was going to get a tattoo that says YOUR NAME on my butt, just so I could bet people that 'I have your name tattooed on my butt,' and win."

"Well," I said, "Brandon wants you to know he thinks that's funny."

It was an amazing impromptu reading, with an incredible number of validations from Brandon to his mother. But in fact, Angela didn't need me to know her son was still around. She didn't need me to understand that Brandon was still joking, still laughing, still connecting people from the Other Side.

One afternoon, while Angela was cleaning her kitchen, she thought about Brandon and felt sad.

"Okay, kid," she said aloud, "Mama needs another sign."

Later that evening, Angela headed upstairs to the kitchen. When she hit the stairway, she heard the Bose radio playing a song. She hadn't remembered leaving it on.

"It was playing one of Brandon's favorite songs: 'See You on the Other Side' by Ozzy Osbourne," she recalls. "I knew it was Brandon. I asked him for a sign and he sent it to me right away. I thought, *How cool is this! Thanks, B, love you!* Then I just stood there on the stairs and listened to the lyrics of the song."

But I know I'll see you once more
When I see you, I'll see you on the other side

Thirteen years after Brandon passed, on the anniversary of his crossing, Angela was driving home at the end of a long day. "I'm always looking for signs, especially on his birthday and the anniversary of his death, and when something special is going on with his friends or family. But I hadn't noticed any signs that day."

Then, at a stoplight, she glanced at her trip odometer. It read 134.1 miles.

"I thought, well at least that's close to our number," she says. "I kept driving home and kind of kept my eye on the trip meter."

When she finally pulled up to her home, she stopped at the top of her driveway, by the mailbox.

The odometer read 137.8.

"Oh well," she thought, "that's *really* close."

Then she pulled into the driveway, opened the garage door, and rolled on in.

"When I finally stopped, I looked at the meter again," she says.

It read 137.9.

"I sat in the car for a while and said out loud, 'Good job, B! Love you too!'"

Life and death are one thread,
the same line viewed from
different sides.

13

GHOST CALLS

SUZANNAH Scully had a great job in the corporate world. She'd spent ten years learning the ropes, working hard, impressing people, and getting promotion after promotion. Her future looked impossibly bright. And then—she quit.

"People looked at me like I had three heads," Suzannah says. "I had achieved success, so why would I just throw that away?"

The answer was simple—curiosity.

Growing up in the Bay Area, Suzannah had lots of big questions—about life, death, everything. "The people around me were all very logical, practical thinkers," she says. "Meanwhile, I had this great curiosity, and no one could answer my questions."

When she got older, Suzannah finally found some of the answers in a book—*Journey of Souls* by Michael Newton, PhD. Newton, a master hypnotherapist, regressed twenty-nine subjects in time so he could access their memories of past lives. His book is about how people in a super-conscious state can describe in detail the journeys their souls have taken between lives here on earth.

"When I read that book, it was like someone pulling back the curtain for me," Suzannah says. "I remember reading it in bed and turning to my husband and saying, 'This book explains the whole meaning of life!'"

Suzannah read more books about the afterlife and our soul journeys, and began looking at the world in a different way. With her new perspective, she focused on how we choose to spend our time here on earth.

At work, Suzannah was the colleague others came to see with their problems. "They'd come into my office and close the door and tell me their hopes and dreams," she says. "I found that I really enjoyed talking to them and helping to steer them toward something more fulfilling." Somewhere along the line, Suzannah realized she could do the same thing for herself.

So she quit her job and became a life coach.

"My life changed tremendously," she says. "I woke up every day excited about what I was going to do. I was passionate about helping people make a major shift in their lives."

One of her most crucial skills as a life coach, she has found, is the ability to stay open to signs and messages. "We are trained to tap into our intuition," she explains. "As a life coach, I have to trust what I feel. So if something pops into my mind while I'm talking to someone about their lives, I've learned to follow that something, even if it feels kind of weird."

An example: Suzannah was in the middle of a session with a client when an awful screeching noise distracted her. "There was this crazy bird squawking and squealing outside my office window," she says. "It was like this bird was just complaining, complaining, complaining about something. I tried to ignore it, but then I just stopped the session and said, 'I'm sorry, but I have to pay attention to this bird—it's squawking like crazy.'"

Suddenly her client began to cry.

"She told me, 'Today is the seventh anniversary of my father passing away,'" Suzannah recalls. "She said that her father would have used the same word—*squawking*—to describe how much she was complaining right now."

That led to an important emotional breakthrough for the client. "And if I hadn't felt comfortable acknowledging the bird," Suzannah says, "the whole moment would have passed. Sometimes our bodies tell us things before our minds know it. So we have to stay open to signs and messages that are not obvious statements and words. When one of my clients says something and I get the chills, I know we're onto something really big. I just *know*. So I say, 'Stop. What you just said there. Let's talk about that.' And then I'll see the emotion on their faces."

A few years ago, Scott Dinsmore quit his Fortune 500 job, too.

Scott had read Suzannah's inspirational blog online and called her for advice. They realized they shared an interest in the road less taken, and quickly became friends. Not much later, Scott and his wife set out on a year-long journey around the world, visiting twenty cities before reaching Tanzania, where they would climb Mount Kilimanjaro.

On the sixth day of the eight-day climb, Scott and his wife were just two thousand feet below the nineteen-thousand-foot peak when they heard a cry from overhead. Someone was yelling, "Look out!"

A boulder the size of an SUV was hurtling down the mountain. Scott's wife dove for cover, but before Scott could move, the boulder struck him. No other climber suffered so much as a nick that day.

But Scott was killed.

He was just thirty-three years old.

"It was shattering when I got the call," Suzannah says. "I literally collapsed to the ground. It made no sense. How could someone so full of life, so in *love* with life, suddenly just not be here anymore?"

Scott's blogs about his journey, as well as a TED Talk he gave that had millions of views, made him a star in the world of inspiration and achievement. "He lived more in his thirty-three years than most people do in a lifetime," his father said. Two months after his passing, Scott's friends staged an event at San Francisco's Palace of Fine Arts to celebrate his life.

"That day was so much like Scott," says Suzannah. "Everyone got up and gave these incredibly inspiring speeches. It was a beautiful, joyous occasion celebrating Scott and his legacy."

When it was over, Suzannah returned to her car and checked her cellphone, which she'd had on silent for the ceremony. She saw there was one missed call from a number she didn't recognize, as well as one voicemail. She played back the message.

"Nobody talked or said anything," she says. "It was just fifteen seconds of the most beautiful, peaceful, ethereal music I'd ever heard. And then it just ended and there was nothing." Suzannah redialed the number, but a recording told her it had been disconnected.

In other words, the call seemed to come from nowhere.

"I knew immediately that it was a sign from Scott," she says. "I just knew it without a doubt. We had this very special connection, and we bonded over the fact that we both took unexpected paths. The music on the message was so soothing, and it lasted for just a little while and then it was over. Nothing like that had ever happened to me."

Since receiving that ghost call, Suzannah has occasionally seen missed calls from strange numbers on her phone, and when she's redialed the numbers they are always disconnected. "It only happens when my phone is on silent, so I don't hear the call and pick it up," she says. "I've never gotten another voicemail with music, but I do get a lot of missed calls from nonworking numbers. And I think, *Okay, there's Scott, saying hi.*"

Suzannah, who hosts a popular podcast, invited me on as a guest not too long ago. During our interview, she put her cellphone on silent. After we were done, she checked it and saw four missed calls, all from the same disconnected number. "It didn't even surprise me," she says. "Of course Scott tried to reach me while I was talking to a psychic medium."

Today Suzannah always talks to her clients about the importance of staying open to nonverbal signs and messages. Signs, she believes, will help you shift your life to a higher, more fulfilling path. Scott Dinsmore named the inspirational online movement he created Live Your Legend.

"That's what we're all trying to do," says Suzannah. "We feel called to something bigger in our lives. We might not know exactly what that is, but we can feel it in our bones."

14

BIRDS OF A FEATHER

CATHY Kudlack considered herself a very lucky woman. She and her husband, Frank, had been married for ten years and had three beautiful children. "Frank was a cop, and he had the driest sense of humor, and he made me laugh all the time," Cathy says. "He adored his kids and he was a great dad. I just loved him so much."

Then, tragically, Frank was diagnosed with cancer. He crossed two years later, at the age of thirty-nine.

Cathy never remarried—the loss was very hard for her to handle. "I could never find anyone quite like Frank," she says. "We always had an easy way of communicating with each other and I never wanted anyone but Frank to have a say in raising our children. So I just raised the kids by myself."

And yet, Cathy says, she often feels that she's not alone—that Frank is somehow still with her.

"I feel his presence," she says. "Sometimes it's just a feeling. Sometimes he finds a way to say hello."

One morning, while Cathy was getting ready to go to work and her daughter Jeanette—who lived with her—was putting her young children on the school bus, Cathy heard an awful racket outside.

"I walked outside and there was a bright-red cardinal sitting in my birch tree," she says. "And this bird was screaming. Just squawking about something. Jeanette came out and I said, 'Take a look at this bird, it's going nuts.' And you know, that birch tree—my husband planted it when it was a sapling."

Jeanette went back inside, but Cathy stayed out front and kept an eye on the crazy cardinal. The bird refused to leave—or to quiet down. It jumped from the tree to the mailbox, where it continued to complain. Then it jumped on Cathy's car and squawked some more. "It was just looking at me and making a lot of noise," Cathy says. "Finally I went inside to do some chores. I got the garbage and took it around back. And when I was in the backyard, the cardinal flew around the house and sat on the roof of the garage. Just looking at me and squawking.

"That's when I said, 'Okay, that's Frank. Who else could it be?'"

Later that day, when Cathy was at work, she happened to glance at a calendar. When she saw the date, she gasped.

"It was May thirteenth—the anniversary of Frank's death," she says. "This was twenty-nine years to the *day*. And out of nowhere this cardinal shows up and squawks at me for twenty minutes." What's more, the cardinal flew off at nine ten A.M., "which was the *exact* time of Frank's passing," Cathy says. "That's when I knew for sure that it was Frank."

Two years before he crossed, Frank took Cathy to visit a piece of property on Eagle Lake in Pennsylvania. "He already knew he was sick," Cathy says, "but he really wanted to buy the land. He said, 'I want to take my son fishing on this lake.' Did Frank like to fish? No. But he loved spending time with his son."

The Kudlacks bought the property, but before they were able to spend time there, Frank took a turn for the worse, and soon after he crossed. In the months and years that followed, Cathy would take the children there every weekend. "Frank wanted us all to be there together, as a family, and when I was there I really felt his presence," she says. "And when our kids grew up and had their kids, they brought them up to the lake, too. I think we all felt close to Frank there."

Their next-door neighbor on the lake, a wonderful man named Cliff, became a kind of surrogate father to Cathy's son, Frank Jr. "He taught him everything my husband would have taught him—how to fix things, how to paint, all the things you need to know when you own a home," Cathy says. "I think that was ultimately the purpose of our family being there. Even though Frank never knew Cliff, he wanted us there so Cliff could eventually be this wonderful mentor to our son."

After almost thirty years, when the kids stopped coming as often, Cathy started to think about selling the property. "But it was so hard. I was so torn," she says. "Frank wanted us to have this place—he wanted us to be a family there. And we were. I needed to know that Frank was okay with it."

It was right around this time that Cathy's daughter Jeanette reached out to me. She told me the story of the property on Eagle Lake, and how her mother had just made the painful decision to sell it, but was still uncertain if it was the right thing to do.

I connected with Cathy's husband, Frank, right away. He was very clear in his position.

"Your dad says to absolutely sell it," I texted back. "More than anything he wants things to be easier for your mom. So tell her to stop worrying. Also, your dad is joking and saying you can't get rid of him that easily anyway."

And besides, he wanted her to know, it was never the land tying him to the family. "It is the *love* that binds him to all of you," I conveyed to them. "Trust in that."

The next day, Cathy sent me a thank-you note in response.

"I'm looking forward to the next phase now," she wrote. "It feels so good to have the validation that our loved ones still support us. I believe that with all of my heart, but it's still wonderful to hear it from you."

I was moved by Cathy's heartfelt letter.

"I know you don't need me to know that your husband is around," I wrote her, "because you already feel him and he sends you signs and messages all the time. He wants you to be happy and to be open to all that is being brought to you in your next chapter in life—but he is saying that he will send you the sign of an eagle so that you know you have his blessing on the sale of the property."

What I didn't realize was that Frank had already sent the sign of the eagle.

I later learned from Cathy that the day before she'd reached a decision about selling the property, she decided to clean out one of the closets in her home. There were boxes and boxes of papers in it that hadn't been touched in years. Cathy reached deep into the closet and pulled out the first of many folders packed with documents.

"On the cover of this folder was a picture of a beautiful eagle," she says. "I had no idea this folder even existed."

Then it hit her: The property Frank bought for his family was on *Eagle* Lake.

"I thought it must be a sign," Cathy says. "That folder was hidden there for years and years, totally forgotten, and I pulled it out just when I needed Frank to send me a sign about the property. When I saw it, I felt it was him telling me, 'Okay, it's time to let it go.'"

On the day of the sale, Cathy was driving to the dentist with Jeanette. "All of a sudden Jeanette said, 'Mom, look at this!'" Cathy recalls. "There was an eagle flying right by our car window, almost close enough to reach out and touch."

After that, Cathy began seeing eagles everywhere.

"They'd fly over my head or be sitting on a branch where I could see them," she says. "And every time I saw one, it confirmed for me that, yes, Eagle Lake was our special place, and yes, we all felt close to Frank there. But the truth is, we don't need that place. Because Frank is *everywhere*."

Today Cathy talks to Frank all the time. "I'll say, 'How you doing today?' Or, 'Frank, I need your help with this.' And Frank always comes through, with either a sign or a thought or a word that pops in my head."

Although Cathy and her family no longer have Eagle Lake, they still get together. Last summer, Cathy joined her children on Montauk Point for the weekend. "Several of us took a walk by the lighthouse, and I remember it being very peaceful with the seagulls flying around us and the fresh smell of the ocean air. I also remember trying to stabilize myself on the rocks so I didn't fall into the ocean."

All of a sudden, Cathy's daughter noticed that one of the rocks near them had a name written on it. It was the only rock among thousands that had anything written on it at all.

The name written on it was Frank.

"At that moment, I thought about all the people who were walking along the shore with me—Frank's daughter; two of his grandkids, Kingston and Caleb; his sister Nancy; and his future daughter-in-law, Kim. And I knew that seeing that rock with his name on it was Frank's way of letting us know that he was with us there, too. There is not a single doubt in my mind about it."

No matter the method, Cathy is always ready to receive whatever message Frank is sending.

"Every single time, it brings a big smile to my face," she says. "Frank has a really easy time communicating with me. He always did. And he's still the same kidder he was, still looking out for us like he always did. It's very comforting knowing that Frank is still here. He visits me all the time, and that's just a really wonderful thing."

15

STREET SIGNS

MATTHEW Bittan was a bright, funny, outgoing boy with a huge personality and an uncommon curiosity about life. He would often surprise his parents with strange questions that revealed a mature thought process. One afternoon when he was eight years old, his mother was driving him to a store, and Matt grew quiet.

"You know, Mommy," he finally said, "I'm not sure I want to die before you."

His mom, Franciska, was startled. "Why would you say that?" she asked.

"Because I know that if I die before you do, you will die from heartbreak."

"Oh, honey, don't worry about that," Franciska assured him. "You don't need to think about that."

Matt never brought it up again. But Franciska always wondered if, somehow, Matt could feel it in his soul that he wasn't going to be here for very long.

———

Matt was two weeks past his twenty-fifth birthday when he overdosed on drugs and crossed. He'd been battling an addiction to painkillers for several years, but seemed to have finally freed himself from the struggle. He was optimistic about his future, more like his old self than he'd been for a while. But then he had a relapse while staying in a sober living facility in California. His unexpected crossing was a cruel and devastating shock.

"For a long time I felt so incredibly guilty about it," Fran says. "What if I had been stronger? What if I had seen the signs? What if I had raised him differently?"

After his crossing, Fran shuttered herself in her home for five weeks. She didn't want to face anyone, didn't want to talk about Matt with anyone, couldn't bear to resume her life. She was frozen in grief and despair. Finally a friend told her she needed to come to their local school to help stuff backpacks for children in need. Fran says, "I didn't want to do it. I didn't want to talk to anyone. I was afraid that if I opened my mouth, I would start bawling."

But her friend insisted, and Fran finally gave in.

Before she left for the school, however, she did one thing: She asked Matt to send her a sign.

She asked for a hamsa—a Jewish symbol comprising a five-fingered hand with an eye or Star of David in the palm. The symbol is commonly seen as a sign of protection against negative spiritual forces. It also signifies strength and blessings. "It's not something that you see everywhere, so I was afraid I was asking for something too specific, but I asked for it anyway," says Fran. "When I got to the gym of the school I looked around for it, but I didn't see it anywhere. I guess I was hoping I'd see it right away."

Fran spent the next two hours quietly stuffing backpacks with school supplies. "I didn't talk to anyone," she says. "I just packed the bags like a machine." Finally, an older woman approached her to say hello. They talked for a while, and suddenly Fran blurted out that her son had recently crossed. "It just came out—'my son died,'" she says.

"I even told her about how I asked Matt for a sign and hadn't seen the sign. I'd been looking for it everywhere and I hadn't seen it."

That is when the woman pointed toward one of the gym's walls, which was covered with signs put up by the students. The sign closest to Fran—basically right in front of her—had a distinctive symbol drawn on it.

A hamsa with the Star of David in the palm.

"I hadn't seen it," Fran says. "It was right there but I just missed it. And when I saw it, I said, 'Wow, Matthew, that was pretty impressive.'"

The hamsa in the gym struck Fran as an obvious sign from Matt, and yet no matter how much she wanted to believe it, there remained a part of her that questioned whether it was real or just coincidence. Still, driving home from the school, Fran felt as if something had shifted. Like she had flipped a switch, activating the connection. Fran hoped that maybe more signs would follow.

In the car, she punched her address into her navigation app. Fran was pretty certain she knew how to get home from the school, but she used the app just to be sure. Suddenly the computerized voice on the app was telling her to make a left turn. "It was so bizarre," she says. "Turning left would take me out of my way. I mean, really out of my way. It would put me on all these different streets I didn't need to be on. It didn't make any sense, but I made the left turn anyway."

The app steered her through an unfamiliar neighborhood before finally directing her down a dead-end street. When she pulled to a stop at the end of that road, the app inexplicably shut off. "It had never done that before," she says. "I didn't know what was going on."

Fran turned the car around and drove out of the dead end. Just as she was leaving it, she glanced up at a street sign and noticed the name of the unfamiliar street: MATTHEW'S WAY.

Fran stopped her car and sat there for a while. "I just thought, *Oh my God, is this a sign? I mean, it has to be a sign!*" she says. "Matthew's Way!"

———

Ever since, Fran has kept a notebook of the signs Matt has sent her. "He is extremely good at sending me signs," Fran says. "And when you get them, you want to keep getting them. But I didn't want to be greedy, so I basically got it down to asking Matthew for one sign a week. I ask for the hamsa or for his favorite song, 'Wonderwall.' And you know, that song comes on in the weirdest places."

A few months after Matt crossed, Fran attended an event where I read for some of the participants. When she came up to me, I immediately felt Matt's presence.

"Do you have a son who recently crossed?" I asked.

"Yes, I do," Fran said.

"Okay, well, he says he loves the fire pit, and he wants you to know he is there with you all the time."

Fran looked shocked. She explained that she had just recently built a fire pit in her backyard, because Matt loved sitting outside with his family, playing his guitar.

"He says he also likes that you're wearing his necklace," I told Fran.

No necklace was visible around Fran's neck. But when I said that, she reached inside her blouse and pulled out a chain with a beautiful Star of David at the end.

It was clear to both of us that Matt was excited about the connection that still existed between him and his mother.

Sure enough, Matt has kept busy sending Fran lots of different signs. She is always finding pennies on the ground that are from 1991—the year Matt was born. For a few consecutive days she kept waking up at precisely 5:30 A.M., but she couldn't figure out why. Then it dawned on her—Matt's birthday was May 30, 5/30. "As soon as I figured it out, I stopped waking up at that time," Fran says. "It was like Matt waited for me to interpret the sign before he stopped sending it to me."

Nine months after Matt crossed, Fran and a friend took a much-needed vacation. But as soon as she got there, Fran felt racked with guilt. "Matt loved to travel—he went to Australia and Thailand and all over," Fran says. "I know he would have wanted me to get out and see the world again, but still, I felt so guilty because he would have loved to have been there with us. So in my head, I asked him, *Please, send me a sign and let me know you're here with me.*"

Just then, a large man in swim trunks plopped down in the pool chair next to Fran. "I looked over at him, and there on his biceps was a giant tattoo of the Star of David, with the words I LOVE YOU MOM underneath it," Fran says. "The sign couldn't have been any clearer."

More than two years after his crossing, Fran still feels the enduring connection between them. When she wants to feel close to him, she sits by the fire pit out back, and some nights she can practically feel Matt sitting there with her, playing his guitar.

"It's about opening your mind and your heart to the idea that the relationship isn't over when they cross," Fran says. "I've heard about parents who lost a child ten years ago and they're still incapable of moving on, and I understand that, but I would want them to know that they need to find a way to create a new relationship with their child. That's what I am doing now—I am learning how to be in a new relationship with Matt. No matter how much I stomp and scream, I cannot physically bring Matt back to me. But I can find a new way to connect with him, and that's what I've been doing."

The signs that Matt sends Fran, she says, allow her to believe that he is okay. "And that makes it possible for me to live the life I know Matt would want for me."

This is love: to fly toward a secret sky, to cause a hundred veils to fall each moment. First to let go of life. Finally, to take a step without feet.

—RUMI

16

DANCING CANDLES

A NUMBER of years ago, I was getting my hair done at a salon I had never been to before on Long Island. The lovely man who was cutting my hair, Henry Bastos, did not know that I am a psychic medium, and I had no intention of telling him. But while I was sitting in his chair, I sensed someone pushing through for him. It wasn't a very strong signal, and I wondered if I should say anything at all. But it wouldn't go away. Finally I confessed that I was a psychic medium.

He wasn't particularly impressed. He wasn't much of a believer in those kinds of things, he told me. I explained to him how I received messages from the Other Side—and that we have to be open to receiving those messages in order for them to come through. Okay, Henry said, he would try to be open-minded about it. As soon as he expressed this, his grandfather, Hernan, was there with a message for him.

"He is showing me a pocketknife," I said. "It's a pocketknife in a leather pouch. He is saying that the person who has this knife believes they are responsible for his death. But they aren't, and they need to know it wasn't their fault."

Henry was incredulous. How could his grandfather, who'd crossed sixty years earlier, suddenly be there with us, sending us a message for someone else?

"Okay," he finally said, "let me call my mother in Costa Rica and ask her about a pocketknife."

I listened as Henry dialed his mother, Elizabeth, right then and there, and spoke to her in Spanish. When the call was done, Henry seemed upset.

"When I asked her about the knife, she said, 'How do you know about it?'" Henry said. She told him that Hernan had given his uncle Luis the pocketknife before he died. Luis long believed that because he wasn't home when Hernan had crossed, his death was Luis's fault. He carried that guilt for sixty years, until Hernan sent the message through Henry that he had crossed because of an illness, and there was nothing anyone could have done to save him.

Hernan had one more message for Henry.

"He wants me to tell you that he is doing fine, and that he is working every day to build a paradise for your grandmother, and it will be ready for her when she gets there. He wants her to know that they will be sitting on the porch together, enjoying the sunset. He's showing me an image of him cutting up an orange for her with a little knife."

Henry's face turned white, and his eyes started to well with tears. "My grandparents lived in a small house facing the beach, and they always sat together on the porch and looked at the sunset," he told me. "My grandfather would sit there with his little pocketknife and cut up slices of oranges for my grandmother. Everything was exactly how you are explaining it to me now."

Henry had always lived his life in a spiritual way, but now he became a believer in the beautiful cords of light that connect us all. "I understand that there is something waiting for us on the Other Side that is above and beyond what we see over here," he says. "Something that is even more beautiful than all of the beauty here. And that allows me to have a kind of closure about people in my life who are crossing to the Other Side."

One of those people was Henry's beloved grandmother Emma. "My mother worked really hard for the first fourteen years of my life, so I was raised mostly by my grandmother, whom I called Mami Emma," Henry says. "She was my confidante. She was the one who really paid attention to me."

When Henry was twenty, he left Costa Rica to pursue his dream of working in the fashion industry. It took him a while, but he managed to carve out a vibrant career for himself as a hairstylist. When I met him, his grandmother Emma was ninety-nine years old and in poor health.

Before Mami Emma crossed, Henry had promised that he would visit the site of the Miracle of the Lady of Fatima in Portugal and light a candle there in her honor.

"We believe that Our Lady of Fatima helps people heal internally and rehabilitate and not feel terrible pain anymore," says Henry. "My grandmother always told me to pray to her for help in keeping me on the right path."

After his grandmother crossed, Henry booked a flight to Portugal and traveled to Cova da Iria, where a small chapel had been built on the site of the miracle. Henry bought two small candles, then he went to the side of the chapel where people lit candles for loved ones. There were hundreds and hundreds of small candles there, and Henry found space where he could leave two more.

He lit the first one and offered a prayer for world peace, and for anyone around him who needed help and guidance.

"Then I lit the second candle," Henry says, "and I offered the candle to Fatima just for my grandmother. I said, 'Mami, I am here. I am fulfilling my promise to you. And I know that you are here with me right now.'"

There wasn't a breath of wind in the air. All the other candles had small, unflickering flames. But when Henry began talking to his grandmother, the flame on his candle began to flicker and grow, until it went from one inch to nearly ten inches high.

"This flame, I am telling you, this flame was stretching up to the sky and dancing from side to side," Henry says, still moved and surprised by what he witnessed. "I took a photo of it. You can see how high it is. The hundreds of other candles—nothing. But this candle, this flame, it was moving and dancing. And I began to cry, and I cried like I never cried before in my whole life."

Henry didn't want to leave. The flame was still jumping, and he was still crying, and his grandmother's presence was only getting stronger and stronger. "Finally I said, 'Mami, it is okay. This is not goodbye, it is till we meet again.' And when I said that, the flame slowly came down. And then it was like all the other candles. I know it makes no sense, but I have photos of it. Everyone there saw it. It really happened. It was the most unbelievable thing that ever happened to me in my life. It is something I will think about forever."

When I saw Henry after he returned from Portugal, he told me all about the miraculous flame. He showed me the photos, and sure enough the flame on Mami Emma's candle towered above all the others. I told him it wasn't unusual for our loved one on the Other Side to use natural firelight and candles to send us signs and messages. Air and light and wind and fire are all elements that the Other Side can manipulate. Lighting a candle as a way to communicate and connect with his grandmother gave her a great opportunity to send him a message in return.

So that became their sign—a flickering candle.

"It's not like every time I light a candle, I ask my grandmother to play tricks with it," Henry says. "But there are times when I really do need to feel her presence, and when I do I will light a candle, and she will always let me know that she is there."

After a dear friend of Henry's passed away from cancer, Henry was especially saddened because she hadn't made it to see his Christmas tree, as they had discussed. He was so full of grief that he had no motivation to put up his tree that year. Instead he sat in his living room and lit a small candle, and began to talking to his friend.

"I told her that I loved her and I missed her and I knew she was there with me, and then I looked at the candle," he says. "I was expecting it to start moving, but it didn't."

Then Henry sent a message to his grandmother.

"I said, 'Mami, I know you're here, so please let my friend know that I am going to put up my Christmas tree just for her.' And the candle went crazy. The flame started dancing. There were no windows open or anything like that. Everything was perfectly still. But the candle started dancing."

Henry doesn't talk about his candles with too many people, but whenever he lights a candle for his Mami Emma, and it flickers and dances in the windless air, Henry makes sure to mention it to me.

"It is something that is so personal to me and my belief," he says. "It brings me so much peace and so much closure. I feel like I understand how the Other Side works.

"Every time I get the sign, it is this beautiful message of hope and security and unity, of how we are all connected, how our families endure, and how we can always be there for each other in times of need."

17

TURTLES AND MERMAIDS

STEPHANIE Muirragui worked as a bartender in a Japanese restaurant in Florida. Everyone loved her—customers, co-workers, everyone. She was so popular that she was often asked to work double shifts, simply because she drew such a big crowd around the bar. In one twenty-day span, Steph worked more than 120 hours. "She was like a magnet," says her mother, Gio. "Everyone knew her, everyone gravitated to her. She worked so many hours it was like she never got to go home."

After a grueling fourteen-hour Saturday shift, Steph got in her car around two thirty A.M. to head home. She was tired, but also excited because it was her niece's first communion later that day. For some reason, most likely exhaustion, she neglected to buckle her seatbelt.

She fell asleep at the wheel and her car hit a tree. She crossed instantly. A police officer found her cellphone and called her mother, but Gio didn't hear it ring. The police came to her house, but Gio didn't hear the knock. An officer came back later that morning, and this time Gio answered the door.

"Can I come in?" he asked.

That's when Gio knew.

"Steph was such a beautiful person, so loving and caring and generous," Gio says. "She put everyone ahead of herself. So many people we didn't even know showed up at her funeral."

The grief was almost too much to bear. It all seemed so abrupt, so meaningless. "The only thing that helped was that we never stopped telling each other, 'I love you,'" Gio says. "We were so close, and we shared everything." On the morning of the last day they saw each other, Gio told her daughter to be careful.

"She looked at me and she said, 'LudaMom'—she called me LudaMom because I like the rapper Ludacris—'I'm okay, I'm going to be okay.' And that was the last conversation we ever had."

One month later, Steph's college diploma—she'd just completed a major in communications and a minor in marine biology—showed up in the family's mailbox, a sad reminder of a future that would not be.

"It made no sense," says Gio. "All of the love we had between us, and suddenly it all just disappears? Just like that? No. It's not possible. Love like that cannot just disappear."

I met Gio and her husband, Pat, a few months after Steph crossed, at an event sponsored by the Forever Family Foundation.

As the session began, something immediately drew me to where Gio was sitting. Someone was coming through for her, very clearly and forcefully. It was a woman. She shared the story of what had happened to her.

"She passed before her time, and she has regret about that," I relayed. "But she is happy. She is okay. She is telling me she chose your family."

Steph went on to explain what she meant by that. Her parents were both married before, and they each brought children into their marriage. "You brought three kids," I said, pointing first to Pat and then to Gio, "and you brought two. And early on, this caused problems."

Gio nodded. "Our marriage was very rocky in the beginning," she says. "It was a difficult adjustment for all of us, maybe like it is for most blended families. And then we had Stephanie, who came along at just the right time and brought us all together. Just like she always did."

"She was the glue that united her family," I told Gio at the reading, before Steph corrected me, and I corrected myself. "Actually, she is saying she wasn't the glue. *Love* was the glue."

Gio and Pat were crying now. They believed their daughter was there, assuring them she was okay. But like so many grieving parents, they needed more. They needed a way to connect with their loved one. They needed to know the connection between them was *still alive*.

But the thing is—Gio already knew.

She just didn't *know* she knew.

So her daughter, through me, reminded her.

"She is bringing up your necklace," I told Gio, who instinctively reached up and touched it. "She wants you to know that she loves it, and that it is tied to her."

Gio was taken aback. She knew that Steph had never seen the necklace. A friend gave it to Gio after Steph passed, in her honor. But Gio immediately understood *why* Steph brought up the necklace.

Ever since she was a little girl, Steph loved animals. *All* animals. "As an infant, she crawled around in the dirt and looked for insects," says Gio. "She was fearless and daring. She loved anything that was alive, though her favorite were turtles. We had all kinds of pets—dogs, cats, sugar gliders—but her favorite was a little turtle she called Pollo."

Steph loved turtles so much, that became her nickname—Turtle.

In high school, she worked as a caretaker in a dog rescue center. In college, she volunteered at the Loggerhead Marinelife Center—an organization in Florida devoted to turtle conservation. "Her dream was to make a life helping turtles and other creatures," says Gio.

A few weeks after Steph crossed, her family threw a party in her honor, on what would have been her thirtieth birthday. "Pat built this big aquarium with her name on it, and filled it with pink coral and angelfish, which she loved."

Around that time, Gio heard from one of Steph's friends. Steph had encouraged him to pursue a career in art. "He never believed in himself, but Steph pushed him to paint," says Gio. "When she passed, he started making these amazing paintings. He did them in her honor. He said he owed his career to her."

The paintings were all wonderful depictions of mermaids with Steph's beautiful face.

Not much later, a neighborhood group announced a fundraising sale that included a huge painting of a mermaid. "I bought it in Steph's memory," says Gio. "There was even a little turtle in it."

Gio would always buy little turtle figurines for Steph, and after she passed she continued to buy every turtle she saw. And, Gio says, "They just keep turning up."

Gio was desperate to find a way to connect with her daughter. She was searching for the key that would unlock all the love they shared when Steph was still alive. She just needed to find that one thing that would convince her Steph was still with her, and always would be, forever.

But what was it? What was that thing?

It was the most obvious thing in the world.

"When Laura Lynne said that Steph loved my necklace, it all made sense," Gio says. "It was just a simple black leather cord and a gold pendant. But inside the pendant was a silver turtle."

The love that we feel on earth comes with us when we cross. The love we have for one another, and the love we have for all the things we bonded with while we were here. In Steph's case, her passion for animals, and for turtles in particular, wasn't diminished by her crossing. And so now she would be using turtles as a way to connect with her mother.

Turtles would be their sign.

Deep down, Gio surely already knew this. Every time she saw a turtle figurine, or a turtle postcard, or a turtle T-shirt, she thought of her daughter. And in that moment of remembrance, Gio experienced the love all over again! The turtles made Gio feel like her daughter was still with her. Yes, the way they communicated was different now. But the love they felt for each other was as real and vital and *life affirming* as ever.

Everything came into sharp focus for Gio. Her daughter had been speaking to her all along! For example, she shared how, a few months after Steph's crossing, she decided to start going to church after work to pray for her daughter. Her local church wasn't open at that time of day, so she found another one, but it was much farther from her home. On the first evening there, she felt sad and out of place. "I was in this strange building and I didn't know anyone," she says. "It made me feel lost."

Just then, a woman walked into the church and sat in the pew directly in front of her. She was a nurse, still in her hospital scrubs. "I looked at her, and I noticed the pattern on her scrubs," says Gio. "They were turtles. Hundreds of turtles! The church wasn't that full and she could have sat anywhere, but she chose to sit right in front of me."

Gio instantly felt better. "It was the turtles," she says. "They were a message from Steph. And the message was, 'LudaMom, I'm doing okay. LudaMom, I'm still here.'"

I don't believe Gio needed her session with me to understand that turtles and mermaids would be the signs she shared with her lovely daughter. I believe she would have realized that on her own.

But I also believe that it was Stephanie who brought her mother into my path, so that she could speed up the process and let her mother know they were still connected in a powerful way. During our session, Steph came through with so many clear affirmations. She told Gio she loved her turtle necklace, but she also shared that she was amused to see her father wearing shoes, not sandals ("Of course that would make her laugh," Gio says). She loved the aquarium her father built for her, and the chocolate cake her mother got for her, and even the Chinese lanterns the family strung up for the party in the backyard.

"She was letting us know that she was at the party," Gio says.

In fact, Steph was letting her loved ones know that she would *always* be there with them, no matter where they were.

And even though Gio and Steph couldn't physically go on shopping trips together, or sit on the bed and talk for hours like they used to, they could still keep telling each other, "I love you"—just like they did when Steph was still on earth.

Except now, they would use turtles and mermaids instead of words.

If you could sense how important you are to the lives of those you meet; how important you can be to the people you may never even dream of. There is something of yourself that you leave at every meeting with another person.

—FRED ROGERS

18

THE CONNECTOR

I F you are reading these words right now, chances are that you have already saved someone's life, or will one day.

That's right: From what the Other Side has shown me, most of us have the opportunity to save at least one person's life, and possibly even more.

Our lives are all interconnected, and because of this, the things we do to and for one another have far-reaching consequences we don't always get to see (well, at least not until we cross to the Other Side and do our life review, which is when we see and understand *everything*). While we are here on earth, we each follow our own path through life, but our paths intersect with other people's paths, and theirs with ours. And these intersections are very meaningful—they are opportunities for us to play important roles in one another's lives, from offering support and guidance to, yes, saving a life.

What I've seen in my thousands of readings is that the Other Side uses these points of intersection to help steer us to our highest path. The Other Side also enlists people here on earth to be part of our

Teams of Light—people who help guide us toward those paths. I call these people light workers.

Light workers are the Other Side's foot soldiers on the ground, sleeves rolled up, making things happen. They are contracted—without even knowing it—to do the Other Side's work here on earth. They facilitate the flow of ideas and connections and signs among others, sometimes just by being in the right place at the right time, sometimes by bringing their unique skills and gifts to a certain situation. Just as the Other Side sends us all kinds of signs and messages, sometimes the Other Side sends these light workers into our lives.

Who are these light workers?

They are *us*.

Each of us has the potential to be a light worker. We can all be used by the Other Side to make things happen for others, and we often are, even if we're none the wiser about it.

There are some people, though, who seem to have an advanced ability to play this role. People who *always* seem to be in the right place at the right time to play a part for others. They function like old-time telephone operators, sitting at switchboards and slotting phone plugs into phone jacks and making connections happen! They are souls that have entered into a spiritual contract with the Other Side—unbeknownst to them—to do the Other Side's bidding.

They are what I call connectors.

Let me tell you about Jill, a friend who is one of the most magical connectors I know.

Jill is one of those special people who is very comfortable in her own skin. She is kind and quirky and funny and completely open to the world and all its possibilities. When she was twenty-five, she met an Indian guru and had a spiritual awakening. The guru gave her a meditation practice, and Jill went on to travel throughout India having experiences that challenged her notions of how the world works. "I felt my heart opening up and I felt the limits of time and space expanding," Jill says. "I was open to new dimensions of reality."

Eventually, Jill's friends began noticing that wonderfully strange things seemed to happen when they were with her.

For instance, one of her good friends recently lost her husband. Before he crossed, her friend's husband had been reading a book called *Just Kids* by the iconic singer Patti Smith. "So my friend decided that she wanted to meet Patti Smith," Jill says. "She believed meeting Patti Smith would be a sign from her husband."

Not too much later, they took an Amtrak train from D.C. to New York—it was her friend's first trip since her husband's passing. "All of a sudden she came up to me on the train, shaking," Jill remembers. "She said, 'Patti Smith is on this train.' I said, 'You're hallucinating.'"

But Patti Smith *was* on the train, and Jill and her friend got up the nerve to approach her. "I ended up explaining the whole story and told her, 'You are my friend's sign,'" Jill says. "And Patti Smith said, 'I am so happy to be her sign!'"

"I don't know why," Jill's friend told her, "but whenever we get together, signs come."

When another friend's father, who was a well-known actor, passed away, Jill was there to help her through the grieving process. "I noticed all these weird things started happening, with TVs and phones and electronics," Jill says. "I told Susie, 'This is your father's way of communicating with you.'"

Photos of her father that Susie hadn't taken began popping up on Susie's cellphone. When Susie and six friends gathered in her home to reminisce about her father, the windows inexplicably rattled whenever his name came up, then stopped when the conversation was about something else. The song "I Will Survive" kept playing on Susie's car radio. Her cellphone's autocorrect kept changing "does" to "dies" and the name "Alita" to "aorta," which made her think of her father, who died of a heart condition.

"All of this weird stuff just kept happening," Jill says. "I told her to start keeping a list, because this was her dad trying to connect."

Jill drove Susie to her father's funeral, but they got lost on the way back. They drove down unfamiliar streets and finally stopped so they could figure out where they were. They found a street sign—and the name of the street was Susie's father's last name.

"It was very comforting for us both," Jill says. "I'd say, 'You are getting these signs!' I just felt like I knew what they were, and when you know something, you know it. People can believe what they want, but beliefs don't matter as much as experiences do. And all of these things that were happening were direct experiences of connection. They were real."

Jill's friends began to describe her uncanny ability to make signs happen around her. They called it manifesting—as in, Jill manifested Patti Smith for her friend. Jill seems to invite vivid, powerful signs from the Other Side for those around her.

Jill's personal spiritual journey has changed the way she sees the world and made her an ideal accomplice for the Other Side. Her intense meditative experiences, she says, "have allowed me to have different kinds of relationships with people who have passed on. And because of that, I do not see death as an end. I always say, when a good friend is traveling somewhere far away and I feel sad that I can't physically interact with them, that I don't have their physical presence. And that's what I feel death is like. It's like the people we love aren't gone forever, they're just away somewhere far away. Like Thailand!"

Jill devotes a great deal of energy to activism and is a powerful champion for social justice, sustainable development, and education for all. As a friend of hers says, "Jill has tapped into her life's purpose, and through her work she lives in this sweet spot of being a connector, moving forces toward the greater good of humanity. She thrives in all of these worlds, and the connections between them come naturally and effortlessly for her. Synchronicity has become the currency of her life."

Here's just one example of how that synchronicity works:

Recently, Jill got a call from a friend involved with a human rights organization. The group had had a really challenging year financially, and they were struggling to meet their operating budget when an urgent humanitarian situation arose. The situation needed their immediate help. The friend asked Jill if she knew anyone who might be willing to step up to help them generate resources. Jill told her friend, "Let me see what I can do." And then, as Jill puts it, "I kind of sent the message out to the universe."

Within just a few hours, Jill got a phone call from a different friend who wanted to know what they could do to make an immediate impact and help children in need.

"As a matter of fact," Jill said, "I may have just the place."

Jill made the connection, and within just a couple of days an airplane was hurtling through the skies, delivering essential supplies to some very grateful children.

When I heard that story, I marveled at how quickly the universe used Jill to make something magical happen. She is a true light worker, contracted by the Other Side to make vital connections here on earth.

And yet, aside from her heightened sense of spirituality, Jill doesn't possess any superpower that is unique to her.

On the contrary, the abilities that make her such a powerful connector are abilities that we *all* possess.

Just as we can all receive signs and messages from our Teams of Light, we can all be connectors for the Other Side.

Sometimes—as is the case with Jill—we will be aware that we are serving as a kind of conduit for signs and messages. But many times, we won't be aware of it—it will just happen. All our paths extend beyond our own lives and intersect with other people's life paths, creating endless opportunities for us to play meaningful roles in the journeys of others. Our lives aren't just about us—*they are also about our connections to other people.*

We need to understand that we can meaningfully affect others' lives by simple gestures—a smile for a stranger can have far-ranging consequences. I recently read a story about a woman who stopped by a Dunkin' Donuts, saw a homeless man, bought him a cup of coffee, and sat and talked with him for five minutes. That was it—a cup of coffee and five minutes.

She then went to place an order to go, and as she was getting ready to leave, the homeless man pushed a small, crumpled note into her hand, then walked out. The note said he'd been planning to kill himself that day, but their brief conversation—a simple acknowledgment of his existence and his worth as a human being—had changed everything for him, and kept him alive. I have heard many, many other stories like that. Stories about how simple acts of kindness can have consequences far beyond what we can imagine. A smile, a word, a gesture, a gift, can change everything.

And, yes, they can save a life, if they haven't already.

We cross into one another's paths for different reasons. If we approach these moments of connection with open hearts and minds—with the understanding that what we say and do may have an exponentially larger impact on someone's life path than we can even know—we will better honor our roles as connectors for the Other Side.

It has been said that people cross our paths and enter our lives as either a blessing or a lesson. Often, it is both. Either they have something to teach us, or we have something to teach them, or, at best, we have something to teach each other. *That* is how this great chain of light and interconnection works.

And here is one of the most beautiful things about signs and messages: The Other Side *needs our help* to make them strong and powerful. Our Teams of Light need us to be aware and open and receptive, not just for our own signs, but also to help facilitate signs for other people. We are meant to live lives of interconnectedness—put simply, we are all in this together.

"We belong to each other," as Mother Teresa said.

My friend Jill is a remarkable expression of this. But the truth is that we can all be light workers and connectors. The universe is ready to use every one of us. We just have to be ready to join one another's Teams of Light.

Until one has loved an animal,
a part of one's soul remains unawakened.

—ANATOLE FRANCE

19

ALL CREATURES
GREAT AND SMALL

I'M often asked if our pets cross to the Other Side and if they, too, can send us signs. The answer to both is yes. The animals we loved so dearly here on earth are indeed on the Other Side. And once they're there, they can—and do—send us amazing signs.

I have encountered pets in hundreds of readings, and they always appear as happy bundles of light and energy. While they're with us, they are our teachers, sharing profound lessons about unconditional love—lessons they are uniquely suited to teach. And when they cross, they remain connected to us in real and powerful ways, providing hope and comfort and support and, of course, everlasting love.

It may seem strange, but animals can actually be better at sending signs than humans. Why? Because they are beautifully unspoiled. They are unfettered by analytical thinking, so they remain free to engage in the energy of our connection to them—as infants do, before their logical brains kick in.

Because of this innocence and freedom, animals are keenly perceptive to the flow of energy in our universe. The Other Side has taught me that we see only about 15 percent of what is around us here on earth. The rest is unseen energy and light connections. Animals, however, can see much more than just 15 percent. For instance, animals have been known to react days before earthquakes and other natural disasters. Think about it—have you ever noticed your dog or your cat suddenly sit straight up and react to some imaginary noise or event? As if they saw or heard something you didn't? Chances are, they reacted to something very real.

Animals can also sense and see the energy of spirits visiting us on earth.

Not long ago, I read for a woman who had recently and tragically lost her son. In our reading, her son came through and had me tell his mother that the reason their dog acted crazy the day before was because the dog had seen him—or rather, had seen his spirit.

"Oh my God," the woman said. "That happened. That really happened. The dog went absolutely crazy, and we were all like, 'What in the world is the matter with the dog?' We actually wondered aloud if maybe he was seeing or sensing our son visiting us."

Our pets, it turns out, are pretty good at picking up on spirit activity while here—and communicating with, and sending signs from, the Other Side.

One of my former students, Melissa, texted me a story about her beloved dog, Heidi, who lived for twenty-one (yes, twenty-one!) wonderful years. Heidi was a rescue who was playful and loving and liked chasing butterflies. Her crossing was devastating for Melissa. She had been part of so much of Melissa's life journey. Melissa missed Heidi so much that the idea of getting another dog was something she couldn't even entertain.

Two years after Heidi's crossing, Melissa checked her Facebook page and received an important event reminder. That day would have been Heidi's twenty-third birthday. While remembering Heidi, and celebrating her love for her, a beautiful thought formed in Melissa's mind: It might finally be a good time to rescue another dog.

That day, Melissa downloaded an application from a dog rescue organization and took it with her to her job as a lifeguard. "Just as I was filling it out," she says, "a butterfly flew right over my head and danced around. I always connect butterflies to Heidi."

Because Melissa was open to messages from the Other Side, she knew what the butterfly meant. It was a sign from Heidi, giving her a blessing, celebrating with her, and affirming that she was doing the right thing in rescuing another dog. Melissa went on to adopt a new dog, and since then, her life—and the dog's—has been meaningfully enriched.

This is one of the most important tasks our beloved pets on the Other Side undertake—they help us relinquish any guilt we may feel about their loss, and steer us toward decisions that will make us happy and expand our experience of love in the here and now—specifically the decision to get another pet. Just like all our loved ones who cross, our animals on the Other Side want us to be happy.

So if you are facing that situation and wondering if you should get another animal, don't be afraid to ask your pet on the Other Side for a sign.

My mother's connections to the many dogs she has loved over the course of her life are strong, too. Their presence remains in her life long after they have crossed. Lightning was a tiny toy fox terrier— a totally adorable black, white, and tan little guy with crooked legs and inexhaustible energy. My brother had picked him out to be his own dog, but Lightning attached himself to my mom.

"He just decided that I was his person," she says.

My mother brought Lightning on a family vacation to Lake George. She wanted to take a boat out on the lake, so she put Lightning in a second-floor bedroom and closed the door. I was sitting outside on the porch when I saw a dark shape suddenly drop out of the sky and dart across the lawn. It was Lightning! He had jumped out the window and off the balcony and dashed through a meadow, just to get to my mom on the lake.

Another time, my mother left Lightning with a dogsitter whose backyard was enclosed by a six-foot-tall fence. No one thought Lightning could scale a six-foot fence, but of course he did, and he ran away in search of my mother. Since my mother was hours away, my aunt (who is psychic, too) left work to search for the dog. She was drawn to the harbor in Huntington and sure enough saw Lightning walking along the water. She opened her car door and called to Lightning, and he jumped right in.

Lightning lived a long and active life before he crossed. By then, my mother had gotten a second dog—a big Lab named Cassie. Lightning had always slept at the foot of my mother's bed, while Cassie slept in a dog bed on the floor. At bedtime, Lightning would jump into Cassie's bed, and Cassie would look at my mother as if to say, *You see? You see how Lightning is messing with me?* My mother would shoo Lightning out of Cassie's bed, and Lightning would jump up on the bed and settle down to sleep.

The night Lightning crossed, at bedtime, Cassie went into my mother's room but refused to get into her dog bed. "She was clearly agitated," my mother recalls. "I said, 'What's the matter? Lightning's not here, you can go to sleep,' but Cassie just kept looking at me and looking back at her bed with distress in her eyes. She was eighty-five pounds with short legs, and she could never jump high enough to get in my bed, but that night she somehow managed to leap onto my bed rather than go anywhere near her own. She looked spooked. I couldn't see anything, but something had really unnerved her."

Was it Lightning, still teasing her from the Other Side?

The day after Lightning passed, my mother got out of the shower and heard little whimpering sounds on the other side of the bathroom door. Lightning, she remembered, used to stand outside the bathroom and whine until she came out. But Lightning was gone, so who was making these sounds? "I know Lightning's noises," my mother says. "I know all his sounds. And these sounded like him. But of course when I came out of the bathroom, no one was there."

Several months after Lightning crossed, my mother got a new dog, a Chihuahua-poodle mix named Dobby. Dobby slept at the corner end of the bed, in the very spot where Lightning used to sleep. "In the middle of the night I moved my foot and without realizing it, must have accidentally hit Dobby, because I heard her jump off the bed. 'Dobby,' I called, 'come back up, I'm sorry,' but I heard nothing." She knew that Dobby liked to hide underneath the bed if she felt threatened, so she figured that was where she had gone.

My mother tried to go back to sleep. When she stretched out, her foot hit something heavy. She was puzzled—had she left a book on her bed? She reached down to feel what was there, and it was Dobby, fast asleep! She was a little unnerved. "I know I'm not crazy, but I also know that I heard a little dog jump to the floor from my bed. How many times had I heard that familiar noise over the years with Lightning? I lay back down—and then I heard little doggy footsteps going down the creaky floor of the hall—I really did!"

My mother is very open to signs and messages, too, and it didn't take her long to figure out what had happened.

"It was Lightning," she says. "He was trying to tell me that he was still around. And he didn't stop until I finally figured it out. And once I did, the noises all stopped."

A few weeks later, my mother was visiting my sister at her house in New Jersey. As she arrived, she accidentally dropped Dobby's leash and Dobby took off. Dobby was a rescue dog, very insecure and very scared of people. She had never been to this area, so she would not know how to get back to the house even if she wanted to. My mother and sister and a few neighbors searched and searched for her for two days, but couldn't find her. Even worse, it was the dead of winter. After two days, my mother knew she'd have no choice but to go back home to New York because she had to go to work. She was frantic.

"I was heartbroken," she says. "I was driving around, looking for Dobby and crying. I said, 'Please, Lightning, you got lost twice and somehow we found you—and each time it felt like a miracle. Now I need one more little miracle. Please help us find Dobby."

Two hours later, there was a knock at my sister's door—a neighbor who was a runner thought she had spotted a little dog in the nearby woods. She stayed in that spot and called her husband on her cell-phone, and he came and got my mom and sister. They all drove to the woods and started searching. But there was no dog in sight. Dobby was little, very insecure, and liked to hide—and her tawny color would camouflage her. Suddenly, out of the corner of his eye, the man spotted what looked like a little dog swimming toward a tiny is-land in the middle of a pond. Then the dog seemed to disappear. But she had to be there! The neighbor and my mom managed to balance on several fallen logs, making their way to the tiny island. And there, hiding deep in the underbrush, they found shaking, cold, wet Dobby. "She was shivering and freezing—who knows what would have hap-pened if we hadn't found her," my mom said. "And she was so com-pletely hidden that finding her truly was a miracle."

My mom knew Lightning had answered her plea for help. "Light-ning helped bring me my miracle. He helped me find Dobby."

When our pets cross, they want to let us know that they are okay. If they were infirm or in pain and suffering at the end of their time on earth, they want to let us know that they are now pain-free and once again frolicking and jumping and running. And when they cross, they want us stop doubting ourselves or feeling misplaced guilt. Our pets know that every decision we made was made with their best in-terest at heart. They know we did everything in our power to make their crossing as comfortable as possible. They want to assuage our grief and heal our broken hearts. And the way they do this is by letting us know they're still with us.

I've also learned that when it is our time to cross, our pets are often the first ones to come bounding and leaping and fluttering up to greet us. I've seen it time and time again during my readings.

My friend and fellow psychic medium Joanne Gerber recently shared a story about her beloved dog, Louis. Louis was a West High-land white terrier, and he was central to Joanne's life. I had become accustomed to, and looked forward to, all the adorable pictures of

Louis that Joanne posted on her Facebook page. So I was very upset when I read about Louis's diagnosis of a brain tumor, and his crossing four months later.

Louis's crossing was devastating for Joanne, but in the weeks and months that followed, she reported that Louis had come to her several times and showed her that he is happy, mobile, and pain-free.

One night, just a few weeks after Louis's crossing, Joanne was in a horrible three-car accident on Highway 90 in Connecticut. The car in front of her suddenly hit the brakes, and Joanne swerved to avoid a crash. Her car spun out on the black ice into three lanes of oncoming traffic. One car sideswiped her, then a tractor trailer hit her on the passenger side, and her car crashed into a meridian barrier. The airbags deployed, but Joanne remained conscious. She kicked the door open and crawled out onto the snow. Miraculously, she only suffered cuts and bruises.

First responders helped clear the scene of the accident, and a tow truck driver arrived to remove Joanne's mangled car and drive her home. The driver was about to load the rear bumper, which had come off, into the backseat of Joanne's car when he abruptly stopped and asked her if she had a small dog in the back of the car . . . because he thought he saw a small white animal there.

But there was no animal in the car.

Immediately, Joanne knew—it was *Louis*!

"I know that I had angels protecting me," she wrote of that night, "and Louis was one of them."

Joanne's story stunningly illustrates that our pets never stop trying to protect us and make us happy. The unconditional love is still there. Our connections to them remain strong. They will try anything to let us know they're still with us. And if we need a miracle, they might just fetch one, too.

I am quite confident that the most important part of a human being is not his physical body but his nonphysical essence, which some people call soul . . . The nonphysical part cannot die and cannot decay because it's not physical.

—RABBI HAROLD KUSHNER

20

———

GROUNDHOGS

I MET Julie, my editor, not long after she acquired my first book. I came to her office in Midtown Manhattan prepared to read for her, but she quickly told me that she didn't want the reading that day. "I'm already a believer," she told me, "so you don't have to read me to convince me." But my literary agent was there, too, and she insisted that Julie should have a reading with me. Julie reluctantly agreed—but I could tell there was a reason why she initially resisted, though I didn't press her.

We settled in and got started. Somewhere around the middle of the reading, Julie's father came through. I told her he was there with a dog.

"He is showing me a peach," I told her. "I'm not sure what I'm supposed to say about this peach, but that's what he's showing me. I don't know—maybe Georgia? Like a Georgia peach?"

Julie got visibly emotional.

"Georgie Girl," she said. "That's my childhood dog."

Julie's father told me he had information about a different dog. He even gave me the dog's name—Alfie.

"Your father wants you to know you made the right decision about Alfie," I relayed. Then I hesitated for a moment and clasped my hands together. "You know what I'm going to say . . . but your dad wants you to know that you did the right thing. You bought him a good chunk of time, but when it's his time, your father and Georgie Girl will be there waiting for him."

At this point, Julie was a weeping mess. Julie's dog, a fifteen-year-old Tibetan terrier named Alfie, had had risky surgery just a few days earlier. That's why she was initially resisting the reading with me that day. She was raw—and worried about opening the emotional floodgates. And of course she was worried about what she might learn about Alfie's health in the reading.

Her dad's message proved true. The surgery had turned back the clock for Alfie, who recovered quickly and regained his youth and vigor. In fact, he lived a good life for two more years, but then his health began to decline.

So Julie took him to the downtown vet who'd known him since he was a puppy. "I wanted to know if Alfie was in pain and if I was being selfish in keeping him alive," she later told me. She sat in the waiting room with a heavy heart, with Alfie lying at her feet. While there, her eye was drawn to the lost dog flyers posted on a bulletin board on the wall across from her. She got out of her seat and went directly to one poster, for a missing Shiba Inu. "I had the thought, *I wonder where this dog was last seen,* and traced my finger across to that information. The address was the building where my mother had grown up in Brooklyn." Julie texted a photo of the flyer to her sister. "Check out the address," she wrote. Her sister responded, "Incredible—right down to the apartment number!" Julie hadn't even noticed that detail—#1A, the very apartment where her grandparents had lived for nearly fifty years. When Julie was a little girl and the family would visit her grandparents, Georgie Girl would bolt out of the car, run up the steps of the building, make a left, and sit outside the apartment door with her little tail wagging.

"I understood it immediately," Julie later told me. "I was there at the vet because I knew we were reaching the end, and here was an unmistakable sign that echoed what you had told me in our reading. When it was time for Alfie to cross, Georgie Girl, my father, and even my grandparents would be there to receive him."

Now that a channel of communication had been opened between Julie and her father, he would push through occasionally when we had a meeting or a scheduled call. One day, we were on the phone, discussing the upcoming publication of my first book. At the end of the call, I asked her, "Is today some kind of special day? Your dad has been hanging around me today and he's saying there's going to be some sort of celebration, a party?"

Julie paused—I could tell she needed a moment. "Today is my father's birthday," she said. "February second, Groundhog Day."

Julie had a special relationship with her father, who had crossed over some twelve years earlier. "I was his sidekick, his wingman," she explains. "His business was not far from my school, so every day he would drive me to and from school. We got to spend all of this time together, morning and evening. He was solid as a rock—hardworking, reliable, energetic, always in motion. He was as handsome as a movie star, and all his customers adored him."

Julie was in her thirties when her father passed after a long illness. "He never complained; he had such grace. It was like his soul underwent a kind of burnishing, and he found a deep contentment with his life. It was terrible to see this man who'd been so athletic and capable become physically constricted. But what was beautiful about him before his illness became even more beautiful."

A few months after our Groundhog Day call, Julie was at her weekend home in a rural part of Long Island. It was Father's Day, which in the years since her father's passing had become a day that brought up bittersweet feelings. She was doing dishes, looking out the window across the yard toward a farm that is adjacent to the property. Suddenly in her peripheral vision, she spotted a small brown creature emerge from a wooded area and pause in the middle of the yard.

"Come in here and look at this," she called out to her husband and son in the next room. "What is that? A weird-looking cat? Is it a beaver?"

"It looks like a groundhog . . . maybe?" her husband said.

"Google it—what does a groundhog look like, anyway?"

Her son googled it and pulled up a photo of a groundhog sitting up on its hind legs. "Yep, that's it." They looked back to the groundhog in the yard, who'd obliged and struck the exact same pose as the groundhog in the photo.

"Oh my God," she said. "It's Father's Day."

A few months later, a friend from college was visiting Julie and her family for the weekend, and she told him the story of the Father's Day groundhog sighting. She added that I encouraged people to ask for signs from the Other Side—her friend had lost his father years earlier, too—and not to worry about it being too specific; the Other Side can handle specific. While she talked, Julie gazed out her kitchen window, half hoping the groundhog would miraculously appear again. But, she thought, that would be too much to ask.

She went upstairs to make the beds and looked out the window. Two cardinals, a couple, were sitting on a branch directly in her line of sight.

"I'd see them around from time to time," she says. "I called them Mr. and Mrs. Cardinal. They reminded me of my grandparents, who were married for fifty-four years. I acknowledged them and said—out loud, because no one was around—'I'm so happy to see you two, I'm always happy to see you, but today, you know what I would really love? I'd love to see the groundhog again.'"

Julie finished making the beds, walked back downstairs, and went to clean up the breakfast dishes. She stood at the sink and looked out the window. The groundhog was there, waiting for her.

She was afraid to move. She stood stock-still, watching the groundhog make its way across the yard, taking its time, until it disappeared into the bushes.

Though she was a believer, as she'd told me in our first meeting, after the second groundhog sighting Julie was reluctant to ask for her sign on demand—she was afraid the groundhog might be a no-show and she'd be disappointed. But over a year later, after coming through a difficult time, she thought, *I wish I knew that my father was with me now that I've made it through.*

Later that day, she went out for a run on a wooded country road. On her way back, she saw a small, brown creature amble across the road about a hundred yards in front of her. "I couldn't tell if it was a cat or a raccoon or what," Julie says. "I started running toward it, but before I could reach it, it crossed the road and darted into the trees."

Oh well, she thought.

But when she approached the place where the creature had crossed, she saw that it wasn't entirely wooded—there was a small clearing just on the other side of a thicket, and there in the clearing was the groundhog, waiting for her. "I seriously gasped," she says. "We looked at each other for a moment or two—and then it scampered off into the woods."

Julie ran back home at record speed, with a bright-yellow butterfly flying overhead, accompanying her. She was elated—"the world felt like a benevolent place" is how she describes it. She couldn't wait to tell everyone what she'd seen. "I felt the groundhog was an unequivocal message from my dad that he was aware of what I'd been going through and that he was with me. I got over my fear of disappointment. I asked, and he answered, just when I needed it most."

21

HOW TO CO-CREATE
YOUR OWN LANGUAGE

WHEN I read for people, I move myself to a quiet place and consciously shift my energy into a state of total receptivity. I call it opening myself to the Other Side. In a way, I empty myself out—I stop being Laura Lynne—so that I can be a better messenger for our Teams of Light. Everything that comes through me originates on the Other Side; I am simply the vessel.

Getting myself into this state was not always easy. Growing up, I didn't understand the nudges I'd get from the Other Side; in fact, I was scared of them. I didn't *want* to know anything about people, alive or dead, that I shouldn't have had any way of knowing. It took me a long time to understand and accept my gift, and even more time to learn how to use it. Eventually, I got to the point where I could control the flow of information from the Other Side, so that I wasn't swarmed by it twenty-four hours a day.

As I trusted more and developed more, I began to learn the secret language of the universe. As I've mentioned more than once, I came to understand that this language is available to us all—it *belongs* to us all. And I've come to understand that it is part of my journey to awaken others to this possibility. What follows are a few guidelines to help you co-create your own special language with your wonderful Teams of Light. I hope the stories I've shared with you thus far have helped to prepare you to take the first step of opening your mind and your heart to the Other Side.

QUIET, PLEASE

I recommend that you begin this process by giving yourself ten minutes of quiet time. Not ten minutes on the sofa with the TV on, or ten minutes with your cellphone in your hand. I'm talking about *real* quiet. Meditative quiet. The kind of quiet that allows you to clear your mind and shift your energy and disconnect, as much as possible, from your everyday life.

Start by finding a quiet place to sit. That might not be as easy as it sounds—believe me, I know; I've got a husband, three kids, two dogs, and a cat. Close your bedroom door. Run a hot bath. Sit on a cushion, sit cross-legged on a yoga mat, or lie on your back, palms up. If there's noise seeping into your quiet place, put on some soothing music. Try to create the most serene and undisturbed environment you possibly can.

In fact, if you can set aside these precious quiet minutes every day and stick to it, you will begin to learn how to shift your energy and enter into a different state of consciousness by virtue of your intention. It's like what we talked about when we talked about dreams—we're trying to shut down our logical brains. We want to free our consciousness from our bodies. We want to quiet all that frontal-lobe chatter that is often called the monkey mind.

We want to get to a place where we can hear—and connect with—the Other Side.

So find your quiet place. Get physically comfortable. Close your eyes. Take long, deep breaths, in through your nose, out through your mouth. Bring your attention to your breath. Inhale, exhale. Gently push away stray thoughts.

If you feel you need an image to quiet your mind, picture a beautiful shining lake filled with shimmering light just above you, then allow the light to flow down into the top of your head, filling up your body from your feet to the crown of your head. I call this *bringing in the light*.

Do this for a minute, then another minute. Do it until you lose your sense of time. Stay in this peaceful, quiet place. Don't do anything other than savoring the stillness.

I should note that there are times in our lives when we accidentally slip into these altered states without even realizing it. It happens when we perform tasks that are second nature to us, and don't require much thought. At those times, our brains shift into autopilot. Showering is a great example. We are in motion when we shower, taking care of business, but we don't *think* about what we're doing as we do it—it all just sort of happens automatically. This frees up our brains and allows us to drift into a slightly disconnected state.

It can also happen when we're driving on a route that we've driven on a million times, or when we're cleaning a sink full of dishes. Tasks that don't require a lot of active deductive reasoning.

I have heard literally *hundreds* of stories of people who, while taking a shower, connected with loved ones who had crossed. I have had these experiences myself. There is something about the sound of running water that calms and mesmerizes us and allows us to shift our energy. The steady sound of a shower also tends to drown out any other noises, producing a wonderful kind of stillness (not to mention the effect of negative ions, which we'll discuss in a later chapter). We can feel pleasantly isolated in the shower, or we can feel embraced by the warm rushing water. All of this creates an ideal environment for the Other Side to reach out to us—and for us to *hear* them.

I'm not saying you should dash to the bathroom, get in the shower, and start trying to talk to your aunt or uncle who crossed. That is trying too hard, and it's counterproductive. I'm saying that we should be *aware* of what flows in and out of our minds when we are in these kinds of accidentally disconnected states. They are wonderful opportunities for the Other Side to come through, and they give us insight into the frame of mind we'd like to be in when we take step one and ease into our quiet time.

ASK FOR YOUR ORANGE

Step two is asking for a sign that you want. It's really that simple.

Remember when I asked the Other Side to send me an orange, as a sign that I was on the right path? I did that during a quiet moment when I was backstage, and within just a short amount of time I had my orange—in fact, I had thousands of them. So think about what sign you'd like the Other Side to send you, and then just ask for it.

A few tips. You can ask for a sign out loud or just in your head. You can make it a longer conversation between you and a loved one, or you can simply say, "Send me a green monkey." You can use some of the same elements that make up the default signs, since those are easier for the Other Side to use—but with a twist that makes the sign distinctive. Or you can create a sign straight out of your imagination.

Try not to ask for something that is all but impossible or in any way negative. For instance, you might not want to ask to see a jumbo jet land in Central Park. But you *can* ask to see a shiny airplane in an unlikely place (the response to that could be a model plane in a toy store window, or an ad featuring a plane on your Facebook feed, or a paper airplane suddenly and gently hitting you in the arm). So while you don't want to ask for something that is truly absurd and next to impossible, you *do* want to ask for something that is unique and even challenging.

Another tip: Allow for some time to see your sign. Quite often, people will receive the signs they ask for within three days, but they may come in just one day, or a week later. Don't expect to see it instantly—the Other Side is truly amazing, but even our Teams of Light can't make something materialize before our eyes (or at least I don't *think* they can). That said, I've spoken with dozens of people who've actually received a sign within moments of asking for it. Sometimes, the Other Side works *really* fast. But in general, allowing the Other Side some time is a good way to keep ourselves open to the sign, and make it more likely that, when it comes, we will notice it.

Finally, ask for something personal. Ask for something that connects you to a loved one on the Other Side. Maybe they collected porcelain dolphins. If so, ask for dolphins. Or ask for something you like that is personal to you. The point is to make it *your* sign—something that is particular to you and/or your loved one. This will increase the deeply beautiful feeling of love and connection that comes with a sign.

You can also assign different signs to different people on the Other Side. You could ask your grandmother to send you a pink heart with the word LOVE on it—and your grandpa to send a blue hippo. You can ask your spirit guides to send you the number 555. It's all up to you to create the language you will share with them. And the more signs you create and establish, the more fluid the language will become. The phrase *love you more*. The number 333. Neil Diamond's "Sweet Caroline." A bee. The more signs you create, the more expansive the language will become.

So maybe we can't share a cup of coffee with a loved one who has crossed. But we *can* share a lovely moment of feeling close again.

All we have to do is ask.

YOU CAN ASK FOR HELP, TOO

We aren't merely limited to asking for signs; we can ask for help, too. The Other Side is *eager* to help us. And I'm not talking about helping in an abstract way—such as "Help me be a better person" (your teams are going to do that anyway). I'm talking about help with specific things. "I've got a really important test today—please help me stay calm and focused." "My boyfriend and I are fighting—please help me think of what I can say to fix things." "I've fallen into debt—please help me make the moves that will improve my finances." "I need a parking spot close to the store today, please help me find one." Specific help for specific problems. Real, honest-to-goodness help. I've done this plenty of times myself.

So if you feel like you're at the end of your rope and don't know where to turn for help, turn to your Team of Light. Think of it as a prayer if you'd like. Be specific, and be honest. And ask for the help you need.

BE RECEPTIVE

I've written about how we can miss signs sent to us by the Other Side. If we're not looking for them, we can pass them by. But I've also heard stories about people who asked for a specific and challenging sign, received the sign, and missed it anyway. I've seen it happen up close.

Not long ago, my mother asked my father, who'd recently crossed, to send her a sign. She asked for something specific—a purple elephant. She told me that within one day of asking she got her sign in the form of a huge, purple blow-up elephant lawn decoration on a neighbor's front lawn!

A week later, my sister Christine came in from New Jersey. We had a difficult task to complete. We were going to the cemetery and then we were going to order a headstone. My mother drove us to the cemetery. Afterward, we went to get lunch in a nearby town. Later, we had to go back to the cemetery and retraced our route. I looked out the window and saw a huge sign above a new restaurant that I hadn't noticed before:

The Purple Elephant

There was even an actual purple elephant with its trunk turned up to the sky in front of the restaurant! My father had truly outdone himself. He sent my mother exactly what she asked for, in a way she couldn't miss. And yet we all missed it the first time around!

"Mom, did you see that?" I cried out.

"See what?"

I made her turn the car around and drive right up to the restaurant so she could get a nice, long look.

"Oh wow," she said when she finally saw it. "How about that? Looks like a great place to have lunch, too."

The lesson here: We need not just to look, but to *see*.

To do this, we don't need to change anything about our lives except to slightly alter our method of perception.

In the sport of golf, positive-thinking coaches tell golfers to walk down the fairway with their heads held high, fully absorbing the landscape around them, as opposed to hanging their heads and seeing only the grass in front of them. This is designed to get golfers more involved and alert and receptive, and better prepared for their next shot.

We can do the same thing in our everyday lives—we can more fully absorb the landscape around us simply by looking up. It's a small, subtle shift in our manner of focusing, a slight uptick in our level of attention. A commitment to being more *mindful*. If we make that commitment, we'll be much better prepared when the next sign comes from the Other Side.

SAY THANK YOU

It's important that when we do receive a sign, we take the time to express our gratitude. If we asked our grandmother to send us a monarch butterfly, we should say, "Thank you, Nana, for the beautiful butterfly." We should acknowledge the sign and be grateful, either with a thought or with actual words.

Why? Because thanking the Other Side for a sign is a way to honor the powerful connections that exist between us. It is also a way to make the occasion of seeing the sign a *shared* occasion—a moment of joyful communion between ourselves and our loved ones who have crossed. From what I've seen, our loved ones on the Other Side derive enormous joy from connecting with us. It lets them know their presence is still felt, and conveys that they are still acknowledged as part of the lives of their loved ones here on earth. Hearing "Thank you" is the ultimate validation of that.

Perhaps most important, saying thank you for a sign makes *us* feel better, too. It makes us feel more connected and less alone. How can you be alone if you're having a conversation with a loved one who just sent you a wonderful sign? Saying thank you honors the blessing of our interconnectedness, and creates a powerful spark of joy and well-being that travels across dimensions.

SHARE YOUR SIGN

I've spoken with so many people who have received incredible signs and yet not told another soul about it. Maybe they were afraid people wouldn't believe them or would think they'd lost their mind. For whatever reason, they've filed away this amazing experience as their own private thing.

You can do that, of course, and the sign will still be meaningful to you. But my advice is to share your story with the world. If you feel like you want to tell your friends about it, tell them! The phenomenon of signs is not just about us connecting to our loved ones on the Other Side. It's also about us *connecting to each other* here on earth.

If you believe that a sign is real, don't worry about anyone disbelieving you or thinking you're a little off. That's going to happen anyway, with lots of different issues and topics of discussion. There will always be trolls and critics to pounce on any divergent opinion. But here's the thing: If you share your story with someone, you're just as likely to encounter complete acceptance of your experience. Sharing your story may even free someone to finally share theirs! And sharing any joy with someone only increases and spreads that joy. So be talkative. Tell your story. Share your signs.

Most of all, be aware that our lives are not just about our own choices and paths. We influence the world around us and the people around us in very real and profound ways. We play major roles in other people's journeys, which means that how we carry our energy through the world matters. What we choose to share with the world matters. Not sharing these conversations with one another about such meaningful moments in our lives is actually a disservice to our friends and loved ones. We are all on this wild and beautiful ride together. The truest joy of all existence is this very interconnectedness. And the more we honor it by sharing our stories and our energy and our light with the world, the more our existence is enriched.

These are the basic elements that go into co-creating your own unique and special language with the Other Side—mindfulness, openness, stillness, gratitude, energy, communion. A willingness to ask for signs and a willingness to receive them. An appreciation of our interconnectedness and an inclination to share with others our experience of wonder and awe.

In the next section, I'd like to share some stories about people who created and developed a deeply personal language to connect with loved ones on the Other Side, and who discovered that the profound moments of connection that followed helped them navigate serious life crises and make life-changing decisions.

These moments of connection are available to us all. The secret language of the universe does not have to stay secret. The power of signs is unlimited and unrestricted. The password is whatever we want it to be.

PART THREE

NAVIGATING
THE DARK

I have decided to stick to love . . .
Hate is too great a burden to bear.

—MARTIN LUTHER KING, JR.

SIT WITH A PEN AND PAPER AND PLOT OUT ALL THE important moments in your life: your birth, your first date, your first job, career moves, weddings, kids. Draw a circle around each of them and lay them out chronologically in a sequence, from left to right. Then draw a line connecting all the circles. That through line is your path through life.

But I want you to know that this is not the *only* path available to you.

The universe teaches us that we all have several paths that can take us through life, including our very highest, most fulfilling, most authentic path. All the paths will get us from start to finish, but how we get there—how we make our way through life—depends on the path we choose.

The universe sends us signs to steer us toward our highest paths.

Now, jumping from one path to another isn't always easy. Embracing change and confronting the fears that hold us back can be very difficult. Sometimes we refuse to leave the path we're on. It's like wearing a pair of shoes that's a size too small. We can choose to keep walking in those shoes, and eventually we'll get where we're going, but that's not the best choice.

Signs shine a light on our fears so that we can navigate the dark and choose the higher, better path. The stories that follow are about people who heeded the signs that helped them make fateful life decisions—moments when they looked fear squarely in the eyes, then chose the path of hope and love.

22

CAMOUFLAGE, A GUN,
AND A NEW ASSIGNMENT

SEVERAL years ago, I was participating in an event for the Forever Family Foundation on Long Island. It was an intimate gathering in a conference room, with the relatives of ten children who had crossed. When I entered the room, they turned to me all at once, looking at me with a mixture of hope and heaviness. You didn't have to be a psychic medium to see the pain and longing on their faces.

After a few introductory remarks, I briefly closed my eyes, opened myself to the Other Side, and waited to be pulled toward someone. The first one to come through was a boy who pulled me toward his mother and sister on the left side of the room. He had an amazing energy and he had many messages of comfort and solace for them. The reading was happy and hopeful and incredible, and the energy in the entire room shifted. But while I was reading for them, I couldn't help but notice another parent sitting by himself across the room.

He was a big, burly, mustached man in his fifties, wearing a black leather vest, blue jeans, and motorcycle boots. His arms were folded across his chest, and he was staring down at his feet. Once in a while he'd look up and kind of glare at me. His body language suggested he was closed off and defensive and angry, and, frankly, he kind of scared me, but I could also feel that his sharp exterior was a shield against a very deep pain. I knew I was there to try to help him with his pain, but still, part of me was worried about what would happen if I was pulled to him. How would he receive the message the Other Side was sending?

And then, of course, the Other Side pulled me right to him.

It was a very strong pull. I walked over and stood in front of him, but he kept his head down, glaring at the floor. There was so much anger and tension around him, so much negative emotion. I didn't know how to get started.

So I blurted out, "Hi!" in a ridiculously chirpy tone.

He slowly looked up. His eyes met mine. I was taken aback. There was a softness in his eyes that was in stark contrast with his gruff exterior, and it was heartbreaking.

A girl on the Other Side immediately came up on my screen. Older than a little girl—a teenager, or maybe early twenties. She was communicating very quickly, barraging me with words and symbols and images. And what she showed me was awful.

"You have a daughter who crossed," I said to him.

His eyes began to water and he loudly cleared his throat.

"Yes," he said.

"And she crossed because . . ."

I hesitated.

". . . she tells me she crossed because she was murdered."

The man looked down again and didn't say a word.

He didn't have to. His daughter's story poured out on my screen. She had been murdered, and in fact everyone knew who her murderer was—her ex-boyfriend—yet for some reason, he hadn't been charged with the crime. And this, the girl showed me, was a source of agony for her father. The injustice of what had happened was unbearable.

Then the girl showed me something that played across my screen like a film clip. This happens sometimes—a stream of images that is so clear and so vivid, it comes to me like a scene from a movie. The girl showed me her father, alone, in his house, dressed head-to-toe in black clothes and camouflage gear. She showed me several rifles laid out on his bed.

"She is telling me that she tried to stop you all day," I told him. "She was there the whole time and she was pleading with you not to do it—not to kill her ex-boyfriend. But you didn't hear her. You had your guns and you loaded them in your car and you didn't listen. She is showing me that you were determined to find your own justice. She says she was trying and trying all day to get through to you, but you just ignored her."

The man was staring at the floor. The room was silent.

"You were going to kill him that night," I said.

He cleared his throat again and wiped away tears.

"Yes," he said. "I was."

"But . . . but you didn't. You didn't kill him."

He said nothing.

"You heard her. Your daughter says you finally heard her. You were so angry, you were going to avenge her death, but then you finally felt her and heard her and you listened. You listened to her."

He began to cry.

"She wants you to know that you are not meant to avenge her," I went on. "That is not your job. Your job is to continue to love her and honor her life. And she wants you to live your life vibrantly and to be engaged and to choose paths of love that elevate your soul, not paths of anger and hate and darkness that would diminish your light. That wouldn't be honoring her. She says that karma is real and every soul has to take responsibility for their actions. Whether it's here on earth or when you cross, every soul will be held accountable. But that is not your job. And if you had chosen to do it, you would have chosen a path of darkness. You would have created more darkness, not light.

"And now," I went on, "your daughter wants to say thank you.

Thank you for listening to her, and thank you for not going through with it. Thank you for loving her always. She is just so grateful and so happy that you listened."

My reading with this grieving father had a profound effect on everyone in the room, including me. When his daughter came through, she taught us all a very powerful lesson. A lesson about life paths.

In our journey, we may at times get confused and instead of following the highest path, we choose a lower path, one that constricts us, slows us down, leads us to dead ends. A path that takes us away from love and into darkness. When this happens, we end up living what I call a shadow life—a life that is a mere shadow of what it can truly be. One that doesn't reflect our true strengths and potential. One that doesn't allow us to share our true light and love and energy with the world. A *lesser* life.

I have read for people who are stuck in shadow lives, focusing on fear and anger. In many of these cases, I have seen how the Other Side never gives up, and always tries to steer us from the path of a shadow life to a higher path of love and light and meaning.

Why does the Other Side do this? Because our Teams of Light— our loved ones and spirit guides and God energy—want nothing more than for us to be happy and fulfilled. They want us to lead lives that are based on love, not fear.

How do our Teams of Light steer us?

They do it with signs and messages that make their presence known.

Some signs are meant to say hello, or to let us know our loved ones who have crossed are still with us, rooting us on. But other signs are meant to help us make the right choices in our lives. These signs appear when we reach a crossroads—and present a choice between a lesser path and a higher path. These are the moments when the Other Side practically *screams* at us to get our attention and influence our choice.

Here is what happened to the man in camouflage. Consumed by

grief and anger, he was on a path of hatred and pain. If he had followed through with his plan, his actions wouldn't have changed the past, but they would have changed his future. He would have had blood on his hands and on his soul, and gone to jail, and seen his own life ruined.

This is what his daughter was trying so hard to tell him—he was not meant to avenge her loss, because that is not our job here on earth. Our job is never, ever to follow a path of hate. Our highest and brightest life paths are *always* paths of love.

His daughter understood that it was her job to steer him toward that higher life path. The sign she sent him was not a visual sign. It wasn't a bird or a rainbow or a license plate. It was what I call a clairaudient and clairsentient sign. Clairaudience is when we hear something through means other than our worldly sense of hearing. For instance: A word or a phrase in our head that isn't our own. A thought that isn't our thought. A voice that isn't our voice. Have you ever had something relevant and surprising just pop into your head—something that seemingly came out of nowhere?

It didn't come from nowhere; it came from the Other Side. Clairsentient signs might be a gut feeling we can't shake off. We may have an ineffable sense that a loved one is present. We might clairaudiently "hear" our loved one's voice in our thoughts.

This man's daughter reached out to him over and over again on that fateful day, when he was at a crossroads, but he either didn't receive the messages or didn't acknowledge them. Yet she persisted. Even after he'd loaded his rifles into his car, she kept sending him the same message over and over.

Don't do it. This is not how to show your love for me.

And finally, *finally*, he heard her.

As he explained to all of us in that room, "I heard her. I heard my daughter tell me not to do it. I felt her there with me, telling me not to do it."

He listened to his daughter! He opened to her message! He heard her just as if she'd been there with him—which, in a very real way, she was.

And because he did, he wasn't doomed to live a shadow life locked away in a jail cell with a mark on his soul. With his daughter's help, he chose a higher life path—a path that gave him a chance to turn his terrible grief into something good.

In fact, he was already doing just that by deciding to attend the meeting, and having his daughter come through and teach us this powerful lesson.

Like the people in the incredible stories that follow, we all face choices that affect the trajectory of our lives and the lives of others, crossroads that suggest different life paths. What we need to understand, and what this man's brave daughter teaches us, is that *we are not alone at the crossroads*. We do not have to make these hard decisions by ourselves. Our Team of Light tries so hard to get through to us in these difficult moments. They are determined to not let our fear or grief or uncertainty stand in the way of our highest life path.

In these moments, we need to listen to and honor the signs the Other Side is sending us:

- A phrase or idea that pops into our head
- A gut feeling we can't shake off
- The voice of a loved one who has crossed
- The sense that your loved one is present

The signs are there! They will always be there! The Other Side will never stop sending us these incredible signs. They will never stop trying.

So we must stay open to them, and really look and listen for them and allow them to guide us toward our best, happiest, and highest life path. Because time and again I've learned that the choices we make, and the energy we embrace, impact not only our own life path but also the collective path of love that we are all on together.

23

BABIES AND BEARS

FEW life decisions are as consequential as the decision to have a child. That's because children change *everything*. I should know, I have three of them, and they are the absolute loves of my life, my greatest joys, my most treasured blessings. I cannot possibly begin to imagine my life without Ashley, Hayden, and Juliet—it's simply unfathomable to me. They are the very best decisions I ever made, along with marrying my wonderful husband, Garrett.

Nevertheless, these decisions can be frightening, confusing, and overwhelming. That is why, when we're making them, it is so helpful to turn to the Other Side.

And often, without us even needing to ask, the universe and our Team of Light will step in to guide us. That's why the universe sends us lots of timely and powerful messages about babies. It happens in many of my readings. While people are unsure about a lot of big life decisions, there is a special urgency and gravity that comes with the decision to have a child. Lots of profound emotions enter into play, as well as a potentially frightening sense of finality. After all, we can quit a job, but we can't quit our kids. In my experience, our teams on the Other Side know just how harrowing this decision can be, and that's why they send us signs and messages to support us in making this decision.

The stories that follow show just how consequential and life altering these amazing signs can be.

When Clayton and Natali Morris met for the first time, millions of people were watching.

Clayton was one of the hosts of a popular morning TV show, and Natali was one of his guests. "She walked onto the set, and she just knocked my socks off," Clayton remembers. "I was instantly dumbfounded by her, and I think I spoke really quickly through the whole segment."

"I saved the tape," says Natali, who was then an editor at a news website and a co-host of an influential technology podcast. "I remember looking at Clayton like, *I'm supposed to know you, but I don't know how.* It's amazing that we have that moment on film." (I call that feeling soul recognition.)

Just a few years later, another hugely important moment for Clayton and Natali would also happen live on air, in front of millions of people—including me. And this time, it involved the decision to have a child.

Clayton and Natali had not yet talked about getting married when Natali first got pregnant. "It was a surprise for both of us," she says. "I was thirty-one but I still remember thinking that I was too young for this. I worked a lot, and my career was a big part of my identity. Having a child felt like going through the looking glass."

They decided to have the baby, and in time their lovely son Miles was born. But Natali's mixed feelings during the pregnancy filled her with guilt. "Early on, Miles needed some medical treatment, and I wondered if the problem had been caused by trauma in the womb," she says. "Because we weren't married, and because I'd been unsure, the pregnancy felt traumatic to me, and that made me feel even more guilt."

Years later, when Natali and I crossed paths, I did a reading for her in which the Other Side showed me the image of a doctor's office.

"Why are they telling me all this stuff about a doctor?" I asked her.

Natali then described her ambivalence and the guilt she felt over it.

"That's why the Other Side pointed it out," I said, "because the guilt is a toxic thought you need to get rid of. Your son came to heal you, to make you a family, to point you in the right direction. So get rid of the guilt you are carrying. Just let it all go."

Natali and Clayton got married in city hall in Manhattan three months after Miles was born. "Since I worked the weekend shift, I was home with him a lot in the early months," Clayton says. "We sort of fell into these roles of mother and father, but we started to realize that we were pretty good at them. We were pretty good parents."

Eventually, they agreed to have another child, and beautiful Ava came along.

"After that," Natali says, "the feeling I had was, *We're done.*"

But Clayton wasn't so sure.

"We both agreed to stop at two, and we agreed that we were this great little unit of four people, and that was enough, but then I sort of started pushing for a fifth member," Clayton says. Natali, too, had been thinking about it, but "my honest feeling was that I really did not want to have another child," she says. "The pregnancies were tough, and I wanted to go back to work, and so I was really struggling with it. I was very, very conflicted. After a while I had to tell Clayton to stop asking me about it."

This is kind of where I entered the picture.

When Clayton was young and growing up in Spring Township, Pennsylvania, he had an innate curiosity about the secrets of the universe.

"As a kid, I ran around in a *Ghostbusters* costume trying to find ghosts everywhere," he says. "Later on, I taped this little show about the paranormal and put the episodes up on YouTube. As I got older, I built up these walls with stress and anxiety about life, and I stopped trying to tap into this space, this curiosity. But I was always open to it."

Natali, a California native, was raised a Jehovah's Witness but left the faith when she was twenty. "I hadn't found any set of beliefs that really worked for me," she says. It was only after she started reading books about the afterlife and consciousness that she began to form a true worldview. "It was like everything I believed about life up to that point had been completely wrong!" she says. "Those books really informed the way I think about my life."

Together she and Clayton explored spirituality by reading more books, studying meditation, and just "trying not to limit our ability to connect with the world vibrationally."

It was that desire for more connections, more openness, that brought Clayton and Natali to my book *The Light Between Us*. "As soon as we finished the book, we both said, 'Oh, she should be on the show!'" Natali remembers. But before Clayton could suggest it to anyone, his producer sent out an email to all the show's hosts the very next day: "So who wants to interview this psychic medium Laura Lynne Jackson?" the email read.

"I'll do it," Clayton quickly wrote back.

The day of the taping, I arrived at the show's studio in Rockefeller Center. Just before airtime, I settled onto a sofa across from Clayton on the stage. Natali wanted to be on set for the interview, so she stood behind the cameras, listening intently. Both Clayton and Natali were looking for—hoping for—the very same thing: some kind of sign about having a third child.

When we started taping, Clayton and I talked about the book for a while, but the Other Side had a different game plan. Someone came through very forcefully, and their message was very clear.

"Okay, I'm going to start reading for you," I told Clayton. "You have two children now, right?"

Clayton said that he did.

"Okay, well, I see a third light waiting for you."

Behind the cameras, Natali burst into tears.

"I'd been so scared and so resistant, but as soon as Laura Lynne said those words, it didn't feel scary anymore," she says. "I was standing there laughing and crying because I knew that was what she would say."

But there was more. The being pushing through from the Other Side was Clayton's grandmother, Alma. She gave me her name to give to Clayton as an affirmation, and she also showed me something about a new pair of boots. It was like she was poking fun at Natali about them.

"Laura asked Clayton if I'd just bought boots, and of course I was wearing a new pair of knee-high black boots I'd just bought," Natali says. "But I knew Clayton would point out that they were very similar to these other black boots I already had, so I was trying to hide the shopping bag from him. And then Alma came through and talked about them."

More important, Alma showed me the fear and uncertainty that both Clayton and Natali were feeling.

"She is here and she is saying you're scared, you think you can't run your family or your careers with another child, but it's going to be great, so just do it, just have the third child," I told them. "If you choose to do it, it will be beautiful. But don't *not* do it because of fear."

Just four weeks later, Natali was pregnant again.

"This time, I made myself enjoy the pregnancy in a way I hadn't before, because I trusted in what was happening," she says. "I had faith in our decision. I let go of all the fear and uncertainty. And it was our third child who fully healed me. This persistent little soul came along and healed me."

Their third child—a glorious little girl—was born. But neither Natali nor Clayton could settle on a name. Clayton's co-hosts were set to announce the birth live on air, but with just a few minutes to go before the broadcast, the couple *still* hadn't picked out a name.

"I was in the lobby of the hospital, about to go up and see Natali, and I just stood there with my cup of Starbucks and took a deep breath and waited for a lightning bolt," Clayton says. "And then one hit me."

Upstairs, in her hospital room, Natali also had a name pop in her head. "I was having breakfast and I just came up with it and it felt right," she says. "And then Clayton burst in and said, 'I know her name.'"

He told her a name. She told him a name. It was the same name.

"So with just a few minutes to go I texted the name to my producer, and then they went on the air and announced the birth," Clayton says.

That's how the world was introduced to Eve Morris.

Since Eve's birth, Clayton and Natali have both been even more open to signs from the Other Side. Recently, Clayton was struggling with the decision to stay at his TV job or leave to start his own real estate investment business. "I've always felt that my spirit animal is a bear, because I see bears a lot, and every time I see one, something amazing happens," he says. "You know, I'd see a bear and I'd have a great deal happen within an hour."

The day he finally decided to leave the show, he called in to work to share his decision with his producers. "And within moments of the call—*moments*—I was in my car and this enormous black bear just walked right in front of me on the street," Clayton says. "I just stared and watched him go. It was the universe validating that the choice I had just made was on my highest path."

Today Clayton and Natali are living truly beautiful and authentic lives together. Now that they have navigated and mastered their own fear and uncertainty, they are both true light workers.

They didn't need me to tell them a third child was on the way— all they needed was to trust in what they already felt inside. They needed to recognize which choice was the path of fear and which choice was the path of love. In the end, every choice we ever make while here on earth comes down to choosing a path of fear or love. It is our job to recognize the difference—and choose the path of love. That is always our highest path.

"We let go of fear and allowed what was supposed to happen to happen, and when we did it changed everything—our finances, our family dynamic, our future," says Natali. "It's about trusting the signs and trusting what the universe is trying to tell you.

"We make things happen when we realize we have the power to make them happen," she adds. "We can all create magic in this world, we just have to believe that we can."

24

FLICKERING LIGHTS
AND SPARKS

How do we know if we're doing what we're meant to be doing in this life? How do we find our higher purpose? How do we know if we are on the right path?

Many of us search for the meaning in what we're doing and wonder if we're living our very best lives. Danielle Perretty wondered these things, especially when she found herself at a crossroads. "I was in a situation where I began to ask myself, *Am I using my skills, my passions, to help people?*" she remembers. "I wanted to feel like I was making a difference in the world. I wanted to feel like everything in my life was aligned the right way."

It's not that Danielle was in dire straits or had hit rock bottom — in fact, from the outside looking in, her life seemed wonderful. She had a job that she loved, a boyfriend she loved, and her future looked bright. She didn't feel like there was any glaring need she had to address, or any great opportunity she had missed. For the most part, she felt she was on the right track.

"It wasn't anything overwhelming or overpowering," Danielle

says. "It was just this sense, this little calling. Like a tiny whisper that was saying, 'You can do more. You can *be* more.'"

So Danielle listened to the whisper.

And when she did, nothing was ever the same again.

Danielle first heard the whisper when she was at a design conference in 2010. At the time, she was working as a marketing director for a respected product design and development firm. She was also living with her boyfriend of ten years, and they were planning to get married and start a family. At the conference, Danielle ran into a friend, Angela, and the two shared a ride home. During the ride, Angela told Danielle about a psychic medium she'd been seeing—me.

Not much later, Danielle reached out to me. She'd never thought about having a reading, but she felt the need to connect—it was the first whisper.

In our first reading, Danielle's grandmother—Sally, as she was known—came through. Sally had been an important figure during Danielle's childhood. Her parents divorced when she was five. "I spent a lot of time alone—writing, hiking, listening to music. Nature was my solace." And she had Sally, whom she calls "a person of great joy and happiness and light. She was more of a mother to me than a grandmother. We'd spend weekends together, and we'd bake things and play games and tell stories and sing songs. She was creative and fashionable, and she had such great energy and enthusiasm for life and for the people she loved."

Sally crossed when Danielle was sixteen—and now, nearly twenty years later, she was trying to reconnect. Sally pushed through in the reading, not even waiting for me to begin the process of clearing the way for her.

"She is very protective of you," I told Danielle. "She is watching over you all the time. She says, 'Do you remember how we used to hang out together on the weekends?' Well, she says you still do. She is with you every weekend."

Sally was also very insistent about relaying her message. "She's a real spitfire," I told Danielle. "It's like she's stomping her feet, saying, 'Enough already, we want your life to go forward. You need to be more forceful, more verbal, and less patient.'"

Danielle understood what Sally was talking about: her boyfriend. Their relationship wasn't perfect. He was having trouble committing. Every time they talked about getting married, something would come up to delay it. "I was beginning to realize that he wasn't evolving and growing and on the same path as me," Danielle says. "But even so, I loved him. It's one thing to break up and leave someone when you're over it and ready to go. It's a very different thing to break up with someone when you love them but realize you have to move on if you want to grow."

Danielle struggled with whether to leave her boyfriend until finally, she found the courage to go.

Because of a downturn in the economy, Danielle lost her job. Her bosses were very kind and gave her a generous severance package, but even so, it came as a total shock. "At almost the same time that I left a relationship of ten years, I got laid off from a job I had for more than eight years," she says. "All of a sudden I was on my own."

When we had our next reading, her grandmother had a very direct message for her.

"This is not a mistake," I relayed. "This is not random. The universe took you out of your safe space. The universe did this on purpose. It is leading you to your highest path."

Hearing those words didn't ease the pain or take away the fear. Not right away, anyway. But after a while, it began to make sense to Danielle.

"It was the universe giving me a clean break," she says.

Danielle traveled for six months, then came back and started looking for a new position. Very quickly, great offers came in. "I got a few from companies in Boston and others from San Francisco, and they were all amazing offers," she says. "The kind of jobs you'd be crazy not to take." She settled on one of the firms, and instructed the recruiter who was working with her to negotiate a higher salary.

Then a friend of hers asked her a simple question. "He said, 'If money wasn't an issue, what would you want to do with your life?' No one had ever asked me that before, and it made me think."

In fact, Danielle had a secret passion.

She'd always thought of nature as a safe haven. She'd been a vegetarian since the age of twelve and took care to live in a conscious, healthy way. When she allowed herself to dream, she thought about how to help people strike a perfect balance in their own lives. She dreamed of her own line of fresh juices and of becoming a yoga instructor.

"When I thought about starting a juice shop and teaching yoga, I just got very excited, but at the same time I told myself, *Oh, you're never going to do that*," she says. "I never once realistically considered doing it. I was single, I couldn't afford it, I'd have to do it all on my own—I put up all these walls. And that's where the dream stayed— buried behind walls."

Instead, she focused all her energy on the job offer. One evening she was on the phone with her recruiter, who was telling her about the firm's counteroffer. "It was a lot of money," Danielle says. "Everything was lining up for me to take the job."

But during the phone call, she heard a pop. "I looked over at the outlet and saw smoke and sparks flying out of it," she says. "Sparking and smoking, like an actual fire. And the weird thing is, nothing was plugged into it."

She told the recruiter she'd think about the offer and hurriedly hung up. As soon as she did, the sparking stopped.

The next day, Danielle pressed the firm for a better offer, and that night the recruiter called back with an even more enticing counteroffer, including a lucrative bonus. And then the socket started smoking and sparking again.

Similar things had happened before—the lights in her apartment would flicker and dim, lightbulbs would unexpectedly burn out, she'd go to a friend's house and the lights would start to flicker there.

"I would also get a lot of ghost phone calls," she adds. "The phone would ring and no one would be there, and when I'd call the number back it would be disconnected. That happened all the time."

From her talks with me, Danielle had become more and more open to signs from the universe—and in particular, to signs involving electricity. The Other Side often communicates through electromagnetic force—the physical interaction between electrically charged particles and magnetic fields. Because of its fluidity, this force is easily manipulated—if not precisely, at least noticeably. In my experience, ghost phone calls, flickering lights, full blackouts, and sparking outlets have all marked interactions between the Other Side and us.

Danielle came to believe that Sally was using electricity to get her message through, because along with these perfectly timed occurrences came the feeling of a download. "The fact that it happened during the phone calls with the recruiter—that was Sally letting me know she was there and pushing me to get it going, get started on a new adventure," she says. "It was Sally wanting me to have a more joyous life. She had always watched over me, and she was still watching over me. She wanted me to be happy and fulfilled."

Danielle turned down the job.

Then she began dismantling the walls that she'd erected between her life and her dreams.

Today, just two years after those unusually charged phone calls, Danielle is the owner and manufacturer of a line of juices called Beacon Blend. "A beacon is a guidepost, and that's what my grandmother was and is for me," Danielle says. "And that's what I want my business and my life to be: a beacon of wellness and joy." The Beacon Blend logo is based on a necklace that Sally used to wear. Danielle has created a product of pure wellness. And that is a really beautiful way for her to honor her grandmother.

Building her business from scratch—while also teaching yoga classes several times a week—has been difficult and, at times, pretty scary. "I'm strong in marketing and I have a plant-based diet, but I don't have a business degree," she says. "I don't have a business partner. I didn't really have any money except for my savings. I had to make a leap into the unknown and basically jump off a cliff. And every day, there was a new cliff to jump off."

What helps Danielle push through, she says, "are the signs. The signs from my grandmother. I have these rough days when I really want to hear from her, and I'll ask her for a sign, and she always comes through. The lights will flicker. The phone will ring. She always lets me know she is there with me, watching out for me. She gives me strength."

What really helps, too, is that Sally is always on the job.

"I started to ask her to send me elephants," Danielle says. "And around the time I started my business, someone randomly gave me a little elephant figurine for good luck." Being open to these signs — "and learning how to trust in them" — has forever changed Danielle's life.

"I feel like I'm able to share a kind of lightness with the world," she says. "We all have the ability to rebuild our entire lives. Our lives can be something so much bigger and more beautiful than we ever even realize. And it's all up to us. We need to ask ourselves, *How do I really want to build my life?*

"And when we come up with the answer," Danielle says, "the universe will back us up and root for us to succeed."

25

BOWS AND CLOVERS

AMY, a young singer and musician from California, woke up one Friday morning feeling sick. She tried to get on with her day, but she just couldn't shake her nausea and exhaustion. Then she threw up.

"And, you know, I *never* throw up," Amy says. "I think that's when I knew. That's when I said, 'Uh-oh.'"

Amy drove to the pharmacy and bought a pregnancy test. Not much later, she had a result—she was pregnant.

"I looked at the little stick and I said, 'This has to be wrong,'" she remembers. "So I went to the store and got another test."

The result of that test was positive, too.

So Amy bought a third test.

And a fourth.

And a fifth.

Finally, after six tests came up positive, she stopped going to the pharmacy.

"I said, 'Shoot, I'm pregnant,'" Amy recalls. "Then I thought, *Okay, well, I'm not going to keep this baby.*"

That night, Amy had a terrible nightmare that armed militants came and stole her baby. She spent the next two days curled up on her sofa crying. She avoided contact with just about everyone for the next two weeks. "It was a dark, horrifying time," she says. "I was terrified. I went back and forth about having the baby and not having the baby. I wanted to keep it, but the idea of keeping it was totally out of the question. I was so lost."

Finally, Amy chose what she believed was her only real option. She called a clinic and scheduled an abortion.

It wasn't that Amy didn't want to have a baby—she did. It's just that the timing was terrible. Only a year earlier, her father—a powerful TV producer—had gone into the hospital with pneumonia. Twenty days later, he crossed. "I was devastated," says Amy. "He was healthy and he really took care of himself. It was extremely confusing and unfair and painful."

Around that time, Amy was also in the process of ending a two-year relationship. "I didn't like the way he made me feel," she says. "He was really bad for me. I hung on because I always thought we might get married and have children. But that was never going to happen."

Amy struggled with grief and depression, and she turned to alcohol for solace. "I was in a horrible place," she says. "It was a really shaky time. In a way I felt like I was a child who couldn't take care of herself. It was the worst time of my life."

A few months later Amy's aunt gave her a reading with me as a gift. Amy was driving when I reached her for the reading; she pulled over and we got started. Her father, whom I would later learn was a commanding presence here on earth, was also pretty bossy on the Other Side. He came through right away and gave me a series of affirmations to share with Amy, so she could be sure it was him.

"I told Laura Lynne about what I was going through, and what a hard time it was for me," Amy says. "I said that I wanted to get married and have a baby, but that was now feeling like it was never going to happen. That's when Laura told me my father was laughing. He said, 'Amy, you're going to have a baby much sooner than you think.' I said, 'Okay, Dad, that's not funny. Don't even joke about that.'"

Three months later was the day Amy woke up feeling sick.

"I honestly didn't see any way I could keep the baby," she says. "People would tell me, 'You can do it, babies are beautiful,' but all I could think was, *I can't do this by myself. It's too hard. It's too scary.*" Even her brother told her, "You are not keeping this baby." That, says Amy, "was such a painful moment. I felt so much pressure not to have the baby."

Even after she decided to terminate the pregnancy, the terror and the confusion continued. "Something was telling me to have the baby, even though I knew it would be a terrible idea. I was so torn— I felt like I was going crazy, like there was no one in the world who could understand what I was going through."

With just a few days to go before her appointment, Amy sent me an urgent email asking for another reading. My schedule was completely full, but I felt the pull to call her. What's more, I knew the reading was meant to be a gift from her father. It would be complimentary. I set up a time for us to talk. What I didn't know was that the reading was set to take place one day before Amy's scheduled appointment at the clinic.

Amy told me she was pregnant and that she didn't believe her ex-boyfriend would be there for her in the future. She asked me what she should do. She was desperate for an answer—any answer. I told her what I tell everyone—the choice was hers and hers alone. She had to be the one to decide which life path to follow.

Then, on my screen, I saw the connection between Amy and her unborn child—between her soul and the child's soul. I saw that they were linked on a deep level, a soul level. The Other Side was showing me the consequences of Amy's decision. "Having this baby can be a beautiful path for you, but it's not the only path," I told her. "You have to make the choice, but you have to make the choice independent of your boyfriend. The baby is linked to you. If your boyfriend steps up, great, but if he doesn't, you need to understand this is not about him, it's about you and the baby. It's about how your souls are connected." Amy needed to ask herself what was motivating her choice. If it was fear, it would always lead her down a lower path. But if she followed a path of love, she would find her highest path.

There was something else I needed to tell Amy—about her father. He was pushing through and letting me know that he'd been sending Amy lots of signs and messages, but she just wasn't receiving them. She was too caught up in her fear and confusion. He showed me a gift box with a big blue bow on top.

"Your father is sending you a message," I told Amy. "This baby can be a gift to you. Search yourself and trust your pull. Don't let the roar of fear prevent you from hearing whatever that voice inside is telling you to do."

Amy admitted she was having trouble receiving signs from her father. Even now, after her father had come through, I couldn't be sure she'd truly heard what her father was trying to tell her. It was like she needed to get a sign directly from him.

I told her to keep looking for the signs, that her father would send validation of his message to her directly. I told her to remember that he'd shown me a gift and a bow. I reminded her that she was loved and supported by the universe—that she was not alone. She had a Team of Light from the Other Side around her always.

Two hours later, Amy drove to her friend Sue's home. Sue was standing over a table, putting flowers in a vase, preparing it for a friend's upcoming wedding.

"I looked at the vase and my mouth dropped open," Amy says. "There was a big, beautiful bow tied around it. A huge blue bow."

Inside her, she heard a quiet little voice get a bit louder.

Yes, the voice said. *Yes.*

Amy immediately got on the phone and called the clinic.

"I canceled my appointment," she remembers, "and I told Sue, 'I am having this baby.'"

The signs continued throughout her pregnancy. She would see two children walking toward her with gifts in their hands, each box topped with a bow. Amy began establishing a more concrete language with her father, and asked him for her own sign—the song "Sweet Caroline," which they used to sing together. The first time she asked for it, it was the first song that randomly played on her iPhone.

And she asked for clovers. Her father was Irish, and Irish clovers seemed to be everywhere when Amy was growing up. Now she wanted to see them again. He obliged, sending them in advertisements, on billboards, even actual clovers Amy found flat on the ground, with no clover patches in sight.

"My dad was talking to me," Amy says. "He'd been talking to me all along. He was telling me I had made a beautiful choice to have this baby."

Amy gave birth to a healthy boy she named James. "He had this adorable dimple, and he was this perfect little man, and I loved him right away, except it was a new kind of love, so deep and so profound," she says. "I nicknamed him my little Buddha, because he's so happy and smiling all the time."

Even so, their first few months together weren't easy. James, says Amy, is a handful, and she and James's father are no longer a couple—so she is raising James as a single parent. "There are days when I talk to my father out loud and say, 'Dad, please help me with all of this, please send me signs so I know you are watching over us and helping protect us,'" she says. "There are days when I'm still really scared."

On those days, Amy thinks about the connection between her and her son, and also the connection between her son and her father. "The way I see it, James spent time with my father in heaven before he came to me," she says. "So whenever I get really sad, I think about that. I know this baby has spent time with my father, and that makes me very happy. I feel like my dad is saying, 'I wasn't ready to leave you yet, so now I'm sending you this child who is a gift of love in your life.'"

My reading with Amy taught me another incredible lesson about the way the universe works.

Sometimes our highest path takes us away from someone we romantically love or think we love, simply because they aren't ready to change paths with us. We need to realize that even if we choose a path that doesn't include them, that doesn't mean we no longer love them, or that our time together wasn't "the right path." We cross into each other's path for a reason—to teach each other useful lessons and help each other grow. But sometimes, in order to keep growing, we have to venture onto a new, higher path by ourselves. And that is okay. You can love someone and *still* not be meant to spend your whole life with them.

Amy's relationship with her child, however, is different. They are connected on a deep soul level, and if they didn't meet in this life, they would have met in another. By choosing to have him now, Amy honored that special connection—independent of her fears about the future. She made a decision based purely on love. And when we make decisions that are love-based and not fear-based, we move on to a higher life path.

Today, says Amy, "I feel that my father sent James to me, and honestly, in a very real way, he saved my life. I truly feel this baby saved my life."

Amy's child has also rekindled her connection with her father. After losing him so painfully when he crossed, and then struggling to find him when she needed him most, she is now reconnected to him in a way that allows their relationship to continue to grow. "No matter how hard things get, I have some really strong angels, and I have my father," Amy says. "He was a boss on earth, and he got things done, and he never took no for an answer, and now he's helping me be the same way in my life."

And when things get really challenging?

"I just talk to my dad and ask for a sign," says Amy. "And when he sends it to me, it makes me feel like I have an in with God."

26

RAINBOWS

O F all the signs sent to us by the Other Side, few are as beautiful and dramatic as a rainbow—a fantastic spectrum of colors stretching across the sky. For most of us, the sight of a rainbow is an exhilarating surprise, a tiny burst of magic in an otherwise ordinary day. Whenever I see a rainbow, I know the Other Side is trying to tell me something—or if not me, someone, somewhere. That's because the Other Side *loves* using rainbows to catch our attention.

Rainbows make great signs because they are relatively rare. So when we see one, we really and truly take notice. And double rainbows are even scarcer; seeing one can feel like spotting a unicorn. What's more, rainbows are created when sunlight reflects and refracts through droplets of rain in the sky, and the Other Side is very good at manipulating light. Plus, rainbows are light and bright and lift our spirits. Throughout history, many cultures have seen rainbows as powerful and positive messages of love and hope. In Norse mythology, a rainbow is even considered a supernatural bridge between humans on earth and gods on the Other Side.

In my experience, rainbows are spectacular signs sent to us by our Teams of Light on the Other Side. Rainbows have come up in dozens of my readings and in many stories I've heard about signs. One of those stories in particular stands out, and I'd like to share it with you. It's a story that defies all logic, but nevertheless is true.

I know, because I was in the middle of it. And I watched it all unfold in the most magical way.

A few years ago, Susan and her three sons flew from California to New Orleans to visit her husband, Marc. Marc was a production designer who was working on a film that was shooting in the city. The family had planned a lovely long weekend together.

While Marc took the boys on a boat trip, Susan went into town and stopped by a voodoo museum. On a whim, she allowed a man who worked in the shop to read her tarot cards. "He had just come back from Haiti, and seemed very kind, so we sat down and he laid out all my cards," Susan says. "Every single card was about death or dying. It was very scary and intense."

Susan could even see that the tarot reader was surprised.

He asked her, "Is your husband okay?"

She told him Marc was fine.

"I feel like he has a headache," the reader said. He looked at the cards again and added, "What I can tell you is that you are going to go through the biggest transformation in your life. But in the end, you are going to be okay."

Susan was spooked. But she shrugged it off and, the next day, the whole family flew back to Los Angeles. A few days after that, Marc returned to New Orleans to finish the movie.

Marc was healthy and vibrant, and had no major health issues, but on the very morning he returned to New Orleans, on the way to the movie set, he suffered a brain hemorrhage.

Six days later, surrounded by his family, Marc crossed.

Susan was devastated. Her sense of loss was unbearable. "I had incredible friends and incredible support, but those months were such a dark, terrible time," she says. "Actually, it wasn't months; it was more like two years."

It was during this period that Susan's friend Jill—the connector we met in chapter 18—called to arrange a phone reading for Susan.

At the very start of the reading, Susan's husband came through. He knew his crossing had left her in a really dark and lonely place and how hard her life had been. But he had a plan to change all that.

"He is saying there is another relationship waiting for you," I told Susan. "He says you aren't necessarily ready for it now, but he wants you to know that you are not meant to be alone. You are meant to live vibrantly, and he wants to help you live that way. He is going to organize it from the Other Side."

Susan was startled, and understandably so. She'd just lost her husband; the last thing on her mind was another relationship. And yet here was her *husband* telling her he was going to set her up on a date.

Marc's message was very straightforward. He was going to help Susan find the happiness she deserved, but it wasn't going to happen right away. In fact, he said, it was going to take four and a half years from the time of his crossing. Susan accepted what Marc was saying, but I could see she didn't really believe it. The mere thought of entering into a new relationship must have seemed to her like a betrayal of the love they shared.

I understood why she would feel that way, but I also know that's not how the universe works. And that's not how our loved ones on the Other Side look at it. They want us *to be happy*.

When we cross, we take the love we felt on earth with us. And once we're on the Other Side, that love only intensifies. But even as it grows and grows, it never becomes possessive. We don't take love away from one person by giving it to another person. On the Other Side, there is an *abundance* of love, and so love is not a zero-sum game. So for Marc, seeing his wife, Susan, share love with someone else would not be a betrayal, or even a suggestion that her love for him, or his for her, was being diminished in any way.

On the contrary—by living a life filled with love and vibrancy, Susan would be *honoring* the love she shared with Marc. She would be giving him the greatest gift he could ever ask for—seeing her on her highest life path.

I have read for many people who were terrified that any new relationship would hurt a loved one who had crossed. And every time, the wife or husband on the Other Side came through forcefully to explain how this is simply not true. In fact, they not only approved of a new relationship that would lead to true happiness and fulfillment, they very often played a big part in making that relationship happen!

Still, my reading with Susan was the first time someone on the Other Side explained to me in advance how they were going to play matchmaker. So I was curious to see how it would play out.

A few weeks later, I was in Los Angeles, and I met Susan and Jill for breakfast. Susan didn't ask me any more questions about our reading, but I felt someone pushing through for her. It wasn't her husband Marc—it was someone else. I was getting an R name.

"There is something coming through very strongly," I told Susan. "His name . . . his name is Randy."

"Randy?" Susan said, completely stumped.

"Yes, Randy. He is standing here, and he's not leaving. He says he knows you."

Susan thought about it for a moment. Then she said, "Randy D.?"

"Yes!" I said. "He is standing here. And he is here with Marc. They are standing together."

"That's really odd," Susan said. "Randy passed away seventeen years ago. I don't really think about him very often. He was married to my good friend Barbara. Wow—I haven't spoken to Barbara in a while . . ."

"Well, he's here and Marc is saying he is going to enlist Randy to help find a man for you."

I could tell Susan wasn't sure what to think. She said she still talked to Barbara, Randy's widow, a few times a year, but she hadn't connected with her recently. Really, there wasn't any reason Marc would team up with Randy on the Other Side.

Moments later, Susan's cellphone rang. She looked at the number, and her face froze. It was Barbara—just wanting to catch up.

Now Susan really didn't know what to think.

But I did. Randy was the second piece of the puzzle.

Four and a half years is a long time to wait, so to keep Susan aware of his presence in her life, Marc began sending her signs. In our reading, she had already mentioned how she suspected he was sending her signs—and one sign in particular: rainbows.

"Marc's favorite song was 'Over the Rainbow,'" she says. "He loved to play it on the piano. After he died, we went to Hawaii, where Marc and I were married, to spread his ashes. I remember standing in this beautiful spot on the beach spreading his ashes, and looking up and asking Marc, 'Why aren't you sending me any signs? I want a sign.'"

Just a few minutes later, a beautiful rainbow appeared across the sky.

But Susan wasn't impressed.

"I said, 'Marc, this is Hawaii, there are rainbows all the time. Is that really all you got? You're an artist! You can do better than that!"

Just a few minutes after that, Susan looked up at the rainbow again. By then it had changed. It wasn't just a rainbow anymore.

It was a double rainbow.

"And then I said, 'Well, okay, that is impressive, Marc.'"

Now that they had their sign established, Marc got really creative. Susan wanted to have a memorial service for Marc at Sony Studios, where he had done so much wonderful work. She tried to book the date for the service, but construction in the parking lot was disrupting events. So she settled for a later date.

On the morning of the service, Susan and Jill drove to Culver City. Along the way, Susan looked out the car window and saw a dazzling sight—the biggest, most vibrant double rainbow she had ever seen in her life. Susan and Jill knew immediately that Marc was guiding the way. "The rainbow was so amazing, it made the news the next day," she says. "When I saw it, I just started crying."

But that was only Marc's opening act.

When they arrived at Sony Studios and pulled into the parking lot, she saw the construction that had delayed the service. It wasn't a new building or additional parking spaces.

It was a rainbow. A gigantic, towering rainbow.

"I was astounded," Susan says. "They built it over the parking lot as a tribute to *The Wizard of Oz*, which had been filmed there in the 1930s. And as soon as it was completed, I could have the service. We couldn't have the service until the rainbow was finished!"

The rainbow was 188 feet across, ten stories tall, built on a hundred-thousand-pound steel truss and covered with 648 brightly colored aluminum panels. It wasn't just any rainbow; it was a glorious Hollywood rainbow that took ten cranes and 115 people to build—just like one of the many sets Marc had designed on that very lot.

And it was there, in the very same lot, just waiting for Susan to see.

Three and a half years after Marc crossed, Susan hired an architect for a job she was designing. They became friendly, and one day the architect told Susan about another client of his.

"I'm building a house for him in Seattle," he said. "I really want you to meet him, I have a feeling you two would like each other."

Susan was polite but firm.

"I said, 'No, I'm sorry, I'm not ready, I don't want to meet him.' And that was that. We dropped it and moved on to something else."

But a year later, the architect called Susan out of the blue.

"He said, 'Hey, my friend from Seattle is here in Los Angeles, I really want you to meet him,'" Susan recalls. "And once again I said, 'No thanks, I'm not interested.'"

"Come on," the architect said. "Let's just all meet for dinner and have a good time. Nothing more than that."

So Susan joined the architect and his friend—David—for dinner.

They got along. They had a lot in common. They talked about art and architecture and their travels and their families and lots of other things. After dinner, David asked Susan if he could call her once he got back to Seattle. She said that would be okay. A few days later, he called. The day after that, he called again. "He called me a lot," Susan says. "We had all these wonderful conversations. And then one day he was in Hawaii, and he sent me a text. The text didn't have any words, it was just a picture."

David sent her a photo of a beautiful double rainbow—even though he knew nothing about the significance of rainbows in her life.

"That's when I said, 'Whoa, okay, I better pay attention to this.'"

Not long after, David came to Los Angeles again, and he and Susan went out on a date. Then a second date, and a third. Susan visited David in Seattle, and he proudly showed her his collection of motor-cycles. When Susan had to travel to San Francisco, David met her there.

"We had a great time, and then we went our separate ways, me to Los Angeles and David to Seattle," she says. "But on the way to the airport, two more rainbows appeared in the sky. Two separate rain-bows in two different places. I took pictures of them. I have photos of all the rainbows I saw during that time. I'd look out my bedroom window and I'd see a big, giant rainbow right there. Or I'd be driving, and I'd turn a corner, and I'd run right into a big rainbow. They were showing up in ways that I couldn't possibly miss them."

It was right around this time that I happened to be in California and met up with Susan again. To be honest, I'd forgotten most of the details of my reading for her, but when I saw her it jogged my mem-ory. I asked her if she remembered the amount of time that Marc had told her to wait before she met the man.

She said yes—four and a half years.

"And what about Randy?" I asked. "Has there been a Randy con-nection?"

"No, no Randy connection," Susan said.

The next morning, Randy's widow, Barbara, just happened to call her again to say hello.

"And you know, one of the first questions she asked me was, 'Are you seeing anyone?'" Susan says. "I said, 'Yes, this guy, but you wouldn't know him.' And I told her his name."

There was a silence on the phone. Finally, Barbara said, "I *do* know him."

"How do you know him?" Susan asked.

"He was Randy's good friend. They used to ride motorcycles together. In fact, he has one of Randy's motorcycles."

Susan was stunned. She had seen the motorcycle. David had shown it to her when she was in Seattle. And now she was learning that it was Randy's motorcycle. The Randy connection! Finally Susan told Barbara about everything that had happened—the reading, having Marc say he was setting her up, learning about Randy, and finally, meeting David.

"Yep," Barbara said, "that sounds like something Randy would be involved in."

"It was astonishing," Susan says now. "It was like this incredible puzzle with all these pieces that had to fall into place just right. So when I heard that David and Randy had been friends, that's what tied everything together. I knew that Marc and Randy were working together on the Other Side."

Susan was right. Marc enlisted Randy to help him with his mission: steering Susan toward a new relationship that would help her grow and engage in life fully again. The Other Side is capable of brilliantly orchestrating connections for us here on earth, and what happened to Susan is beautiful evidence of how involved our loved ones are willing to get in leading us to our highest paths. "I mean, no one could have known all the things they needed to know to pull this off," Susan says. "David is very logical and not a believer in signs or anything like that, but when I called him and told him about Randy, even David agreed there was no logical explanation for it. He knew no one in the world could have made it happen."

We humans have a tendency to stick to paradigms, or models of reality, that we know and understand. And when something challenges our existing paradigm, we look for ways to make it fit, so it will make rational sense. We look for logical explanations. But what is the logical way to explain Susan's truth? Even if someone googled Susan and Marc and David and Randy and learned everything about them, how could they possibly use that information to make such a plan fall neatly into place? What happened to Susan isn't google-able!

The only people who could have pulled the strings and brought Susan and David together in such a magical way are Marc and Randy, working together, on the Other Side.

A funny thing happened not long after Susan realized that she and David were meant to be dating—she stopped seeing so many rainbows.

"I'll still see one here and there, but it's different," she says. "They aren't as prominent. And I feel like that is Marc pulling back a little bit. It was like he held my hand all the way through it, and now he is giving me the space I need to move forward. And everything has been so free and easy with David. It all feels so incredibly natural. And that is Marc pulling back at just the right time."

That is how the Other Side works. Our Teams of Light will hold our hands through the darkness like a parent walking their child to school on the first day of kindergarten. But they will also let go when they need to, so that we can freely do what we need to do to get on our highest life path.

Okay, but what if I hadn't been there to tell Susan about Randy, or about Marc's plan? Would she still have ended up dating David?

I believe she would have, for one reason—the signs.

Susan established her sign with Marc—rainbows—before we ever met. And Marc confirmed that sign in ways Susan simply couldn't dispute. A giant rainbow in a parking lot? The very parking lot Susan had to drive through on the day of his service? And then, after Susan's architect introduced her to David, David texted her a photo of a rainbow. That made Susan sit up and take notice. Even if she hadn't heard about Randy from me, she likely would have eventually discovered that David was buddies with one of her friends who crossed years earlier, and surely that would have been very meaningful to her.

In other words, Marc would have found a way to put his plan into action with or without me. Sometimes the Other Side uses someone like me—a psychic medium—but most of the time, they don't. They use whatever they can, wherever they can find it. They put rainbows in our path, and even in parking lots.

27

TINY WHISPERS

WHEN we get a sign from the Other Side, it is not a directive. Signs are not mandates to take a particular course of action. While they can act as guideposts or nudges of love and support from our Teams of Light, we each have the free will to choose our own paths, lessons, and experiences. Ultimately, our free will empowers us. We are the ones who decide what we do, not some external force. The choice will always be ours.

What the Other Side *does* try to do is make us realize that, deep down inside, we often already know what we need to do to find our highest path—we just need to trust it. We should not allow our fear to overpower our free-will choices. Our Teams of Light are often just trying to get us to open our minds and our hearts to an answer that is already inside us.

That's what signs do—they *affirm* that we are never alone on this earth, that we are always surrounded by our own personal cheerleading squads, and that our Teams of Light are tirelessly rooting—and patiently waiting—for us to do the things we need to do to live the best, most authentic, most purpose-driven lives we possibly can.

All signs are messages of love. And every decision that will lead us to our highest path is a decision based on love, not fear. So when we acknowledge and honor the powerful signs we receive from the Other Side, we allow them to guide us on a path of love, instead of making decisions dictated by fear.

This knowledge is already in our hearts. If we think about it long enough, we can know which of our decisions are love-based and which are fear-based. And when we're really torn between the two—when we cannot distinguish between the love-based path and the fear-based path—that's when the Other Side tries to send us signs. Signs are the directional arrows that point toward the highest path.

But sometimes, these signs are not external. Sometimes, signs aren't even physical things. Or a spoken word, or a piece of music, or the wind.

Sometimes signs are just a tiny whisper in our hearts.

Sarah and David Rathke met in a bar. He was a bartender, and she was ordering a drink. "What's funny is that the first time I ever saw him, he looked familiar to me," Sarah recalls. "I wasn't sure why, he just did."

They flirted and dated, and six months later David proposed. "It was freezing outside, and I told Sarah I wanted to show her a boat in the harbor, because I wanted to propose by the water," David says. "And when we got to the dock, all of a sudden Sarah turned to me and asked, 'How much do you love me?' I couldn't believe it. There I was with a ring in my pocket about to get down on one knee. It was the perfect setup."

They got married, and in the next few years had two children, both boys. Life with Luke and Daniel was an endlessly wonderful blessing, but also expensive and chaotic. "We live in Northern California, which is very expensive," says David, a chief revenue officer

(Sarah is a classical musician). "We're not trust-fund kids. We drive a minivan. We started talking about having a third child, because Sarah really, really wanted a daughter. But it wasn't an easy decision. To be honest, I wasn't jumping up and down about the idea of having another child."

"And I wasn't going to pressure him if he really didn't want to do it," Sarah adds. "It's not something you can force someone to do."

They were both torn. They didn't want to say yes, but they didn't want to say no, either. And time was also a factor: Sarah was thirty-nine.

Finally they decided to just do it. But even then, they weren't convinced they were making the right decision. So even after they made it, they didn't rush to get pregnant. Fear was holding them back.

It was right around then that I met Sarah and David at a wedding. I was in a really great and festive mood, and I had a couple of drinks, and when I have a couple of drinks, a weird thing happens. I seem to have trouble keeping the door to the Other Side "shut," so to speak; I get especially receptive to it. So when I found myself in a group with Sarah and David, I had no way of stopping David's father from coming through.

"Your father died suddenly, didn't he?" I asked David.

He looked startled and replied, "Yes, he did."

"And his first name started with an R?"

"Yes."

"Okay, well, your father is here, and he wants me to share some things."

Oddly enough, David's father, Richard, showed me shoes, pajamas, and teeth. He had me tell his son that even though David was wearing a fancy pair of dress shoes, he ought to invest in a decent pair of sneakers.

David smiled. He was wearing Gucci loafers and he did indeed need new sneakers.

Then his father told him that while he was at it, he ought to get rid of his ripped pajamas and buy a new pair of sweatpants.

"His PJs have this giant rip down the side, and he'd worn them for ten years, and he wouldn't let me throw them away," Sarah explains.

Then Richard told his son to see a dentist right away. "He says you have an issue with a tooth in the back right side of your mouth, and if you don't get it fixed soon it will turn into a big health problem," I said.

But David didn't have any teeth issues.

Still, he booked a cleaning for the next week, just to be safe. And when the dentist examined him, he quickly asked David a question.

"Are you free this afternoon?"

"Why?"

"You have a tooth in the back that is severely vertically cracked, and I want to send you to an oral surgeon right now for a root canal. If you don't do it soon, the tooth could become infected, and it could affect your heart."

My brief reading with David turned out to be hugely significant for him. Not just because he got his tooth fixed in time, but because of how it affected his relationship with his father, who had a heart attack and crossed when David was just twenty-one.

"After my father died, I spent the next twenty-three years building a box around him," David says. "I didn't think about him or talk about him all that much, and I expected that box to be in place forever. It was just too tough otherwise. So I built the box."

But when his father came through with signs and affirmations, "the box burned down," says David. "It just went away. That's when I knew my father was still with me."

During our brief reading at the wedding, David asked me to pose a question to his father. Or rather, he joked about it.

"Let me guess," David said at the time. "My father thinks we should have a third child."

"He sees a third presence in your life," I told David and Sarah, "and there is a lot of positivity around it. He says to tell you that it will be a girl—and he is telling me that you want a girl. He also says that if you wait until you can afford it to have another baby, it will be too late. But if you have this child, you will never be able to imagine your life without her in it."

Then David's father squeezed out one last message for his son. "Tell him to get on a treadmill and lose some weight."

To David, that sounded just like his father.

I remember that after all these wonderful messages for David came through, he had a question he wanted me—and not his father—to answer.

"When my dad passes me advice from the Other Side," he asked, "is it like he's still here on the planet? Or is it like he is omnipotent? Because when he was here, he got a lot of stuff wrong."

"On the Other Side, your father can see everything in totality," I explained. "So he sees all these things and he wants to pass along some of these things to you, if they are important for your well-being. But it is not absolute. There is the concept of free will. You have choices that you need to make."

In other words, nothing David's father had relayed to him was an imperative. Nothing was an order. David's father didn't take him to the dentist—David had to drive himself there, he had to decide to go. The signs and messages and affirmations from the Other Side were meant to steer him in that direction.

"For me," says Sarah, "hearing his father come through with all those messages is what did it. David's father was just so positive about another baby. We both completely embraced the idea, and within a month I got pregnant."

When David and Sarah's third child—precious little Emily—came along, everything changed. "She is just so happy and smart and beautiful and playful, and David is absolutely smitten with her," Sarah says. "She brought a new and different energy to the whole family. She sort of softened up the boys, and they adore her now. It was true—we really can't imagine our life without Emily in it."

Months after they named their daughter Emily, David and Sarah learned something about his great-grandparents from another relative. "I hadn't known anything about them, but then we found out that my great-grandmother's name was Emila, and my great-grandfather's name was Emil," David says. "It's like Emily was always our destiny. This was always meant to happen."

That is how the universe works—souls have deep connections and unique contracts that span centuries, exist back and forth in time, and bind us in ways we can't really understand. The brilliant cords of love that ran through generations and generations of David's family, and Sarah's family, brought the two of them together (remember how Sarah felt like she already knew David even though they'd never met?) and eventually brought Emily to them. These connections are ancient and everlasting, and they already exist in our hearts, even if we're not always aware of them.

After all, David and Sarah made the decision to have a third child *before* they met me, and *before* David's father, Richard, came through. All Richard did was affirm what they already knew in their hearts.

Sometimes, the sign *is* the whisper in our heart, the deep and undeniable pull, the inherent *knowing* that the answer is already there.

"All of these connections that run in and out of our lives, with people here and with people on the Other Side: They are very real, and they lead to real emotions and real changes in our lives," says Sarah. "If we are open to this, it will truly enrich our lives. Because life is so much more than we can see in this dimension."

Marina Romero grew up in a big family, with five children and many more cousins, and some part of her might have imagined that she, too, would have a big family someday. "I was born in Spain, and Spanish families are usually very large," she says. But when she got older, she created a successful career for herself as a teacher and a therapist, and that career consumed most of her time. "The lifestyle I chose was not made for children," she says. "I worked six days a week, every week of the year, and I was very passionate about my work. And so eventually I decided that I would not have children."

Of course, as so often happens in life, things changed. Marina fell in love and got married, and for the first time in her life, she says, "I was with someone whom I felt, *Okay, yes, I could have children with him.* That was a deep feeling in my heart."

At the time, Marina was fifty years old.

Despite her age, Marina and her husband, Samuel, decided to try to build a family. They went to a fertility clinic, and doctors told her she was more than healthy enough to bear a child. At the age of fifty-two, Marina got pregnant and learned she was going to have twin boys.

After forty weeks, however, "my babies died right before they were born," Marina says with sadness. "It was a stillbirth. The doctors said it wasn't because of my age, but they didn't know why it happened. So after that, we were grieving for a very long time. I began to think it was the universe's way of telling me I was not meant to be a mother, and I let it go. We tried to accept that we wouldn't have a child."

A few months later, Marina and Samuel took part in something called a vision quest. They went into the woods and spent several days there, apart from each other and with no food and just enough water to get by. "I think that when I went into the woods by myself, I was finally able to feel the grief of losing my twins," Marina says. "And once I did, I had another very strong feeling. It was the feeling that I wanted to try one more time."

Samuel supported his wife in her decision, and at the age of fifty-three Marina got pregnant again. This time, her doctor learned after twelve weeks that the pregnancy wasn't viable. "That was extremely difficult," Marina says. "We were going back and forth between viable and not viable, between yes, we will have this child and no, we won't. It was very painful."

But even then, Marina and Samuel decided to try again.

They had started the process with several frozen embryos at the fertility clinic. Now they were down to four. "I tried again with two embryos, but I just never got pregnant," Marina recalls. "I don't know why, it just didn't happen. That is when I told myself, *Now it is really over.*"

Marina was fifty-four, and she felt lost in her life. She tried to devote herself to her career, but some days she couldn't work at all. "I was missing my boys who died," she says. "I had no clarity. I was lost, really lost. I didn't know what to do with my life anymore."

As it happens, Marina and I have a mutual friend, Ken Ring, a renowned psychologist and the pioneering researcher in the field of near-death studies. Ken referred Marina to me. In my reading with her, Marina's father, Rafael, came through quite quickly and showed me two distinct souls.

"Your father is showing me two children," I said to Marina. She seemed surprised that the topic of children came up so quickly.

"Yes, I did have two children," she told me. "They died at birth."

"Your father needs you to know it was not your fault in any way," I said. "Their souls' mission was to feel your unconditional love for those nine months of your pregnancy. That was their whole mission and lesson, just to feel unconditional love. They are safe and happy on the Other Side now, and they are with your father. And now . . ."

I paused, because Marina's father was showing me *another* set of two distinct souls.

". . . your father wants you to think about trying again."

"I was shocked," Marina says. "I was completely closed down to the whole process of trying to get pregnant again, but my father was insistent. He said that there were two little souls waiting to come to me, waiting to come into this life, if I wanted to have them. He said that they would be okay with whatever I decided to do, but that they were wondering if I wanted to do it. Because they wanted to be here."

I could tell Marina was confused. She shared what she was thinking: Maybe all her struggles were a sign from the universe that she *wasn't* destined to be a mother—that she needed to abandon her dream. Her father repeated the same message, letting her know that the twins were happy, and that there were two additional souls wanting to arrive.

"He says it will happen," I told Marina. "That is what he is showing me—it will happen if you open up to it."

So Marina went home and told her husband about the reading, and about her father's clear message to her.

"Now it was his turn to be shocked," Marina says.

The truth was, Marina was petrified. She was scared of trying again, fearful that she would lose another child or even two more children. She truly believed the door to her being a mother had closed. But it hadn't. Despite her age, and despite everything she had gone through, the Other Side made it very clear that the door was still open.

Marina and Samuel talked it over at length, and agreed to see a doctor. If the doctor said Marina was still healthy enough to carry a child, then they would go home and think about it some more. Sure enough, the doctor gave them the green light. Then the universe sent a really big sign: The fertility clinic let Marina know they wouldn't be able to store her remaining two embryos past the next three months. "It was like everything was pointing in this direction," Marina says. "I was both very excited and very afraid."

Her fear, however, was not enough to slam the door closed.

On her fifty-fifth birthday, Marina tried one more time to get pregnant. "That night was showered by these beautiful signs from the Other Side confirming the words of my father," she remembers. "We danced and we celebrated not only my birthday, but the arrival of new souls."

This time, Marina got pregnant. And she learned that she was having twins.

Her doctor told Marina everything looked just fine, but as she got closer to the forty-week mark, Marina could not help but dwell on the twin sons she had lost. And when she thought about them, she felt frightened and depressed. "I just could not be sure that these babies inside me would make it," she says. Then, early one morning, her water broke. The twins weren't due for another month, but still, Marina went into labor. Samuel helped her into the car to drive her to the hospital, but before they left Marina looked up at the sky. She noticed that the moon and Jupiter were together, shining brightly and adding to the beauty of the moment. "I felt it was a loving wink from the Other Side," Marina says.

The twins arrived just after Marina entered the delivery room. Two beautiful, precious boys. They were small—one weighed four pounds, the other five—but they were healthy. A nurse cleaned them and bundled them up and handed them to Marina.

When she finally had her twins in her arms, "It was like I went into this other place, this other dimension," she says. "Like I wasn't even on this earth. It was the most pure and powerful feeling of joy I ever felt. And then our relatives came over and everyone was looking at the babies, and I still couldn't believe what was happening. I couldn't believe that these boys were actually *here*."

Miraculously, the boys were born almost exactly three years from the day the other twins crossed.

The boys are named Oceanos and Arthur, and more than two years later they are doing wonderfully. "They are healthy and beautiful and tender and also wild," Marina says. "I am exhausted all the time, but I am so happy. I didn't think it would ever happen, but then it happened. I am a mother now."

The affirmations and messages she received from her father played a part in helping Marina reach a decision. But the truth is, Marina's connection to her father on the Other Side was not especially clear or strong before our reading.

"Even now when I try to communicate with my father, I can't always feel him directly," Marina says. "But the difference is, now I know that he is there. When the boys are really hard and I am very tired, I will tease my father and say, 'You're in trouble now, Dad.' I do it because I believe that if we communicate with our loved ones on the Other Side, our lives will be better for it."

Had Marina never had a reading with me, and had her father not come through so forcefully, would she have decided to try one more time on her own? She simply can't say. Maybe the notice from the fertility clinic would have pushed her to make the decision. Or maybe, somehow, her father would have found some other way to come through with his message of hope and trust and love.

"With the harshness of the stillbirth, and the difficulty of all the other times I tried to get pregnant, I couldn't always hear the deep, soft, tender voice in my heart," Marina says. "It was blocked, and I felt so lost, and I didn't know what to do with my life anymore. But then the boys came along, and not only did I recover my connection to that soft, tiny voice in my heart, but I also realized that this voice can be a channel for our loved ones on the Other Side to connect with us. It is how they can whisper their loving guidance to us."

Elana was set up with her eventual husband, Steven, by a mutual friend with an uncommon knack for matchmatching. "She was very, very good at it," Elana says. "She lied and manipulated to get us together, and she waited us out while we were dating other people, and finally she told me Steven was really interested in me, and she told Steven I was interested in him. And, you know, she was right. Steven turned out to be the guy."

They got married, and when they were in their early thirties, they had a son, Noah. "He was a beautiful child with no medical issues," Elana says. "But when he was around fourteen months, I started to notice that something was different. He wasn't talking, which is okay, but there was something different about the quality of the interactions he was having with other kids."

Eventually Noah was diagnosed as having autism. "He was very high functioning, and he was social and told jokes," Elana says. "But his ability to be calm and regulated, and to deal with any minor frustration, was incredibly limited. He could get very aggressive and have lots of outbursts. Not being able to find his shoes, slamming things, screaming and yelling. He was emotionally fragile."

Elana and Steven had always believed they would have a second child. They both agreed that they didn't want Noah to be an only child. But the complexity of his situation—and the knowledge that it would not get any easier—made them reconsider. "I really wanted Noah to have the typical family experience of having a sibling," Elana says. "But at the same time, I felt like I already had more than I could handle in life. I was overwhelmed by the thought of having another baby, especially since, when you have one child who is autistic, the chances of having another are much greater. To be honest, it was really frightening. So in my mind, I was ninety-nine percent convinced that we wouldn't have another child."

And yet Elana did not want to completely close the door on the decision. After she turned forty-two, it was her husband who suggested they needed to figure it out once and for all. "He had accepted that it was going to be my decision," says Elana. "But he was like, 'Okay, is it yes or is it no? We need to know one way or another. We can't live with this question mark.'" And yet Elana still couldn't decide.

The weekend after she and Steven had their talk, Elana attended a spirituality seminar. One of the empowerment exercises required her to write a letter to God, then write a second letter *from* God back to *her*. "I've always felt like I have a hard time getting messages from the Other Side, because my mind is too active and chatty, and I can't distinguish between a sign and intuition and what's already in my mind," says Elana. "But then I wrote these letters, and when I sat back and read the second letter, the letter from God, I was completely shocked."

The letter from God told Elana that she would have another child, and it would be a girl, and the girl would be named Ahava.

"Even though I wrote it, I was taken aback by what I was reading," she says. "I was really shaken; it was so powerful. I got right on the phone and told Steven, 'We are having this baby.'"

Not much later, Elana got pregnant. She was happy, but "it wasn't a pure happiness," she says. "I was still too scared. It was like I wasn't ready."

After just one month, she miscarried.

The miscarriage gave her even more reason to doubt the feeling she had deep inside—that having another baby was the choice she most truly and honestly wanted to make. "Steven and I went to counseling, and we talked everything over and we tried to just get to a place where we could be ready to do it," Elana says. "I felt one thing in my heart, but then I kept thinking, *What if the fear is right? What if this ruins my life?*"

One of the measures Elana took to find some clarity was to contact me and set up a reading. Her goal in talking to me was simple and clear: "All I wanted was for someone to tell me if I should have the baby or not."

But that's not what happened during the reading. Elana didn't get the straight answer she so desperately wanted. The Other Side provided affirmations and messages, but no one came through to announce, definitively, that she should or shouldn't have another child.

Instead, the Other Side showed me that Elana had a soul contract with her son, Noah. They were meant to be together, but it was a purple contract, and the color purple signifies something that is very complicated and difficult. All of that made sense to Elana, who loves her son dearly and is devoted 100 percent to his care and well-being. But as for having another child, all the Other Side showed me was that the choice belonged to Elana.

"I was told that it would be a free-will choice," Elana says. "That the journey of my life was like a beautiful hike, and the hike would be more beautiful with this other companion, this other soul, but that it would also be okay if I didn't have this companion. It was part of my journey to make the choice myself."

The message was deep and powerful and brightly lit with love. The soul of the child who miscarried was a soul that had traveled with Elana's soul for many, many lifetimes, and they were meant to be together, but if it didn't happen in this life, then it would happen in another.

"You are really on the fence about this," I told Elana. "You're like sixty-forty. And if you do it, the first year will be really difficult. Your whole life will be disrupted for a year. But it really is okay if you decide not to do it. The two of you will be together again sometime. And when you are, it will be very, very lovely. But if you choose to have this child, they are showing me that it will be a girl."

This wasn't quite the answer Elana had wished for. She wanted a clear yes or no. But that just wasn't something the Other Side could give her. The choice was hers to make.

Then Elana asked, "Will she have the same issues as Noah?"

"No," I said, "the soul contract with this child is different. She will not have autism. And you will make the decision soon. Within the next ten days or two weeks."

That weekend, Elana had plans to get on a plane and attend a women's conference with four good friends. "I told myself, 'Okay, by the end of the conference, I will know what to do,'" she says. "'One way or another, I will know.'"

The first day of the conference passed, and Elana was no closer to having the clarity she needed. Then the second day passed, and the conference ended, and Elana still didn't have her answer. She got on a plane and flew back home, and found herself in the airport still confused, still undecided. "I went into the airport bathroom, and I went into a stall, and I said, 'This is it. Something is going to happen to let me know what to do right now. By the time I leave this stall.'"

And then . . . nothing happened. No sign, no message. Nothing. "Okay, then," Elana said to herself, "I guess I just have to choose."

She came out of the restroom and told her friends, "I'm having another baby."

Just like that. Two weeks later, she was pregnant. Nine months later, her beautiful daughter, Ahava, was born.

Ahava is the Hebrew word for "love."

"She is incredible," Elana says of her daughter, who is now three and has shown no signs of being autistic. "She is the absolute light of our lives. And her connection with Steven is this crazy connection. From the moment I told him my answer was yes and I got pregnant, he was reading kids' stories to my belly and kissing my belly and just getting so excited to meet her. And when she arrived their eyes locked together, and now she shakes with joy whenever he walks into a room. They have a very deep soul connection."

Elana's son, Noah, too, has developed a powerful bond with his sister. "The first year was very hard because she had colic, but we got through that, and now Ahava is so strong and so spirited, and she knows how to handle Noah," Elana says. "She is like a little boss with him. They have a very sweet and very loving connection, too."

As for Elana—who was in an airport bathroom stall when she

found that the answer she was seeking was hidden within her all along—Ahava's arrival has been like a prophecy fulfilled. "It was like she'd been hanging out on the Other Side, waiting to see if I would give us the experience of being together in this life," Elana says. "I felt like I already knew her. I felt like I already had her in my life."

Elana had waited and waited to get an overt sign from the Other Side that would let her know which way to go. But the Other Side, as she puts it, "was radio silent on this whole baby thing." And yet throughout the decision-making process—even the times when Elana had all but convinced herself that her answer would be no— she never completely shut the door on having a second child. Why not? Why didn't she just say no?

"Because when I look back on it now, I think I was getting a strong gut feeling for years that I really did want to have this child," Elana says. "In my heart of hearts, I knew there was a daughter waiting for me. But that hope was sitting on one shoulder, and on the other shoulder was the fear. And the fear prevented me from trusting my gut feeling, my inner knowing."

In the end, she didn't need an overt sign or a message from the Other Side. The answer was already there, in her "heart of hearts." All she needed to do was trust in that gut feeling, that undeniable pull, that inner voice.

"I had to believe that God put this powerful desire in my heart, and that I wasn't going to get kicked in the teeth if I said yes," she says. "I had to trust my heart more than I believed in the fear, and that is a hard thing to do. But once I realized the only one who could give me an answer was me, I was left with two scenarios—one that made my heart sing, and one that was a place of terrible loss and despair. And so I trusted the singing of my heart. I trusted that the universe would not steer me wrong."

Sometimes a sign can be just a tiny whisper in our heart. An inner pull, a soft voice, or a gut feeling. All we need to do is learn how to trust it, to remain open to it, to listen for it, and to honor it when we feel it or hear it. This is not always easy to do, especially when we find ourselves going through a dark time. Darkness leads to confusion, and confusion leads to fear. And fear is the enemy of trust and hope and love.

In these dark times, our Teams of Light on the Other Side will always try their hardest to let us know we are not alone. They will do whatever they can to send us signs and affirmations and messages of love and hope. But if the fear is too great, if the darkness is too intense, we might not see these signs. We might not feel the pull or hear the voice. We may be too closed off by grief and despair and fear to be receptive to the Other Side.

But the Other Side will not stop trying. Our Teams of Light will always try to steer us toward the love-based decision and pull us toward the answers that already reside inside our heart of hearts.

For inside each of us, there is a connection to a deep and beautiful wellspring of love and knowing. Sometimes, it's finding a way to be silent enough to hear the tiny whispers that matters most of all.

Who in your life has been such a servant to you . . . who has helped you love the good that grows within you? Let's just take ten seconds to think of some of those people who have loved us and wanted what was best for us in life—those who have encouraged us to become who we are. . . .

No matter where they are—either here or in heaven—imagine how pleased those people must be to know that you thought of them right now.

—FRED ROGERS

28

A GIFT OF LOVE AND
FORGIVENESS

Nor long after I appeared on a TV show to promote my first
book, someone on the staff of the show reached out to me
with a personal request.

"My husband's sister Leslie suffered a loss, and she's been stuck in
her grief for a long time," this person wrote. "She is not living her life,
and we thought you might be able to read for her and possibly help
her."

Even as I was reading the email, I felt a strong pull to speak with
this woman. I didn't know who Leslie was or what had happened to
her, but I knew that she and I were supposed to cross paths. I wrote
back and said I'd be happy to read for her.

Once I'd opened that door, I felt a younger male presence pushing through. I felt a "son" energy coming from him. He made it very
clear that the reading was going to be a gift from him to his mother. I
immediately knew that meant I was not supposed to charge his
mother any fee for the reading. Once in a while, someone from the

Other Side will come through and insist on a reading being a gift. And when the Other Side speaks, I listen.

The reading took place a few days later, over the phone. Right at the start, the same male energy came through. This time, he gave me a J name—Jon. He also took responsibility for his crossing. And he quickly mentioned that his mother's birthday was coming up soon. I asked Leslie if she had a son who'd crossed, and if he had a J name, like Jon. She said she did. I let her know that he was apologizing and taking responsibility for his crossing.

"Well," I told her, "this is your son's birthday gift to you."

Leslie began to cry. Her pain and grief were clear. I sensed that her birthday held some additional meaning to her and to her son, but I didn't know yet what it was. Then Leslie explained why she was so moved by her son's gesture.

"Five years ago," Leslie said softly, "my son killed himself on my birthday. I was the one who found him."

When Leslie was just ten years old, she got a download from the universe that let her know she was going to have two children. The download also made it clear that something would happen to the children's father, and as a result Leslie would live the rest of her life like a nun. It was an odd premonition for a ten-year-old to have, and in the years that followed Leslie, for the most part, put it out of her mind.

But then she went on to have two children, and not long after that their father walked out on the family. Leslie never remarried and devoted the rest of her life to caring for her children. "That's when I understood why I saw the figure of a nun when I was ten," Leslie says. "That was the only way my ten-year-old self could interpret what would happen in my life."

When Leslie was pregnant with her second child—her son Jonathan—she got another download from the universe.

"I had the strong sense that my child wasn't going to live a long life," she explains. "Every ounce of my being told me he would not live a full life. I even felt that I knew when he would pass on—between the ages of twenty-two and twenty-eight. I just had to accept it, and move ahead, and try not to think about it."

Jonathan turned out to be an exceptional boy. He was incredibly smart—his IQ was over 160—and incredibly gifted. He loved to draw and paint, and one of his childhood paintings—a haunting depiction of broken shards of glass—still hangs in Leslie's home. "He loved doing puzzles and reading books and making these little movies with his classmates in them," Leslie says. "He was the sweetest little boy. We had an extremely close relationship."

Jonathan was four when his father left and became an incidental presence in his children's lives. It was a wound, says Leslie, that never healed. "The pain of losing his father never left him," she says. "It tortured him forever." When Jonathan was fourteen, a classmate came over and offered him marijuana for the first time. "It was like the devil himself coming to the door," Leslie says. "Jonathan started with pot, and at seventeen, heroin entered the picture. After that, he was in and out of rehab all the time. He was fighting to reclaim his life."

Jonathan's struggle with addiction was long and painful. There were days when it felt like his life was draining away. On one particularly bad day, Jonathan stayed in his bedroom in Leslie's home and lay listlessly in bed. "He seemed so fragile," Leslie remembers. "He was like a little baby. I brought soup up for him and I spoon-fed it to him. I told him I'd lined up a bed for him in rehab, and he said, 'Mom, I'm done. I don't want to deal with this anymore. I just don't want to.'"

Leslie didn't press him and told him to try to rest. As she gently closed his bedroom door, she thought of something Jonathan had told his grandmother just a few days before.

He had said, "If only I hadn't been an addict."

Leslie had seen her son endure many such moments of despair before. She hoped some sleep would make him feel better, so she turned off the light and went downstairs. Leslie is an accomplished pianist who was working as a piano teacher. That day, she had a girl coming over for a lesson.

Toward the end of the lesson, Leslie heard a loud and startling noise upstairs.

"It sound like someone banged the floor with a cookie sheet," she says.

She excused herself from the lesson and went upstairs with a rising sense of unease. She tried to open her son's bedroom door, but it was locked. She banged on it, but there was no answer. She went back downstairs, where, thankfully, the girl's father had arrived to pick her up. As soon as they were gone, she ran back up to Jonathan's bedroom.

"I banged on the door and called out his name," she says. "Finally, I threw all my weight at the door and forced it open."

She saw her son lying on the floor in the back of the room. His face was covered with blood. Leslie screamed out to no one, "My son is gone."

"I knew from the second I walked in that he was dead," she says through tears. "I called nine-one-one, and ten police cars and three ambulances came over. But I knew he was gone. My son was gone. All I could say to the police was, 'I can't believe this is what happened to my beautiful boy.'"

Jonathan had shot himself in the head. He was twenty-eight years old. And he had chosen to end his life on Leslie's birthday.

"It felt like every part of my body was under attack," Leslie says. "I was in pain, physical pain, every minute of every day. Constant, terrible pain. It was like I was being attacked from the inside out. Basically, I was destroyed."

In a way, Leslie shut down her life. She was still there for her daughter and she still managed to teach piano lessons—in fact, the only time she didn't feel pain was when she was teaching or playing music—but effectively, she shut down her life.

"Because of how Jonathan lived and how he ended his life, and when he chose to do it, I believed he did it to hurt me as much as he could. So I had this terrible guilt and terrible sorrow, and all I could think about was the day he was born, and how little and precious he was, and how he was gone now and I couldn't feel him anymore, and it was just so deeply painful. I was torn to shreds."

Leslie was haunted by another memory—two years before his crossing, Jonathan asked her to make him a fancy multi-tiered French cake for his birthday. "And I remember saying, 'Oh no, that's too hard,' and I didn't make it, and I baked a simple cake instead," she says. "Now I felt such horrible guilt about not making the cake."

For nearly six years after Jonathan crossed, Leslie's pain hadn't lessened. People told her she needed to get over it and move on with her life, but that just made no sense to her.

"I thought, *No, that is not what I need, because no one gets over this,*" Leslie says. "It will always be there, and I have to find a way to take it with me as I go. But you don't just 'get over' it. For example, my brother was constantly trying to fix me and heal me, but that wasn't going to happen, and so our relationship became strained, too. I felt so alone and unconnected to anyone."

Worst of all, she felt no sense of connection to Jonathan.

"People would talk about receiving signs from loved ones who had crossed, but I never felt like I was getting any signs," Leslie says. "I couldn't feel or see or sense anything. It was just this emptiness."

One year after Jonathan crossed, Leslie's father, Tony, became seriously ill. Leslie was very close to him, too, and toward the end of his life she asked him for a favor.

"I told him that I was very worried about Jonathan, that maybe he wasn't in a good place on the Other Side, and that he was angry with me," Leslie says. "I knew my father was going to cross, and I said, 'Dad, when you get to heaven, please find Jonathan, and find a way to let me know he is okay.'"

Soon after, her father crossed. Three days later, Leslie got a text message on her cellphone. It was a photo of her father, with the words

"Everything is fine" typed beneath it. Leslie checked the number to see who had sent her the text.

It had been sent from her father's cellphone.

"It was frightening!" she says. "I mean, this picture of my father did not even exist on my phone, so it's not like it just popped up from my photo file. But how did it come from my father's phone? How could my dad send me a text three days after he died?"

Leslie showed the message to other family members, who were as baffled as she was. She asked if anyone had Tony's cellphone, but no one did. No one had any idea where it was. So Leslie went to her father's house, and into his bedroom, to sort through his belongings. "I couldn't find his phone," she says. "Finally, I looked under his bed and there it was. I turned it on and it had just a tiny bit of power left. Somehow, that phone had sent me his picture and a text message."

There was no explanation Leslie could think of. No explanation anyone she knew could think of.

Leslie accepted the possibility that the inexplicable text message from her father was some kind of sign—an indication that Jonathan was okay. But it wasn't enough to alleviate her crippling sadness.

Five years later, Leslie and I had our reading, and her son came through so forcefully. Jonathan, I realized, wasn't someone who would have a lot of trouble sending signs from the Other Side. He seemed very gifted at communicating. He seemed *powerful*.

The problem was that Leslie was still too consumed by her sorrow to see what might be right in front of her.

One of the first things Jonathan had me convey to his mother was something he neglected to do on the day he crossed.

"Your son never wished you a happy birthday, did he?" I asked Leslie.

"No, he didn't," she said.

"He is saying it now," I told her.

Leslie started to cry again.

"Jonathan is showing me that he struggled with addiction, and that he killed himself," I said. "And he is saying that he understands things now that he did not understand when he was here. He is stronger now. He is saying that he is healed. He has healed so beautifully and so fully. And he needs you to know that none of it is your fault. You were the most important person in his life, and he loves you so, so much."

I could hear the effect Jonathan's words were having on his mother. They were *exactly* the words she needed to hear the most. And in that moment, I could almost feel Leslie begin to surrender some of the burden that she'd been carrying for so long.

"He is also saying that he is sorry," I told Leslie. "He is very sorry that he did what he did on your birthday. He wants you to know that he didn't do it as a way to hurt you. He did it because he didn't want you to ever forget him, and he wanted you to have a link with him so that you would always, always remember him. And your birthday was that link. It was more of a remembrance, more of a way to honor the bond between you, not to hurt you or punish you. He needs you to understand that."

Leslie exhaled and let her tears flow. The connection to her son that she believed she'd lost, she was realizing, was not lost at all.

Jonathan wanted to affirm the enduring bond between him and his mother, and he showed me the sign they shared: a tree with a heart in it. When I relayed this to Leslie, she seemed stumped.

"No," she said, "that's not our sign. I don't remember that."

But Jonathan persisted. He showed me the sign again—a tree and a heart—and this time he showed me a place where I could find it.

Right in his mother's front yard.

"He is saying that the sign is with you *today*," I told Leslie. "He is showing me the front of your house."

While we were still on the phone, Leslie got up and walked to her front door. I could hear her footsteps on the phone. Suddenly she stopped in her tracks.

"Oh my gosh," she said.

As she explained it to me, there was a tree in her front yard, and beside it there was a little ceramic statue planted in the ground.

A statue of a heart.

"All of a sudden it clicked," she says now. "After Jonathan crossed,

I planted a tree in the front yard in his honor, and I put the little heart next to it because trees and hearts always made me think of Jonathan. I don't know why, they just did. And then I guess I just completely forgot about it. Until Jonathan pointed it out to me again all those years later."

Through me, Jonathan led his mother straight to the sacred little space she had created for him, so that he could acknowledge and affirm the sign between them—a tree and a heart. It had been there all along, and Leslie had probably walked past it a few thousand times. And yet she had forgotten it—but Jonathan didn't.

And now he was reminding her, and thanking her, and letting her know that he was still around, still in her heart, as present as the tree.

"That was such a powerful, powerful moment," Leslie says. "I went from feeling like I had no connection to him to *knowing* that he was still with me. And that was the beginning of me going on with my life."

Since our reading, Leslie has stayed open to the signs her son sends her, and as a result she feels a deep and enduring connection to Jonathan that has helped heal her heart. There are times when she actually *feels* Jonathan's presence, as if he were right there with her.

For instance, Jonathan liked coming into his mother's bedroom and plopping down at the foot of her bed and talking with her for fifteen minutes at the end of difficult days—and today, "I can still feel him there, at the foot of my bed, like someone is actually sitting there," Leslie says. "I'll feel him arrive and it lets me know he is doing okay and watching over me."

Another place Leslie feels her son's presence is by the front door. Before he crossed, Jonathan once disappeared for three days, and Leslie worried she would never see him again. Then one evening, she glanced up and saw him standing just inside the front door. "It was like he was saying, 'I've come home,'" Leslie recalls. "It was a very powerful moment and we hugged for a long time. And now I sometimes feel Jonathan standing in that same spot. Sometimes it's like I can actually *see* him there. And it's like he's always arriving, always coming back home to see me."

When Leslie told me she sometimes "sees" Jonathan, I asked her what she meant. When I "see" people who have crossed, I see them as tiny points of light and energy on the little screen that forms in my mind. Some psychic mediums I know see people who have crossed in their human forms, as if they were standing among us. For Leslie, it was something else—something she had a hard time explaining.

"You know," she finally said, "it's like I see him with my third eye."

I understood what she meant. Many cultures and religions have the concept of a third eye that allows us to perceive things beyond the powers of ordinary sight. Basically, it is a figurative representation of our ability to see and perceive things at a higher and deeper level than is common—a shift in our consciousness that opens us to new insights. The ability to see the unseen that is all around us.

This is the very same concept that I've been returning to throughout this book—the shift in our consciousness that happens when we open our minds and our hearts to signs and messages from the Other Side. When Leslie "feels" the presence of her son in her home, she is demonstrating clairsentience—the ability to feel things through means other than our five senses. When Leslie "feels" Jonathan sitting at the foot of her bed, she is sensing the subtle presence of his life energy and consciousness. In the same way, when Leslie says she "sees" Jonathan standing by the front door, she is demonstrating a form of clairvoyance, which is the ability to perceive things through means other than our sense of sight.

I have had these moments myself, and I have spoken with thousands of people who have had them, and I can attest that they are deeply meaningful. These connections happen. They are not imagined. We feel them. We see our loved ones. We sense their presence. We hear their voices. We understand that they are still with us—that they are not *lost* to us.

And when we have these moments, we should honor them and talk about them, not dismiss them.

Before Leslie opened herself up to these beautiful moments of connectivity, she fully believed that she had lost her son—that he was gone forever. But he wasn't. He never will be. Because our souls endure, no matter how we cross. Our life energy lives on. We remain bound by powerful cords of light and love and energy that flow freely between us.

At the time of our reading, I told Leslie that Jonathan was a pretty powerful force on the Other Side. He helped her father send her an incredible message and confirmation through his cellphone, and he somehow pulled the strings that brought Leslie and me together. He also communicated that he was grateful to his mother for agreeing to shepherd him through the world even though she knew he wouldn't be in it for long.

"He says his soul came to earth to learn from you," I told Leslie. "The lesson you taught him was unconditional love."

"His message to me was a message of love and forgiveness and healing," Leslie says. "I was angry about what happened, and that is natural, but now I feel like I am healing, and I still love Jonathan fully and profoundly. We have a connection that will never go away, and now that I know that, I can live a love-based life, not a fear-based life. Because when we connect, all I feel for Jonathan is love."

Today Leslie marks her birthday on May 1, more than two weeks after her actual birthday, April 14. "That day is now Jonathan's day," she says. "It's a day we can celebrate all that he is and all that he has brought us.

"My message to anyone who is stuck in grief and sadness like I was is 'Do not be afraid,'" Leslie says. "Because when you're afraid, you close yourself off. And when you open your heart and your mind, what comes back from the universe is pure love and joy. And you begin to understand that your loved ones are still with you, and there is no blame, no fault, no anger, no guilt, just unconditional love. And that gives you the freedom to go on."

29

SURRENDER

THIS book is a journey toward a new way of looking at our lives. It starts with opening our minds to the possibility of signs sent to us by the Other Side. It moves on to co-creating a language that makes it easier for our Teams of Light to send us those signs. From there, it takes us to appreciating how powerful and life-altering these signs can be. And then we reach the point that can be the most challenging part of the journey—our willingness to trust the universe. The willingness to *surrender*.

To explain what I mean by this, I'd like to share a personal story about a difficult and frightening time for me and for my family. To be honest, I was reluctant at first to tell this story publicly, but I decided to include it here because it shows how I navigated the very journey of this book, how I came to that point of trusting the universe, and how that changed my path.

This is a story about surrender.

It starts on a beach on Long Island, on a beautiful summer day. I was with my three children. Ashley, my oldest, was fourteen. Nothing was amiss; my kids were all healthy and happy and having a typically carefree summer. Ashley was about to start high school, and she was excited about it but also a little nervous.

Ashley was pure sweetness. She was a beautiful, tender, compassionate soul. She was in advanced classes throughout middle school, she took ballet and lyrical dance, she excelled at art, and she made the honor roll. She was also delightful to be around—funny, kind, thoughtful, and loving. She never once lied to me or talked back to me or used bad language. I know I'm biased, but in every way Ashley was the ideal child.

That afternoon at the beach, I noticed a strange rash on Ashley's back. It looked like a row of six thick, horizontal lines stretching across the middle of her back—almost like they had been carved with a knife. I asked her if it hurt or itched, and she said no. Even so, I took her to see the doctor.

"That's weird," the doctor said when she examined her. "It could be a jellyfish sting."

I told the doctor Ashley hadn't been in the water that day.

"Then it's stretch marks," the doctor concluded. "Don't worry about them. They will fade in time."

"Are you sure?" I asked. Ashley was slender, which made me wonder how she could end up with stretch marks. But the doctor stuck to her diagnosis, and I let it go. That is what we do—we listen to authority. She told me not to worry, so I tried not to.

Right around that time I began to notice a subtle shift in Ashley's behavior. She started experiencing bouts of anxiety. She seemed to get easily angry. That summer we'd gone to Disneyland, and we got stuck for about fifteen minutes in a boat on the Jungle Cruise ride, right next to a tribal scene of a man with a big pot of boiling water and a shrunken head on a stick. At the time it was kind of funny, but a week or so later, out of the blue, Ashley became crippled with anxiety about it. She couldn't stop thinking about it, and she spent two days in bed. She was terrified by the idea of cannibals existing in the world. I reasoned with her and reassured her, and finally she seemed to let go of her terror. I chalked it up to her nervousness about starting high school.

By the time her classes began, though, Ashley was already transforming into a different person. I mean a *completely* different person. She was rude and cranky and disrespectful, and for the first time her grades started dropping. She began having acute insomnia and anxiety attacks that would leave her curled up on the floor in a blanket. In the mornings I couldn't get her up for school no matter how hard I tried. Garrett and I decided to take Ashley out of school and have tutors come to our home instead. We had no choice.

Ashley made it through the ninth-grade curriculum, but when she returned to school for her sophomore year, her struggle continued. She couldn't focus on anything and didn't seem to care. At home she'd wrap herself in a blanket and lie on the floor for hours, with her eyes closed or staring blankly. Her anxiety was so acute she could barely function, and she'd miss days and even weeks of school. I was alternately worried to death about her and angry with her. We fought a lot, and that took a toll on the entire family. Something was clearly wrong with my daughter, but no one could tell me what it was.

One day, I had a sudden thought about a memoir I'd read many years before by the writer Amy Tan, called *The Opposite of Fate*. One of the final chapters told the story of her struggle with Lyme disease. Her symptoms had been more psychiatric than physical, just like my daughter's. That Amy's memoir popped into my head felt like a tug from the universe, and I immediately suspected that Lyme disease might be the culprit in Ashley's case. Part of me was already convinced I'd cracked the case. For the first time in a very long time, I felt a surge of hope.

I took Ashley to the doctor for blood work, and they ran the CDC's Lyme screening test, but when we returned for the results, she told us they were negative.

"She doesn't have Lyme," the doctor declared.

I was stunned. I had been sure that was it. But the doctor insisted the results were clear. She sent us home with no diagnosis. We were back to square one. My daughter was in the grip of something insidious and pernicious, and there was no one we could turn to for answers. I felt helpless and hopeless and lost.

We were in a seemingly endless loop of Ashley acting out and our attempts to respond. A few months later, I took her back to the doctor to have her retested for Lyme disease, but once again the screening came back negative. By then, I'd done a good deal of research and I knew the initial test for Lyme was not always accurate. In order to rule out Lyme, we would need more advanced screening, such as the ELISA test or the Western blot test. But when I asked—or rather *begged*—Ashley's doctor about these tests, she told me we didn't need them and she wouldn't order them. When I objected, all four of the doctors in the practice were adamant that Ashley didn't have Lyme. One of them even laughed at me.

At this point, Ashley was suffering from extreme insomnia. She'd stay up until three or four in the morning and be completely exhausted the next day. We arranged for her to be medically excused from attending classes and allowed to enroll in a home study program again. It was so awful to watch my daughter, who had been so vibrant, loving, and engaged in life, suffering and not being able to function as a normal teenager, experiencing all the excitement, joy, and life moments that high school brings. She was missing out on so much. I just wanted her to get better!

But Ashley continued to get worse. Often, she would get angry out of the blue and rage for hours at a time. Her anger would erupt like a volcano in the house. In fact, sometimes she would get so angry she would run out of the house. One morning, in a fit of rage, she did just that. It was rather cold out, and drizzling, and she left with no jacket. I knew she didn't want to talk, but I worried about her safety and warmth and went after her in my car, hoping I could coax her back home—but she kept running and ducking and I quickly lost sight of her. I drove around, hoping to see her. It was early in the morning and the streets were deserted. Finally, I let my instincts take over and steer me (and the car), and it was then that I caught a quick glimpse of Ashley ducking behind a closed Japanese restaurant. There were two driveways to the parking lot, one on either side of the restaurant building. I was approaching the first driveway, but I decided to pass it by and drive down the second one, calculating that I might be able to head her off and get her in the car with me.

But just before I turned off the main road, something strange happened. A white van going in the opposite direction crossed the median directly into my path, sped up, cut the wheel sharply, and turned down the driveway Ashley had just run through. The van disappeared behind the restaurant, which was where I'd seen Ashley go.

My heart was pounding. The van cut in front of me so quickly and so close to me that we had avoided colliding by a mere second or two. What was more, the van seemed to be following Ashley. I quickly pulled into the second driveway, expecting her to have walked the short distance to the second driveway, but there was no sign of her. It didn't make sense. She couldn't have just disappeared. I pulled around the back of the closed restaurant, and finally I saw her, huddled in a corner by the restaurant wall. The white van had stopped just a few feet from her. The driver's-side window was down, and the driver was gesturing with his hand for Ashley to come closer.

"Hey!" I screamed out. "This is my daughter. What are you doing?"

The man in the van seemed shocked to see me. It was early morning, the restaurant was closed, there were no other cars on the road—everything around us was desolate.

"I was just asking for directions," he stammered. Then he sped away.

In that moment, I knew beyond any doubt that if Ashley had gotten into the van, she would have been killed. I just knew it. If I hadn't caught a tiny glimpse of her, I would have lost her. And I knew exactly why the driver had risked heading straight into oncoming traffic and nearly crashing into my car to turn in right behind her. He had seen her, too. He knew the shops were closed and the area behind the restaurant was deserted. He saw an opportunity to do evil.

Ashley got into my car and we drove home, both of us frightened. I was so rattled, I hadn't even looked to get the van's license plate. If I hadn't been clear about what was at stake before, I was certainly clear about it now. We weren't just trying to find out what was wrong with Ashley. We were trying to save her life.

Throughout this ordeal, I'd been working to stay open to the Other Side. It felt especially important because I felt so lost and directionless and needed as much help as I could get. I believed that my Team of Light would come through. No doctor had been able to give me an answer, but maybe the Other Side could.

By then, Ashley had developed severe stomach problems, and we added a gastroenterologist to her team of doctors. He diagnosed her with IBS-C (irritable bowel syndrome with constipation). He prescribed medication, but it didn't seem to work. The situation was only getting worse.

Shortly after the incident with the white van, I was randomly surfing my Facebook news feed when a particular post by someone I'd gone to high school with caught my eye. It included the words "sudden personality change," and there was a link to something called PANS—pediatric acute-onset neuropsychiatric syndrome. PANS is an infectious disease that can lead to inflammation on a child's brain, causing severe anxiety and personality changes. Another disease, referred to as PANDAS, has the same symptoms but is triggered by strep throat. I sat bolt-upright: *Ashley had been diagnosed with strep throat earlier in the year.* PANS and PANDAS, the research said, could make previously lovely children begin to act as if they were possessed.

They were even known as the possession diseases.

The link led me to one of the very few PANS and PANDAS specialists on the East Coast, and I made an appointment right away. She gave Ashley the antibiotic amoxicillin, and within twenty-four hours some of her worst symptoms diminished. Another antibiotic, azithromycin, helped even more.

But even then, we couldn't be sure of what was wrong with Ashley. Not all of her symptoms synced up with PANS or PANDAS, nor did we know exactly which destructive virus had invaded her body. We couldn't be sure the antibiotics alone would cure her, or even keep her symptoms at bay for very long. We were still searching for an answer. The doctor sent me home with a packet that included a seventeen-page article about the disease, which I intended to read when I could find a quiet moment.

Things were getting desperate. Even though I knew the Other Side was in this battle with me, I needed more help. They had led me to the PANS doctor, but now I needed more guidance. I was watching Ashley unravel and lose her life energy—*I was watching the Ashley I knew disappear before my eyes.* I had to find a way to fix her. I had to pull her back from the brink, because if I couldn't, I didn't know who else would.

One morning at home, while I was sifting through the stacks of medical bills and research and test results that had piled up all over our house in the last three years, I felt an especially strong sense of desperation. The thought of everything Ashley had had to go through was too painful to bear. I went to my bedroom, and I quietly closed the door behind me. Then I did something I hadn't done since I was a little girl—I got down on my knees and prayed.

"Listen, God, Team of Light," I said out loud, "I really need help."

Instantly, I felt my father push through on my screen.

My father had crossed only weeks earlier, and since then he'd been incredibly responsive, sending me all kinds of signs. And now, in this darkest of moments, he was there for me again. I raised my hands up to the ceiling—up to God.

"I give up," I said. "I surrender. I need you to show me what is wrong with Ashley. I know there is something more than what the doctors are saying. I know she isn't bipolar. I need you to show me what is wrong with my child. I surrender. Please, *please*, show me what is wrong."

That night, I got ready for bed, completely drained and exhausted. I turned off the lights and then, suddenly, I got a download from the universe. It was clear and specific.

The packet.

Read the packet.

Turn on the lights and read the packet now.

The packet that the PANS and PANDAS doctor had given me was on the kitchen table—I'd forgotten about it. I turned on the lights, sat at the kitchen table, and pulled out the lengthy article, which was titled "Hidden Invaders."

When I got to the middle of the second page, I froze.

Imagine the sound of a car screeching to a halt, followed by complete stillness and silence. That's what this was like. A single word jumped off the page, as if it were lit up by a neon light.

Bartonella

"We all know that cat scratch fever, caused by bartonella, can cause rages and mood swings in patients," I read. It was written so matter-of-factly, but to me it was a blinding revelation.

Bartonella! This had to be it! I opened my laptop, went straight to Google, and typed in the word. The screen came up, and the first thing I saw was a photo. When I saw it, I gasped and started to cry.

It was a photo of the very same rash I'd seen on Ashley's back three years earlier.

Bartonella, I learned, is an infectious bacterium. If it gets into the bloodstream, it can cause intense psychiatric rages and mood swings. It can lead to trench fever, or to the more commonly known cat scratch fever, which can then lead to encephalopathy—a brain disease that can result in permanent brain damage, or even death.

I had my answer. I knew it with every ounce of my being. I would have staked my life on it. My Team of Light brought me to the truth. Ashley had bartonella.

Then I got another download that showed me exactly how and *why* this disease had overtaken her with such force. Ashley had gotten the HPV vaccine a few years before. The Other Side showed me that something in that particular vaccine had damaged her cells—literally infiltrated her "cell doors" and left them unable to close and lock and fight off disease, which meant that whatever attacked Ashley was able to thrive.

I stayed up until four A.M. doing research. When my husband woke up, I told him the Other Side had shown me what was wrong with Ashley. That morning, I took her to see the pediatrician, armed with the packet. I'd even printed out copies of the photo of Ashley's rash and articles from medical journals affirming that bartonella causes anxiety, rages, and mood swings. I handed them all to the doctor and explained how the HPV shot had damaged Ashley's cells. The doctor smiled and shook her head.

"With all due respect, Ashley does not have bartonella," she said. "The HPV vaccine is perfectly safe."

Then she took down a medical book and showed me a passage that said bartonella presented as a three-dot rash, not the kind of rash Ashley had. I tried to show her the articles I had found, but she waved them away. She even let out a patronizing laugh and assured me that I was absolutely wrong about Ashley.

Not all that long before, at this point in the conversation I would have deferred to her authority and given up. But not anymore. This time, I had my Team of Light with me. They had shown me what was wrong, and I knew they were right. And so I insisted that the doctor give Ashley a blood test to screen for bartonella.

The doctor agreed to run the test, probably to humor me. Two days later, the test result came back.

Ashley was negative for bartonella.

I knew this couldn't be right. The Other Side had steered me straight to bartonella as the cause of Ashley's ordeal. So why were the results negative?

"I don't care what the results say," I told the doctor. "I know this is what she has."

Just a few days later, I was talking to my friend Wendy, who happened to have been diagnosed with Lyme disease. She asked me about Ashley, and so I relayed to her what the Other Side had told me about Ashley and bartonella. Wendy gasped. She told me bartonella and Lyme usually go hand in hand . . . they are co-infections. Wendy had been treated by a world-renowned Yale-trained internist who subspecializes in zoonotic infections, Dr. Steven Phillips, located in Wilton, Connecticut. He was actively engaged in research toward a durable cure for Lyme. A very busy man, he had a two-year waiting list for new patients. Two years was too long for Ashley to wait.

"Let me see what I can do," Wendy said.

I knew she was well connected, and I knew she would do anything to help me, but still, this seemed too much to hope for. And yet Wendy got us an appointment to see Dr. Phillips in two weeks.

He read through Ashley's medical history, and he listened as I told him about my certainty that she had bartonella. He asked me if Ashley had recently developed a certain symptom—IBS-constipation—which would be a good indicator of bartonella. My jaw dropped. As I previously shared, Ashley had come down with it just a few months earlier.

"This is textbook bartonella," he said. "I'm also going to test her for Lyme. They often go hand in hand."

This time, he ran the more advanced ELISA and Western blot tests for Lyme through the labs at Stony Brook University, as well as a specialized test for bartonella through Galaxy Diagnostics, a laboratory in North Carolina and the most specialized testing facility for it in the country.

When the results came back, they showed that Ashley had tested positive for Lyme disease and highly positive for bartonella. In fact, the levels were so high, the doctor believed she'd likely had it for the past three years.

Three years! Exactly the span of Ashley's ordeal.

He immediately put Ashley on a treatment for Lyme and bartonella, and ultimately the parasites that often accompany those infections. The medication she took had its own hellish side effects—she experienced intense pain in her bones and muscles, and once even felt like bugs were crawling inside her body—but all of her psychiatric symptoms disappeared. The antibiotics seemed to get her anxiety under control, but the exhaustion and brain fog that had now taken over were a constant battle.

That is when the Other Side intervened again. Another dear friend led us to a second brilliant doctor, Kristine Gedroic (an M.D. with three different board certifications: family medicine, medical acupuncture, and integrative medicine), located in Morristown, New Jersey, who had cured my friend's son of Lyme and restored him to health. A cellular test conducted by Dr. Gedroic revealed even more. But before she tested Ashley, she asked me to write up Ashley's medical history—her symptoms, and what I felt was wrong. I wrote exactly what the Other Side had told me. Then Dr. Gedroic ran a cellular blood test. When we met with her to get the results, she sat down with a look of astonishment on her face and said she had never in her life seen something like this: What I had written down was exactly what the tests had revealed. There was a very high level of aluminum inside Ashley's cells. And it was a type of aluminum specific to vaccines: Gardasil, the shot Ashley had received for HPV. The doctor went on to explain that the aluminum stuck in Ashley's cells had damaged her mitochondria and thinned the membranes of her cell walls—what I had been shown as her "cell doors" in my download!—allowing whatever bacteria and viruses were present in her body to run rampant. Her cells literally couldn't shut their doors against the infections. Her immune system couldn't keep up. The doctor prescribed a protocol of IV treatment to restore the health of her cells and flush the aluminum out at the same time, as well as numerous herbs and naturopathic treatments to treat any Lyme, bartonella, and parasitic infections that were present.[*]

---

[*] I am not anti-vaccinations at all. I feel they are extremely important; I have always vaccinated my children and will continue to. For whatever reason, this one particular shot was problematic for Ashley.

It was an astonishing moment.

Ashley began getting better. She was improving. More and more, we saw the same sweet, loving girl we'd been so afraid we'd lost. Her fatigue, bone ache, and brain fog also lifted. Her sleeping patterns regulated.

Not long ago, Ashley took her ACT test—a college entrance exam that lasts nearly six hours. For the past three years she'd barely been able to focus on anything for longer than a few minutes, but she aced the ACT.

As of this writing, we are not out of the woods just yet. Ashley has her ups and downs, and we all need to stay vigilant. But she is incredibly strong, and her force of will is amazing. She continues to improve, and I am so proud to see her fighting back and regaining those unique and special parts of herself. I couldn't possibly have more love and admiration for her than I do, and I'm humbled by the beautiful, generous power of her spirit. We still have a way to go, but we are getting there. I am certain that Ashley is going to be okay.

And I am certain the Other Side will lead me to what I need to know to make sure that she is.

Sometimes the Other Side sends us cardinals and rainbows and groundhogs. Other times, it sends signs that are more internal—gut instincts, pulls, dreams, random thoughts. Tugs from the universe in one direction or another.

I am not implying that the Other Side will always fix everything for us. That's not how the universe works. There are doorways and passageways we cannot avoid, no matter how hard we fight to heal a wound or cure a disease or mend what's broken. Parents who fight as hard as or harder than Garrett and I did still lose their children to terrible afflictions. There are no guarantees that the Other Side will deliver a miracle. But what we can be certain of is that in our darkest moments, we are not alone. We have a support system in place. We have forces on our side that are determined to help and guide us—

which is why it's so important for us to always stay open to the extraordinary reach of our Teams of Light.

If I look at it all in retrospect and lay it out like a big floor plan, I can see how the Other Side was guiding me toward the right answer — from Amy Tan's book, to the Facebook post, to the PANS packet, to Wendy, to Dr. Phillips, to Dr. Gedroic. The trail was there for me to follow. There were detours and wrong turns and narrow misses, but the Other Side never let me lose the trail. The universe just kept pulling me in the right direction.

This story is a story about the power of surrendering. The power of putting ourselves in the hands of the Other Side. I believe that when we fully trust in a higher power, something truly profound and life altering happens. Because in that moment we are not only collaborating with the Other Side, but also honoring our dependence on it and recognizing our interconnectedness.

It doesn't matter what we call this higher power. I grew up Lutheran and I have always believed in God. When I got down on my knees in my bedroom and prayed to God, I could feel my Team of Light and my father who crossed there with me, too. My conception of God is different now than the one I had as a child; at this point in my life I can say that it has expanded. The concept of a higher power has different names in different cultures and belief systems — and there are a host of different ways of honoring it. The names and rituals matter much less than the basic belief that a higher power exists. It is there, loving us, available to us, everywhere and all the time. But it's up to us to be open to it, and to trust it, and to finally plug in and surrender to it.

My daughter Ashley's harrowing journey, and ours along with her, is all part of the universe's plan for us. We are learning lessons in love and hope and faith and connection, and it is leading us to the people we are meant to be connected to in our lives.

None of us is alone. No life is meant to be lived solitarily. No existence is unimportant or meaningless. We are all connected to one another, and to the forces of light and love on the Other Side. And through these connections—through these binding cords of light between us—we achieve a spiritual wellness and personal authenticity that make us far more potent and influential than we ever could be without them.

That is the power of surrendering to the Other Side.

GONE FROM MY SIGHT

I am standing upon the seashore. A ship, at my side,
spreads her white sails to the moving breeze and starts
for the blue ocean. She is an object of beauty and strength.
I stand and watch her until, at length, she hangs like a speck
of white cloud just where the sea and sky come to mingle with each
    other.

Then, someone at my side says, "There, she is gone."

Gone where?

Gone from my sight. That is all. She is just as large in mast,
hull and spar as she was when she left my side.
And, she is just as able to bear her load of living freight to her
    destined port.
Her diminished size is in me—not in her.

And, just at the moment when someone says, "There, she is gone,"
there are other eyes watching her coming, and other voices
ready to take up the glad shout, "Here she comes!"

And that is dying.

—HENRY VAN DYKE

PART FOUR

STAYING
IN THE
LIGHT

Love is the bridge between you and everything.

— RUMI

ALL AROUND US, EVERY DAY, THERE IS A SECRET language. This language helps us understand some of the most confusing parts of our world. It helps us understand why certain people come into our lives. It helps us see meaning where before there was darkness or confusion. It helps us navigate loss. It helps us know we are watched over and more loved than we can ever fathom.

It also teaches us that we are all part of the fabric of one another's lives. We weave a magical tapestry of meaning and love and forgiveness and hope and light with one another. We belong to one another. Our relationships matter greatly here on earth, and they continue past bodily death. Love is the unbreakable tie.

Understanding the secret language of the universe helps guide us onto our highest path, and reassures us that we are not alone. Not ever.

And here is a truth. Once you open your mind and heart to perceiving this secret language, you will begin to see it everywhere.

Everywhere.

30

HOW TO SHINE BRIGHTLY

HERE is a simple question: What is a chair made of?

Well, a chair can be made of wood, or plastic, or metal, or really anything solid.

Okay, but what is a chair *really* made of? What is the wood made of? Or the plastic or the metal?

All of these things are made of matter, a scientific term for anything that has mass and volume—anything, basically, that takes up space in the world. Whatever we refer to as a physical thing is considered matter.

Okay, but what is *matter* made of?

This one's easy—all matter is made up of atoms.

And atoms themselves are made up of particles called protons, electrons, and neutrons. Protons and neutrons are made up of other particles called quarks and gluons. There may be other, even smaller particles, but these have not been identified yet.

What we do know, however, is that the principle attribute of *all* of these things—matter, atoms, protons, electrons, and quarks—is the same. That attribute is *energy*.

Scientists who study quantum physics believe that all matter is energy—that atoms themselves are nothing more than constantly swirling fields of electric energy. Albert Einstein's famous equation $E = mc^2$ is fundamentally an acknowledgment that there is no real difference between matter and energy. "Mass and energy are both but different manifestations of the same thing—a somewhat unfamiliar concept for the average mind," Einstein remarked in 1948. Everything that we can see or imagine—in other words, the whole universe—is made of energy.

Which means that chairs are actually made of energy. They may look solid and unmoving to us, but they actually comprise tiny atoms endlessly spinning and vibrating in a tornado of energy. The chair has no actual physical structure, because atoms are not made of physical things. The structure of the atom itself is an invisible field of energy.

Which leads to the natural conclusion that we, too, are made of energy.

It is really easy for us to forget this basic truth, and to think of ourselves as strictly physical beings—arms, legs, eyes, hair. A body with a soul. But the truth is the other way around.

We are all souls with bodies.

And our souls, like everything else in the universe, are made of energy.

In fact, our bodies actually emit light. Scientists have proven that in pitch darkness, we emit biophotons. While imperceptible to the human eye, these biophotons can be measured by sensitive instruments. We are, quite literally, beings of light.

Whenever I talk to people about signs, I always begin by trying to make them aware of their own energy.

Think about it—don't we all know someone who can "change the energy" in a room just by walking in? Don't we all know people whose positive energy practically announces them before they even arrive? And don't we all know someone whose negative energy can stick to us like mud?

Because we comprise energy, we also *give off* energy. And the energy we give off can have a real and profound impact on someone else's energy and life. The way we carry and share our energy may be invisible to the naked eye, but it is as real as a handshake. We all bring a particular energy to every encounter in our lives.

And what I want everyone to understand is that *this energy matters*, not just to us, but to everyone in our path. Even our thoughts matter, for they are energy, too.

This energy matters because we are all connected to one another in very real ways. We are hardwired to seek and crave connection.

And yet we sometimes lose this feeling of interconnectedness. We allow events in our lives to diminish our energy. But we can control our energy. We can dial it up.

The way we do this is by *shifting* our energy.

To shift our energy, we need to be more aware of how we handle and project our energy. Here is one simple way we can put this into action. Try waking up tomorrow morning and resolving to smile at ten different people. That's it—just smile at them. The person who holds a door open for you. Your boss. The receptionist at the gym. The barista who makes your coffee. Just give them a big smile, and then watch how that smile shifts the energy between you. Notice how it affects *their* energy, and your own, too.

Practice creating energy shifts and see how it feels. If a driver is signaling that he wants to get into your lane, wave him in. If someone at the deli seems cranky and overwhelmed, give him a kind word. If you see a mom whose kid is having a meltdown in a store, give her a reassuring smile.

This is how we shift our energy into the positive. It is a way of honoring the great blessing of our interconnectedness. And when we do this—when we shift our energy—we become more receptive to the energy of others and to the energy of the universe. The more we do this, the more we "open" our energy, the more likely we are to be open to all things, including beautiful signs from the Other Side.

Because the way we elevate our lives is by elevating our energy.

There are practical steps we can all take to move ourselves into a more elevated physical, mental, and spiritual place—a place that will allow us to get better at asking for and receiving powerful signs. Let's explore some of these practical steps here.

THE IMPORTANCE OF ART

This book isn't just about our connection to the Other Side; it's also about our connection to one another here on earth—and one of the most brilliant ways we honor this connection, and grow together, is through art.

Throughout history, societies have made the biggest leaps forward in times of great art. Think of the Renaissance, an explosion of growth and invention that started in fourteenth-century Florence. I believe this is because *art shifts our energy*. Art opens us up to new ideas, new possibilities, new energies. Great works of art have a special magnificence and vibrancy, and that beautiful energy can shift our own. Works of art hold and impart a very special energy even *centuries* after their creation. Music and the visual arts can heal and restore people in ways that not even medicine can. In fact, there is a psychological practice of healing through art called art therapy. Consider how we feel when we listen to a song that moves us. The mere act of listening shifts our energy. Often just the *thought* of listening to music we love is enough to excite us and make us feel happy and alive. When we engage with art, we are plugging ourselves into the very flow of the light of the universe.

I also believe that all artists connect with and collaborate with a Team of Light on the Other Side in the creation of their art. For example, J. K. Rowling, the author of the Harry Potter series, has spoken about how the initial idea for the boy wizard—in fact, for nearly all of the story and mythology that would make up her seven Harry

Potter novels—came to her in a flash moment while she was stuck on a train between Manchester and London.

"The idea for Harry Potter fell in my head," she has said. "I didn't have a pen and was too shy to ask anyone for one on the train, which frustrated me at the time, but when I look back, it was the best thing for me. It gave me the full four hours on the train to think up all the ideas for the book."

What an astonishing thing! To have such a magical, consequential idea just "fall" in your head! But here's the thing—even though J. K. Rowling received a download from the universe from which she fashioned Harry Potter, she still had to do her part. Art is always a collaboration.

No artist ever works alone.

All of art is a collaboration between those of us who bring it into being here and those who send us creative light and inspiration and energy from the Other Side.

I remember taking my children to a bookstore at midnight for the release of one of the Harry Potter books. It was an *amazing* scene. There were scores of people in Harry Potter costumes, waving wizard wands, bubbling over with excitement and anticipation. There was so much joy and vibrancy and positive energy on the street outside the bookstore, it actually made me cry. I thought, *Look how J. K. Rowling has brought us all together! Look at all the happiness and merriment! And this scene is playing out all over the world, in thousands of bookstores in dozens of countries! Look how we're all united by this! What a magical moment of connection!*

And yet, despite this truly awesome display of the power of art, we, as a society, don't value art as much as we should.

Our society mandates that children take gym classes, for instance, because we appreciate the connection between physical conditioning and a healthy life. But art? No—we don't mandate art classes. If children are lucky, they have art squeezed into their schedules.

That's a mistake. Art is the way we tell the collective story of all humanity, but it's also one of the most powerful ways we connect with one another here on earth. To deprive ourselves of this connection is shortsighted and costly. To ignore art is to deprive ourselves of all the light and energy and brilliance of an artist or a period, because a great work of art is like a portal to that time and energy, even if it was made centuries ago. Why would we ever want to cut ourselves off from that kind of enduring positive light and energy? Why wouldn't we want to be part of the telling of our own history?

The energy and vibrancy of art has a profound effect on us all, and moves us into a place of higher receptivity to signs and ideas. If we choose to tap into this power, we will be rewarded. Maybe we do it by painting a landscape. Maybe it's sculpting, or playing piano. Maybe it's simply going to a museum or listening to music or reading a poem. Art in all its forms is a kind of dialogue between us and the entirety of existence, past, present, and future. *It is us elevating our lives by elevating our energy.*

Art can also open our hearts and minds. Consider the musical *Hamilton* by Lin-Manuel Miranda. The musical is a vibrant way for us to revisit our history, while it invites us to explore what kind of legacy we want to create in our own time. The musical asks fundamental questions of us—both on an individual level and collectively. Remember the song "History Has Its Eyes on You"?

In my life, I have always felt a deep connection to art. Music, for sure, has always been hugely important to me. It was the way my father and I communicated: by singing songs together. I will admit that I'm not the best singer in the world—I would love to come back as someone with a beautiful, heavenly voice—but I still love to sing. The act of singing—the vibration, the sound waves—is magical to me. It transforms me. My singing voice may lack pitch and tone, but that doesn't mean it can't shift my energy into the positive!

Besides music, I have also made it a point to buy and display art that really speaks to me and inspires me. I can tangibly feel the artist's energy in each piece, creating a powerful link of ideas, exploration, and beauty.

Try it for yourself. Try it when you're feeling down. Go to a museum, or a movie, or a play. Sing a song or read a poem. Open yourself up to the vitality and brilliance of the exchange. I am counting on the fact that you will feel your energy shift.

We've all been given the great and beautiful gift of art, and we should be mindful of this gift. If we are, art can and will change our energy, and our lives.

GRATITUDE

Because we all comprise energy, we give off energy. We emit vibrations—the oscillation of electric waves. What the Other Side shows us is that the two highest and purest vibrations we can achieve as human beings are love and gratitude.

People who are pessimists are energy magnets—they tend to perceive only the negative energy around them. But experiments have shown that if you sit pessimists down and have them write out a simple gratitude list—finding the one or two (or ten) things they are honestly grateful for each day—you can shift their energy from negative to positive in a matter of weeks (studies have shown that practices become habits when they are performed on twenty-one consecutive days).

Sheryl Sandberg, the COO of Facebook, has written and spoken about the transformational impact of gratitude. In 2015, her husband, David—the father of their two young children—died unexpectedly of a cardiac arrhythmia while working out on a treadmill. His death was shattering for her. During the darkest moments of her depression, a psychologist friend suggested she try something counterintuitive.

"He suggested that I think about how much worse things could be," Sandberg said in a 2016 commencement address at UC Berkeley. "'Worse?' I said. 'Are you kidding me? How could things be worse?'"

Her friend's response: "Dave could have had that same cardiac arrhythmia while he was driving your children."

Sandberg's reaction was one single word: "Wow."

In that instant, she felt what she called an overwhelming gratitude that she still had her children. And that gratitude, Sandberg explained, "overtook some of the grief. Finding gratitude and appreciation is key to resilience . . . and counting your blessings can actually *increase* your blessings."

Through this one mental maneuver—thinking about what she was grateful for, rather than thinking about the tragedy of her husband's death—Sandberg was able to do what she thought was impossible: alleviate her grief, if only for a while. She shifted her energy into the positive. It sounds simple, because it *is*. The simple experience of feeling gratitude palpably shifts our energy.

Negative thoughts are like stinky bits of trash thrown into our energy field (with some being bigger and stinkier than others). Now think of positive thoughts as lovely flowers surrounding us. After a while, we are sitting either in a stinky energy dump or in a fragrant meadow. It's easy to choose which energy field we want to be in, because we choose—and control—where we direct our thoughts. We choose which thoughts to embrace.

So give it a try. Make a gratitude list. Start with one thing a day. Then keep going. Write down something new every day. Remember the twenty-one-day rule, which will help you make it a habit. By the twenty-second day, you should wake up automatically looking for things to be grateful for, instead of hunting for things to feel bad about.

THOUGHTS MATTER

This concept is proven by the notes on gratitude above—but the same is true of all of our thoughts—they matter greatly to our quality of life.

Thoughts can be both exhilarating and terrifying, because thoughts imply action, and action leads to change, and change is incredibly powerful. We can feel terrified of the power we have to

change the direction of our lives. And because this is true, we sometimes allow negative thoughts to stop us from changing or moving
forward. We tell ourselves, *I'm so stupid*, or *I'll never be happy*, and
these thoughts become our reality. The subtext in our head—our
thoughts—becomes our actual truth.

But they are *not* the truth—they're just thoughts. And we can
learn to shift and elevate them.

How? How do we shut out that horrible, negative voice in our
heads that likes to tell us how worthless or doomed or unlovable we
are?

We don't. We don't stop that voice.

We talk *over* it.

Here's how: The first and most important step is to be mindful of
when that negative voice pops up. If you wake up and the voice says,
Ugh, today is going to be such an awful day, and you let that thought
just hang there while you get ready for work, you've already predeter-
mined your energy level for that day. You've accepted this negative
thought as a truth.

But it *isn't* the truth. So the next time you hear that negative voice,
identify it and immediately talk over it. Say, "No, actually, today is a
gift. Being alive right now, right this second, is an incredible gift. And
I am connected in a profound way to all things in the universe, and
my presence holds power and magic, and today will be a beautiful
exploration of this connection and of all that I am capable of. Today
will be a *wonderful* day."

That's it! That's all you have to do. Just by thinking it, just by saying it, you've already shifted your energy. That's how simple, and
powerful, thought energy is. So be mindful of the negative voice, and
remember to talk over it, and be aware of how your energy shifts.

MANIFESTING

I am so pulled to discussing this concept, I could write a whole book
about it. But for now, I just want to share my belief in the incredible

power of manifesting—the harnessing, owning, and directing of our energy to create a future that is worthy of us. And here is an important fact to be aware of: We are always in a state of co-creating with the universe!

Now, to say that something is manifest is to say that it is clear and true. Not that it *will be* clear and true, but that it already is. So by manifesting, I mean being open to and mindful of our conversation with the universe about our future, and what the truth of our future is. This conversation needs to be *specific*—we need to share our complete understanding of the life path we desire. The conversation also needs to be embraced *as if it has already occurred*—and thus be in the past tense. Because we are not talking to the universe about what we *hope* will happen.

We are talking to the universe about something that we *know* will happen.

I used to be skeptical of manifesting. Then I had my own direct and powerful experience with it. About a year before I wrote my first book—before I even thought about writing a book—a friend of mine asked me to come to a class about manifesting with her. She was going through a divorce, and she wanted to manifest positive change in her life. I didn't really know much about manifesting, but I wanted to be a good, supportive friend, so I agreed to go.

During the class, the instructor had us flip through stacks of magazines and cut out images and words that reflected what we wanted our futures to be, or that simply tugged at us. In the next class, we would glue the images on a piece of paper, thus creating our own personal "vision boards." We were asked to approach these images not from a place of wishful thinking, but rather from a place of gratitude—as if they had already happened to us.

The whole thing seemed ridiculous to me, but I went along with it anyway, and I found myself cutting out some pretty outlandish and improbable things. One of the first things I felt pulled to cut out was the phrase, "*New York Times* Bestselling Author." It was crazy, nonsensical—I had no plans to write a book! But I cut it out to put on my vision board anyway. I even remember the thought that tried to weasel its way into my head as I cut it out: *What? Who do you think you are to cut that out? Ha ha ha.*

I never made it to the second class, when we were supposed to create our vision boards. Instead, I tucked the words and pictures I cut out in an envelope and put it in a drawer.

Fast-forward one year. I was still a high school English teacher, and I was on hall duty when I got a download from the universe that I would be writing a book about my understanding of how we are connected to the Other Side and one another. It was not a suggestion; it was a directive. It came to me as a done deal. Within twenty-four hours of the download, by mere coincidence, I was connected with a series of people, including a literary agent and a writing partner, and soon after I got a publishing deal to write the book.

And eventually my book, *The Light Between Us*, became a *New York Times* bestseller. I'd manifested what was on my vision board.

I remember stumbling upon the envelope shortly after the book made the bestseller list and marveling at its contents. When we are open to manifesting—to co-creating with the universe—the universe will often dream an even bigger dream for you than you did for yourself.

I want to encourage you to open yourself up to a conversation with the universe about your future.

Step one is the thinking—identifying the areas in our lives that we'd like to change for the better, and specifying *how* we'd like them to change. Next comes the visualization. Get some magazines that resonate with your energy, find a pair of scissors, and cut out the words and phrases and images you feel pulled to. Then paste them on a piece of paper. Display this somewhere you can see it every day. Take a picture of it and make it the wallpaper on your phone or computer!

Now comes the writing. Experiments have shown that people who write down goals are much more likely to achieve them than people who don't—and this resonates when it comes to manifesting, too. So sit down and write a letter to the universe. Write the letter as if the things you want to manifest have already happened. Write,

"Thank you for bringing me that new and safer car by this May or sooner." Or, "Thank you for bringing me the promotion, and having me feel fulfilled and valued at my job, by October 1 or sooner." (Note: You always want to say "or sooner" with time frames, and "or more" when it comes to money, to allow for the universe to co-create with you and bring it to you in a more divine time or way than what you are even aware of.) Write the letter as if your desires are already a clear and true reality! Express gratitude as if they have already happened. Be as specific and detailed as possible. This may sound kind of silly or simplistic, but I wouldn't be sharing it if I didn't believe in it—and if I hadn't personally experienced the incredible power of manifesting. There is an energy in writing that is far reaching and undeniable.

Next step: Share your manifest with a friend or friends. Manifesting with two or more people amplifies the manifest! I find that when small groups of people get together, amazing things can happen, simply because we're all focusing our thoughts on the same thing for a few minutes. We are *pooling* our energy. Sharing the experience with others amplifies the power of manifesting because our collective thoughts are powerful (remember the phrase "there's power in numbers"?).

And finally, the hardest step, the one everyone struggles with: Let it go.

Release it into the universe. Don't try to micromanage the "how" of it. I know this sounds counterintuitive, because, after all, how can anything happen if we don't *make* it happen? But what I've seen is that if we are truly open to this conversation, *the universe will figure it out for us*. And because the universe can surprise us with much more than we ever envisioned for ourselves, it's important that we trust the universe to make it all happen somehow. It is important for us to honor this co-creation.

I'll give you an example: Say you want to write a screenplay and sell it to a production company. How do you manifest that? Well, sit down, get clarity in your thoughts about it, visualize it happening, then write that note to the universe. Thank the universe for letting you be the one to write this beautiful story, and for finding it the perfect home with the perfect studio, and for allowing you to explore your amazing gifts as a writer, and for using this screenplay to elevate you and your place in the world. Specify the date on which you want all of this to happen by ("or sooner"). And then *trust* the universe to make it all happen.

At some point you'll have to work your butt off and write the screenplay—but you also need to trust the universe to steer you down the right path.

If we are mindful of how the process of manifesting shifts our energy in real and positive ways, we can elevate ourselves to a higher and more receptive place. Manifesting can work in all areas of our lives—from romance and careers and money to where and how we live and the families we create.

TRAVEL

Energy doesn't just reside in us—it resides in the places we live and congregate. And because we're all different, the energy of every place is different. When we travel, we drink in the energy of every new place in a way that can be transformational. Traveling infuses us with new energy and enhances our sense of being connected to the wider world. This energy, these cords of connection, stay with us and elevate us even after we leave.

Traveling is more enriching than I can explain. When I was in college, I chose to spend a year abroad studying at the University of Oxford in England—an experience that utterly changed me. My time at Oxford filled me with the energy of the thousands of scholars and artists who came before me, and in a very real way shaped who I became—a teacher.

We've all been to places that had "great energy"—a restaurant, a campsite, a college town, or the like. A place where everything seemed to be more vibrant and defined and alive. Well, that "great energy" is real, and it's waiting for us.

Once there, I would encourage you to be mindful of how you feel. Notice how the energy of the place affects your energy. Take note of the unique character of this new place, be it a museum, a library, or a park, and stay awake to the ways it shifts your own energy.

NEGATIVE IONS

Negative ions sound like something we should try to avoid, but in fact they are just the opposite. Negative ions are good!

An ion is an atom or group of atoms created by the loss or gain of an electron. A negative ion is the type of ion created by an electron *gain*. These ions are brought into being by natural forces, such as air, water, and sunlight. In places where there is a high concentration of negative ions, we can actually sense them. One example is the particular feeling in the air after a rainstorm. Another is the sudden sense of calm that comes over us when we're around gently moving water or the ocean. Or the warmth we feel not only on our skin but on the inside when we're bathed in sunlight. Many of the wonderful, surprising, inexplicable surges of energy we sometimes feel in certain places are the work of negative ions.

Practically and scientifically speaking, negative ions actually clear the air of odors, bacteria, pollen, mold spores, and other particles. Think of how fresh and clear we feel when we're taking a shower. That's because the showers in our homes are natural producers of negative ions. Rainstorms do the same thing, which is why we can feel exhilarated when we get caught in one. Traveling to Niagara Falls and standing near its mighty spray, for instance, would give us a *huge* blast of negative ions. Being on the beach or out on a boat in the ocean or on a dock on the bay or the shoreline of a lake can shift our energy. Even just standing near a *fountain* can have a positive effect on us.

Trees, too, give off negative ions and suffuse us with this energy — pine trees in particular. Taking a hike through the woods is a fantastic way to clear our energy and reinvigorate ourselves. I try to take a trip to the Adirondack Mountains every year, simply because I feel drawn to the magnificent trees and the beautiful lakes. The swirl of negative ions fills me with a wonderful, renewing energy.

Negative ions aren't something we spend a lot of time thinking about, but they are an easy way to elevate ourselves and our energy. Let me put it this way: We carry our energy with us the way our clothes carry mud that we've rolled around in. If our clothes get muddy, we take them off and wash them—but if our energy is negative, we might not do anything to clear it away. We might carry this energy "mud" with us for days on end.

Negative ions cleanse us. Some office buildings in Europe actually pipe negative ions through the ventilation system, and as a result their workers have fewer sick days and report greater feelings of well-being. We can even buy portable negative ionizer machines for use in our homes and cars. But there are simpler ways to introduce negative ions into our lives. Take a walk through the woods. Jump into the ocean. Or when you take a shower, simply notice the way the water runs and splashes. *Focus* on the water. Just this simple act of mindfulness can invigorate us and shift our energy in surprising ways.

SMUDGING

The ancient practice of burning herbs during prayer and cleansing ceremonies is called smudging, and it's still practiced today. Lots of cultures use burning herbs as a method of purification, including Native American cultures. Yet while smudging dates back to the prehistoric days and spans time and civilizations, there is more to it than just ancient wisdom and tribal superstitions. Scientific experiments have shown that the smoke from burning plant matter such as dried sage clears away harmful bacteria in the surrounding air. The fumes act as an air purifier, which can help with lung, skin, and brain function. The benefits of smudging are very real.

Just as smudging rids the air of negative things, it can have the very same effect on our energy. When we direct out thoughts and assign the smoke the role of purifier, it can indeed purify our energy. Often we carry with us the patina of people we've come in contact with who, well, may have a rather negative energy. So it's a good idea to regularly clean our own energy, and smudging is a great way to do it.

What's more, it's something we can easily try at home. Do a little research and find out what works for you. Bundles of dried herbs tied by strings and called smudge sticks are even available on Amazon. I have burned dry sage—an herb whose name derives from the Latin word for "healing"—and I have found it to be an excellent way of clearing away negative energy and shifting my own energy into the positive.

Sometimes small rituals like this can remind us to consistently clean, clear, and honor our energy.

MOVEMENT

Any physical activity that releases our kinetic energy is another great way to shift and elevate ourselves. We are all light beings stuffed into physical bodies. Sometimes that can get a little uncomfortable, and our energy can pool and get stuck. Kinetic movements help unstick our energy and rev us up. Running or dancing or playing sports all help clear away negative energy and reinvigorate our souls. Certain activities, such as yoga, take it a step further. They combine movement with a gradual ascent to a semi-meditative state, both of which are powerful energy shifters. Yoga also balances what I call our BMS—our body, mind, and soul triangle. The art of acupuncture and the exercise of tapping our meridian points accomplish the same thing by hitting on the energy points in our body, and releasing and clearing this energy.

The idea is for us to find ways to create joyful movement in our lives, as a way of tending to our energy and elevating into more receptive states. Using movement to help balance and release energy is a wonderful tool!

FOOD

Something else we need to pay serious attention to is the food we eat. Think about it—eating is actually the most intimate thing we all do here on this earth. It is taking something into our bodies and making it a part of us. Unfortunately, many of us don't give much thought to what we eat or how it makes us feel.

As a result, we consume masses of sugar and preservatives and chemicals and caffeine and other substances that slowly destroy our bodies and create imbalance within. However, some of us are more aware of how bad eating habits can negatively affect our energy level; that's why we continually resolve to eat better and healthier foods. We understand that if we change what we eat, we change our energy. And when we change our energy, we change who we are—and we change our lives.

Listen, I don't want to lecture you, but I truly believe that being more conscious of what we eat is of the utmost importance. We need to eat healthier, less processed foods. If we are so moved, we can even experiment (if we haven't already) with what it's like to eat only nurturing foods—foods not tied to the negative energy of something being killed. If you're a meat eater, consider putting Meatless Monday into practice—just try one day a week with a plant-based diet. See how it makes you feel.

Our diets, of course, are a totally personal choice, and I'm not here to judge anyone. I just believe the more mindful we become of what we put into our bodies, the more we will experience gratitude for our meals, and the more we will honor our bodies and the energy we bring into them.

Over the years I've opened my eyes to the dangers of the food industry. I would encourage you to watch the documentaries *What the Health?* and *Forks Over Knives*. I have also been guided by what I've learned from the Other Side. My advice would be for all of us to become more educated and more conscious of what we choose to eat, and why.

SLEEP

When our cellphones run out of battery power, we recharge them by plugging into a power source. That's what happens when we sleep—we are not only letting our physical bodies rest and heal, but we are also plugging our souls into the energy of the Other Side.

We all have a deep soul connection to the Other Side, our true home. But our souls need to have this connection recharged and re-powered. Sleep is when this happens. Sleep is an altered state of consciousness during which our brains aren't bombarded by stimuli and our bodies are able to restore and replenish all our vital systems.

But sleep is also when we sync up with the Other Side. It's when we have vibrant dreams full of symbolism and meaning—dreams that, as we've discussed, can carry signs from the Other Side. Sleep gives our Teams of Light an opportunity to impart the answers we need. Haven't we all said, "Let me sleep on it"? We say this for a reason—because when we sleep, we plug into the Other Side, and our teams have an easier shot at sending us the signs and directional arrows we need to find our highest paths. Think about it. I bet there have been times when you've woken up with great clarity about an issue that was preoccupying you.

Sleep is also when dream visitations from our loved ones happen. That's because sleep is when the filters of our brains are turned off, allowing direct connections to take place. These dream visitations are often powerful and vibrant. They feel like *experiences* rather than just dreams, and they stay with us long after we wake up.

So, as hard as it may be to do, be protective of your sleep. Try to get as much of it as you can. The National Sleep Foundation in Washington, D.C., suggests that adults sleep an average of seven to nine hours a day (down from the eight to ten hours that teenagers need). It's a goal we're not always going to achieve, but the closer we get to it, the better—especially if we want to shift our energy and become more receptive to the Other Side.

PRAYER

I have come to understand, through the many readings I have done and by witnessing and experiencing things on my own path, the incredible power and importance of prayer. Whenever we consciously direct our thoughts to the Other Side, that is prayer. And whenever we pray, the Other Side always—*always*—hears us. Prayer is an intimate conversation. We may pray individually or with others, aloud or silently, formally or informally. Prayer is not just reserved for places of worship. Prayer is always available to us, at all times of the day and night, whenever and wherever we are. It may be a quick, silent prayer for strength before facing a difficult situation; a prayer of hope or healing for a friend; a prayer to help gain clarity on a situation; or one of forgiveness. There is no right or wrong way to pray. It is an instant cord of light and connection that we may access at any time. And here's the thing: It always strengthens us.

When I pray, I direct my thoughts to God energy—and also to my spirit guides and loved ones on the Other Side. The very act of prayer links you to something greater than yourself, linking you to a great chain of light and love and connection. In fact, often in readings, those on the Other Side will thank the sitter for the prayers they have sent. When we pray, it is a beautiful form of music to the Other Side. Praying strengthens us and connects us, always. So pray, and pray hard. And know that you are always heard.

MEDITATION

When I read for people, I slip into a state of stillness and inner awareness in which my own sense of self melts away and I listen to the Other Side. As I've noted throughout this book, you don't need to be a psychic medium to enter this state of being. Anyone can access it via meditation.

Meditation is an exercise designed to help us reach a higher level of spiritual awareness. Another way to define it is slipping into a place where we can fully appreciate what is happening in the present and *only* in the present. Many, many studies have proven the benefits of practicing meditation in some form—it lowers stress, chases away depression, makes us less irritable and reactive, and improves the quality of sleep, to name just a few of the benefits. Other studies have shown that teaching schoolchildren how to meditate has a decidedly positive impact on their health and performance. His Holiness the Dalai Lama has said, "If every eight-year-old in the world is taught meditation, we will eliminate violence from the world within one generation." That is quite a powerful statement from a very wise man.

In fact, one celebrity, Goldie Hawn, has embraced this idea. Her philanthropic program, Mindup, helps kids from pre-K to eighth grade learn how to meditate, both reducing stress and improving relationships at home.

Clearly, meditation can be a very beneficial practice, but I understand it can also be kind of intimidating. I hear a lot of people say, "Oh, I can't meditate, because my mind wanders all over the place," or "I don't have time to meditate," or "I don't know *how* to meditate." And certainly, long-form meditations are not for everyone. I once attended a three-day meditation and silence retreat, and honestly, I found it very challenging. I kept getting psychic and mediumistic downloads for the instructor and my fellow students.

But I have seen that a ten-minute meditation, or even a three-minute meditation, can have the same positive impact as a three-hour session. In fact, scientific studies have shown that a seven-minute meditation can be just as beneficial as a longer one. And these shorter meditations are the ones that align best with my energy.

So how do we meditate? Do we need to sit in the lotus position? Do we need a mantra? Do we need to chant?

No, no, and no. Meditating can be as simple as feeling our pulse with our finger, or focusing on our breathing. Meditating is about reflecting rather than reacting. It is about achieving and appreciating a moment of true mindfulness. It's about being absolutely *present*. It's about learning to be less triggered by our environment and more reflective. And we don't need a lot of tricks or techniques to make that happen. Closing our eyes and being still and quiet and in the moment is, essentially, meditating. There is even something called a walking meditation where you literally walk throughout the whole meditation.

Of course, the deeper we get into it, the more powerful the benefits can be. We can get started by reading a book about meditation, or taking a beginner's class, or downloading a meditation app.

One of my favorite meditations came from the great spiritual thought leader Deepak Chopra. A few years ago, he was a speaker at an event where I also gave a speech, and I watched as he led a roomful of six hundred seasoned and hardened professionals in a remarkable five-minute mediation. As I remember it, Deepak asked us to close our eyes, touch our thumbs to our forefingers, and focus on our breathing for a minute—deep breaths in through the nose and out through the mouth. He then asked us to form a phrase in our minds: "I am [your first and last name] and I work as [your occupation]." He asked us to slowly repeat this phrase in our minds and focus on the way it served to identify who we are.

Then he asked us to repeat the phrase but leave out the final part and use only our first and last names: "I am ____ ____." He asked us to be aware of how this, too, defined who we are.

Then he asked us to repeat this phrase but leave out our last name: "I am ____."

Then he asked us to leave out our name altogether, and simply repeat "I am."

Finally, he asked us to repeat just "I."

And in this way, we all moved gently away from the trappings of our noisy, self-centered lives and toward a simpler and more elemental understanding of our place in the world—as beings of light and energy connected to all the other light and energy in the universe.

I was astonished both by the simplicity of Deepak's meditation and by how powerful it was. Those five minutes shifted my energy in a very profound and lasting way. They changed how I approached the rest of the day and even the rest of the week. They also changed the entire collective energy of the room. Before the simple meditation, the energy had been charged and somewhat frenetic. But after five minutes of meditating, I could feel everyone's energy flowing together collectively, like a giant wave lapping the floor.

Meditation is also our way of tuning in to and listening to the Other Side. Deepak Chopra described it this way: Prayer is when we direct our thoughts to God/the universe; meditation is when we listen back. It is not unusual to get downloads of information from the Other Side while meditating, because it creates a beautiful space for us to "listen back."

That is the magic of meditation. It's one of the most effective ways we can shift our energy, listen for messages from the universe and our Teams of Light, and live more meaningful lives. Making room and space in our days for meditation just may bring clarity and layer it with meaning, and in the process change our lives.

Being mindful of all of the concepts explored in this chapter can shift our energy dramatically. They are simple, practical methods that allow us to be more clear-minded, elevate our energy, and be more open to receiving messages from the Other Side. They are ways of acknowledging that we are all souls with bodies, comprising light and energy, and that restoring and replenishing this soul-body connection impacts the workings of our minds and, in turn, the choices we make.

I believe that the earth is a school, and we are all students. And I believe we are here to learn continually how to elevate ourselves, how to help other souls, and how to share our powerful light and energy with the world. We are all learning a collective lesson in love. The tools discussed in this chapter can help each of us shine our brightest light and be fully open to the connections to our Teams of Light, and to one another.

Being open to these lessons, and being open to the gentle directions of our Teams of Light, is how we become the very best version of ourselves.

31

SHINE ON

I F there is one theme that runs through all of the stories in this book, it is that *we are all connected.*

We all belong to the same beautiful tapestry of existence, and our lives are all woven together to create the magical experience of life.

None of us are alone, or solitary, or unimportant—we're all part of something that is vastly bigger than ourselves but, at the same time, comprises each of our individual energies. We belong *with* one another and *to* one another. We are forever interconnected, and these connections are more awe inspiring and more powerful than we can even fathom.

In these pages, I have shared some examples of signs sent to us by the Other Side to convey this message of love and connectedness. But really, I could have shared a thousand more. Hardly a day goes by that I don't hear about someone's remarkable experience with a sign, or experience one myself. The signs are everywhere, every day. I can't help but notice them.

What I would love is for us all, collectively, to start noticing and talking about the signs and messages we get—in order to celebrate, honor, and share the stories of connection with one another.

Sometimes, we do.

I have even found evidence of the secret language in the most unlikely of places: Twitter. I remember scrolling through my Twitter account one day and seeing proof of the secret language revealing itself in the feed of *The Tonight Show Starring Jimmy Fallon.*

Producer Mike DiCenzo took to Twitter the day after Jimmy Fallon returned to the show, after taking time off when his mom, Gloria, had passed.

Jimmy had shared a special memory of his mom with the studio audience in the warm-up before the show taped. He recalled how, when he was a little boy, he and his mom had a secret code between them. "She would squeeze my hand three times and say 'I love you,'" Jimmy said. "I would squeeze back, 'I love you, too.' Last week, I was in the hospital, and I grabbed her and squeezed her hand and said, 'I love you.' I just knew we were in trouble."

On Twitter, his producer explained that the singer Taylor Swift had not been scheduled to appear on the show that night, but the crew wanted to do something special for Jimmy—and since Taylor had been in town doing *Saturday Night Live,* they asked if she would be a guest on the show.

"She said yes with zero hesitation," DiCenzo tweeted.

On the show, Taylor decided to sing a song she'd never performed before, called "New Year's Day."

"Suddenly, she sings the line, 'Squeeze my hand three times in the back of the taxi,'" DiCenzo tweeted. "I nearly gasped. Tears. I think everyone in the audience started sobbing. I could see Jimmy silhouetted at his desk dabbing his eyes with a tissue. We all lost it. It was a beautiful coincidence in a beautiful performance. 'Hold on to your memories, they will hold on to you,' Taylor sang."

When she was done singing, Taylor stepped away from the piano and into Jimmy's arms, hugging him tightly.

Mike DiCenzo described Taylor's song as a "beautiful coincidence." But it wasn't a coincidence at all, was it? It was the secret language of the universe revealing itself fully on national TV. It was Jimmy Fallon's mother delivering a message of love to her son, letting him know that she was still with him, that she was still squeezing his hand—and encouraging him to hold on to his memories.

And she used Taylor Swift to do it.

How truly magical.

It's not just on TV that you might see evidence of signs and the secret language. Sometimes you might find they are right next door.

Or at least that proved true for my sister, Christine, when her neighbor Kathleen called her one day to ask her to share a story with me.

Kathleen had read my book *The Light Between Us,* in which I first discussed how loved ones who have crossed can send us signs. Kathleen—whose mother had recently crossed—decided she wanted proof.

Kathleen's Irish American parents had raised her in a large, loving home in the Bronx, and she was extremely close with her parents all her life. When her mother crossed last year, Kathleen struggled with her grief, especially on holidays, when the tradition had been for everyone in the family to get together. When Kathleen decided she was going to open her mind and heart to creating a new language of signs between her and her mother, she thought long and hard about what to ask for. And she came up with the perfect sign: Irish soda bread. Her mom used to bake Irish soda bread and hand it out to friends and neighbors.

Now here's the thing—it was nowhere near St. Patrick's Day, a time when you might be more likely to encounter Irish soda bread. Kathleen had given her mother quite a challenge. Would she be up for it? Would the secret language work?

That night, Kathleen was scrolling through her Facebook feed. Right there, in the middle of her feed, she saw a post from a neighbor, featuring a photo of something that looked very familiar.

Kathleen responded to the post and asked her neighbor, "Is that Irish soda bread? It looks delicious!"

"Yes, it is Irish soda bread!" her neighbor responded. "I'll save you a piece!"

There it was! Her mother had managed to conjure up Irish soda bread, right on her computer screen! "I was in shock," Kathleen says. "I was so impressed by what my mother had done to get through to me."

The next day, Kathleen went out front to fetch her mail. She saw a box in her mailbox and opened it.

Inside the box was a big, beautiful piece of Irish soda bread.

"I hadn't thought that my neighbor was actually going to send me a piece. I thought that was just an expression," says Kathleen. "But sure enough, there it was, right in my mailbox."

Kathleen went inside, sat down with her mother's little Yorkie terrier (whom she took in after her mom passed), poured a cup of her mother's favorite tea, and enjoyed the lovely piece of Irish soda bread. She knew what it meant. It meant her mother was still with her. She couldn't doubt that now, because Kathleen's mother didn't just send a picture of or the words *Irish soda bread* as a sign. She delivered a piece *right to Kathleen's mailbox*!

I love when others share their stories of signs with me. It can happen at any time—and it happened one night when my husband and I were out to dinner with our good friends Paul and Pam.

Their infant son, Griffin, tragically crossed more than twenty years ago. Still, I knew that Griffin remained a part of their family; he is always in their thoughts and hearts. Then Paul shared a story with us over dinner.

Right after Griffin's crossing, Paul and his family had a service, and afterward came home to sit shiva—the traditional seven-day mourning period that is the Jewish custom. Paul noticed a praying mantis clinging directly to the kitchen screen door. Strangely, it seemed to almost be looking at him. He dismissed it, until he saw it in the same spot the following day, and the day after that, too. The praying mantis stayed with Paul and his family until the shiva period ended. And then, mysteriously, it vanished.

Although praying mantises are rather rare, and spotting one is even rarer, something interesting started happening to Paul and his family. It seemed they were being followed. "Whenever my family is together or we're having a special moment or talking about something important, a praying mantis shows up," says Paul. "It's a constant theme in our lives. And whenever we see one, we always say, 'Oh, hi, Griffin.'" At the outdoor reception after his nephew's wedding, Paul spotted a praying mantis right beside him on the sofa where he and his family were sitting. He saw one on a curtain inside his home on his youngest son's birthday. He found another on the gate at his hotel on a trip to Italy.

One day, Paul was in his office in Midtown Manhattan, talking to someone on the phone about a difficult decision he had just made, after considerable struggle. He felt he had made the right decision, but he also felt like he could really use some reassurance. Just then, he looked out the window of his office, and there clinging to the outside of the glass, looking straight in at him, was—you guessed it— a praying mantis. Now, this would have been amazing anyway, but what made it even more incredible was that Paul's office was on the twenty-eighth floor!

"Praying mantises will just show up and hang around like it's no big deal," says Paul. "I was sitting on a park bench with a really good friend when one showed up and sat right between us. I held out my hand and it walked into it, and I held it for a long time. My friend said, 'That is crazy.' I said, 'No, it's not. It's Griffin.'"

What makes me even happier is that Paul is at ease sharing his story, over dinner and a glass of wine—all the while seeing the beauty and meaning in it. Griffin's sign is being received loud and clear.

I really love meeting new people, and when I do, I love to share stories with them. This is true wherever I go, and especially true when a stranger asks me what I do for work. Some people have such incredibly warm and positive energy, and meeting them is a beautiful blessing. This is true of a nurse named Kelly, who works with one of Ashley's doctors.

When I told her that I am a psychic medium, she shared with me that her mother, with whom she had been extremely close, had crossed when Kelly was just nineteen.

"Gosh, I just wish I could know that she was still around me and still with me," she said. "I wish she had had the chance to meet my daughter. I miss her so much."

I told her that her mom was absolutely around her, watching her, and not only knew about her daughter but watched over her, too. I told her that she never needed a psychic medium to have this validated—all she had to do was ask for a sign.

"Make it specific," I said. "Ask her to send it to you so that you know she is around and watching and knows about everything that has gone on in your life. And after you ask her to send it, trust that you will get it. Say, 'Universe, I am ready to receive a message from my mother.' You will see—the sign will come." I told her that sometimes it might take a little while to receive the sign, so she should be patient, because the Other Side would work hard to make it happen.

That night, in the car on her way home, Kelly let it all out. "I was driving and yelling, 'Universe, I'm ready!'" Kelly later told me. "But then I couldn't come up with a good sign. Nothing felt right. It actually took me two more weeks to come up with the right sign."

One day, Kelly recalled a happy memory of her parents taking her trick-or-treating on Halloween when she was three. She even found a photo of it. "My parents were dressed as Raggedy Ann and Andy," she says, "I decided that that would become my sign. It was appropriate, too, because my mom's name is Ann and my dad, who also crossed, is named Andy. So I asked my mom to please send me Raggedy Ann. But I didn't tell anyone what my sign was. I kept it to myself."

Kelly waited patiently for her sign. Two weeks later, she walked into the lunchroom at her clinic and chatted with a co-worker, Mary Ann.

"Mary Ann mentioned that her next-door neighbor had passed away, and she started telling me about her, and it went on for a while and I was listening but sort of half listening," Kelly says. "Then she causally mentioned that her neighbor's name was Ann, and her husband's name was Andy, and that everyone always called them Raggedy Ann and Andy."

Kelly froze. "I was in shock. I turned my back a little so she couldn't see that I was crying. As soon as she left I broke down in tears. I mean, nobody talks about Raggedy Ann and Andy anymore. They're from another time. But she said their names, and I had absolutely no doubt it was my mother sending me a sign, because it was so direct and clear. It was my mom telling me, 'I'm here, I'm with you, I'm part of everything you do.' It was so exhilarating. I felt like I won the lottery."

One of my favorite things to do is teach workshops and give public talks. Even if I'm addressing a larger group, I feel personally connected to each individual's energy in that group. It's truly wonderful when people I've crossed paths with feel that connection, too, and reach out to share their stories.

Recently, Ted, a man who attended a large speaking event I did, followed my suggestion to ask his Team of Light for a very specific sign. "I always felt a bit stuck in my career, and I was having some doubt and uncertainty," Ted wrote me in an email. "So my fiancée and I planned a trip to California to expand our career options. That's when I remembered your advice and decided to give it a try. I tried to think of something specific, and for no real reason at all, a Yankees baseball player popped into my head. Bernie Williams. He wasn't even my favorite Yankee, but I'd always been a fan. I asked my guides to send this to me as a sign that the trip was a good idea and that I was headed on the right path."

One night before he and his fiancée were to leave, Ted looked around his room for paper to make a Valentine's Day card. He found an old notebook that he hadn't touched in years. "I went to tear out a page, and as I did, something fell out of it," says Ted. "It was a baseball card of Sammy Sosa. I thought, well, that's weird—it's not Bernie Williams, but maybe that was the best my guides could do." Ted put down the notebook and started to leave the room when, out of the corner of his eye, he saw something else on the floor. "I hadn't seen it, and I'm not even sure how I missed it, but I picked it up and it was another baseball card," he says, "and this card was Bernie Williams."

An old baseball card falling out of a notebook—some will say that's all it was. But to Ted, it was much more than that. "It was the most amazing sign," he says, "and it helped me so, so much. It helped me know not only that I was on my highest path by deciding to expand my career options, but that I had a Team of Light rooting me on the whole way!"

Sometimes I happen upon stories that share evidence of signs and the secret language in books I am reading. And I don't mean books written by psychics or mediums—just regular books. One such story turned out to describe one of the most profound and powerful signs I've ever heard about.

It involves Dr. Neil Spector, a Duke University oncologist and cancer researcher who shared the story of his sign in his book, *Gone in a Heartbeat: A Physician's Search for True Healing*. I bought the book because it was the memoir of a doctor who discovered that he had undiagnosed Lyme disease. The Lyme went untreated for so long that it damaged his heart. I was so moved by his book that I reached out to Dr. Spector and asked him if I could share his story here, and he graciously agreed.

Neil was a perfectly healthy, athletic man in his early thirties. One day, out of the blue, he began having strange cardiac episodes.

"My heart would start racing to two hundred beats a minute for thirty seconds or more," Neil recalls. "As a physician I knew something was wrong, but we just couldn't diagnose it. Over the next four years I had thousands of these episodes, and I also had extreme fatigue. I went from running ten miles a day, six days a week, to basically not being able to walk ten yards without feeling exhausted."

He was finally diagnosed with third-degree heart blockage, and had a pacemaker and a defibrillator implanted in his chest. But something didn't feel right about the diagnosis, and after several years he began having trouble walking up hills. During a routine hospital procedure to check for infection, he felt something was terribly wrong with his heart. As an oncologist, he was no stranger to illness and its effect on the body. "I felt like I was dying," Neil says. The medical staff was alarmed. They called his wife and told her to get to the hospital as soon as possible.

Something was *very* wrong. The doctors estimated that Neil had only 10 percent of his normal heart function.

"I really should have died," he says. "I had a severely damaged heart and barely detectable blood pressure. The odds of survival were very low."

He made it through the episode, but over the next few days, "I was literally dying," Neil says. "My organs were shutting down, and my heart was barely pumping. It was like trying to sail a boat on a completely windless day." A doctor told him that if he didn't get a heart transplant, he would be dead within three days. "That was actually the most peaceful moment I have ever had in my life," he says, "because I knew it wasn't my time to die. If I had been meant to die, I would have died already."

Incredibly, a heart became available for transplant in thirty-six hours. After twelve hours of surgery, the transplant was deemed a success. The next day, "my young daughter, Celeste, came into my hospital room," Neil remembers, "and I told her, 'You know, we can't just call this Daddy's new heart. Let's come up with a name.' And Celeste said, "I know! Heavenly Precious. It is a precious gift, and it came from heaven. So let's call it Heavenly Precious."

And so they did.

According to protocol, the recipient of a donor transplant must wait one year before contacting the donor's family. After that waiting period passed, Neil sent a letter to the family of the anonymous donor and shared his gratitude. "I'd been counting down the days," he says. "I felt a tremendous obligation to thank them for their sacrifice, and for literally giving me the gift of life." He wrote an emotional letter. It took six months for a response to arrive, but finally, there it was—a letter from his heart donor's family. It came from his donor's widowed husband—Neil's heart had belonged to a woman named Vicky.

"It was incredibly moving," Neil says. "Number one, he said he was thrilled that his wife's heart could help me to continue my efforts to help other people as a doctor. But then, at the end of the letter, he said he was moved beyond tears and joy when he heard about the name my daughter came up with for his wife's heart—Heavenly Precious. He was thrilled because, for all of their marriage, he had called his wife by her nickname, which was Precious."

Precious!

Neil was shocked. He kept reading the letter. "The husband wrote that when he learned the name my daughter gave the heart, he felt it was his wife, communicating through our daughter, to let him know that she was okay, and that his Precious was Heavenly Precious now."

Think about that. What are the odds? Heavenly Precious. Precious in heaven. Could that just be a coincidence? Or would a man of science see it as a sign from the Other Side?

"I believe deeply in science," Neil replied. "But I also believe deeply in things we cannot prove."

In fact, as a physician caring for patients who are nearing death, Neil has a unique perspective on our passage from this life. "I've learned so much from my patients and how they embrace their journey," he says. "I have always believed that the body and soul are different, and I have seen, in my sickest patients, in the moments when their bodies are ravaged, the beauty of their souls burst through. In their eyes, in their energy, in all their kindness and love. I have seen a kind of light emanating from them, and it reinforced my belief that there is something beyond our physical body—that we are not our bodies; we are, instead, our souls.

"What we know about the universe can fit in a thimble. That is how I embrace life, as someone who doesn't know all the answers," Neil says.

Separate and apart from our physical bodies, he believes, "We are all energetic beings. There are people here who are sensitive to this energy, and to our collective energy. Maybe we all have that ability, but we get caught up in the physical here and now—you know, our car is making a funny noise, or the mortgage is due, or whatever—and we focus on that and turn away from the energy of others, and from our collective energy."

If, instead, we stay open to this energy—to the way our lives and our energy interconnect with those of others—we can identify less with our physical bodies and more with our spiritual selves. "I have received so much visual confirmation that we are more than our physical bodies, and knowing that has brought me such peace," says Neil.

This is how Dr. Spector marries his spirituality and his science: by appreciating that we are all energy, and that our energy is connected to the collective energy of all beings. And within this remarkable flow of energy among us all come miraculous moments of inexplicable and life-affirming connection.

On his final day on earth, the visionary inventor Thomas Edison woke from a coma. He opened his eyes and looked upward, his face reflecting something like awe. Then he spoke for the first time in a long time, and said six words.

"It is very beautiful over there."

Almost exactly eighty years later, another visionary, Steve Jobs, lay on his deathbed. Just before crossing, he looked lovingly at his sister Patty and at his children and at his life partner, Laurene. Then he looked past them all, to a place only he could see, and he uttered six final words.

"Oh wow. Oh wow. Oh wow."

At their moments of crossing, when their loved ones on the Other Side rushed to greet their souls, and the embracing light of all creation washed over them, they found the words to convey the sheer wonder of what awaits us, in our true home on the Other Side. In an instant, they experienced how truly interconnected, how truly bound by love and light, we all are. And this revelation was simply dazzling.

Here on earth, it can take a little time to accept the universal truth that we belong to one another and are responsible for one another. But that is why we are here—to learn lessons together. Earth is a school where we are all learning a collective lesson in love.

Through my readings, I have learned that when we cross, this truth becomes instantly apparent to us—just as it did to Thomas Edison and Steve Jobs. The best way I can describe this experience is to call it an instant truth download.

When we cross, we can instantly access every other person's entire lifetime of experience in a millisecond. Think about that. I mean, it is almost unfathomable to us here on earth—knowing everything there is to know about a person in an instant. But that is what happens on the Other Side, where we no longer have physical bodies and where we communicate in a way that is telepathic, consciousness to consciousness. For when we no longer have our bodies, what separates us from others? What separates our experiences from theirs?

Nothing.

What I've seen in my thousands of readings is that this transmission is instant and complete; when we cross we understand perfectly that we've always been connected to everyone else, and that we've always been part of everyone else's journey through time.

We realize that, as beings of light and energy, we are all connected to the same massive current of love that powers the universe and infuses everything with meaning.

For now, however, this truth is something each of us must learn at our own pace. And being open to signs from the Other Side brings us immeasurably closer to this beautiful truth.

The moments of connection that happened to the people in this book can happen to you, too—they are likely *already* happening to you. This is not an exclusive club. The life-altering power of signs from the Other Side is available to us all. It is part of the beautiful package that each of us is born with.

You see, we deliver messages to one another all the time. We are all mediums. Knowingly or unknowingly, there are times when we all serve as messengers for the Other Side—as "angels on earth," if you will. Not just some of us—*all* of us. Each of us matters greatly to other people and to the universe—a universe that is always pulling us toward our best and brightest lives.

Why?

Because we are all born worthy.

Each of us is born with the great gift of light—the radiant force of our love and energy and uniqueness. Each of us is born with the ability to shine this light on the world, to help others navigate their own life paths. Each of us is born with our own completely unique set of skills and attributes that contribute to the universal life force. Each of us is born with an innate ability to make a meaningful difference in the world, regardless of who we are or what we do. This is not something we have to petition for, or hope to get. It is our birthright. We all share it. *It is what makes us who we are.* While we are born with this amazing gift, it is up to us to unwrap it. It is up to us to uncover our light and shine it brightly in the world.

Shine brightly, and shine on.

This is where signs and messages from the Other Side come into play. Opening our hearts and minds to receiving signs helps us unwrap our gift of light, because these signs reveal the truth of the universe—that none of us are alone, that we're all in this together, that we are interconnected in consequential ways. All of the signs and messages described in this book illustrate this truth.

When we begin to accept and honor these signs, we get closer to understanding the path to true power and true success and true happiness in life—discovering and shining our unique light, and using that light to inspire and assist others on their life paths. Ultimately, we rise together.

I'd like to relate one last experience that really hammered this message home for me.

It involved my son, Hayden, who plays the trumpet in his sixth-grade school band. One evening there was a concert planned, and Hayden was told to wear a particular uniform—black shoes, black pants, white shirt, and tie. But Hayden is anti-uniform. He's anti a lot of things, actually, because he's willful and unique and independent-minded. The night of the concert, he insisted on wearing his red sneakers and no tie. We went back and forth about it, but in the end, I gave in, and he wore his red sneakers and no tie.

Garrett and I settled into the auditorium for the concert, not really sure what to expect. Then the children came out (all of them in their matching outfits, except one) and began playing a beautiful song with African rhythms. Honestly, I was floored. Some children played clarinets, and for a while the lovely sound of clarinets filled the auditorium. Then the clarinets gave way to the flutes and in turn the flutes gave way to the drums.

And then Hayden and his fellow trumpeters played their instruments, and they were so good, too, and then all the sounds came together, everyone playing at once, and the result was breathtaking—a true symphony of distinct sounds and movements and melodies all blending to create something bigger and bolder and more beautiful than any one instrument could produce. Watching Hayden play the trumpet in his red sneakers, and hearing him mesh so wonderfully with his bandmates to produce something so magnificent, moved me to tears.

As I listened to the music, I had a download from the universe: *We are all distinct instruments, playing our separate beautiful notes, and it is our job to play them as best we can—but when we all play together, we produce a magnificent symphony that lifts us all and makes sense of our individual roles.* It is only together that we can create something bigger than ourselves, something truly astounding.

And so right there, in a middle school auditorium, the beauty of our interconnectedness shone through. If we all play our best notes—if we all choose our highest life path—then together we can create something beautiful. But we've all got to practice our notes. We are all here to learn the same lessons of love and forgiveness and acceptance. If we practice together, if we help each other learn, then we discover how we can change and enrich the world around us in the most magical ways.

The signs are there. The messages are there. The butterflies and dragonflies and hummingbirds and playing cards and rainbows and soda bread and trees with hearts are all there, waiting for us to see them. Our loved ones on the Other Side are hard at work trying to steer us to happiness, and our Teams of Light are plotting ways to move us onto our highest paths. These things are happening around us every day, and it is up to us to be open to them—to be *mindful* of them.

Because when we are mindful, we will see things we haven't been able to see before. And once we see them, we will never be able to unsee them—nor would we ever want to.

ACKNOWLEDGMENTS

This book is here because of the love, support, effort, and light
of so many people, both here and on the Other Side. There
are too many to list, but here is a start:

Alex Tresniowski—Your patience, kindness, dedication,
endless support, and skilled artistry helped bring this book
into being. You are a light in this world, with one of the
kindest hearts I know! I am so grateful to you!

Jennifer Rudolph Walsh—I continue to be awed and
inspired by the force of light that you are in the world, and
all that you do and create. You make miraculous things happen,
and I am so blessed that the Universe allowed me to stumble
into your path and be guided by you. You are a rock star
in every way—the greatest agent, friend, and teacher
I could ever hope for!

Julie Grau—I am so lucky to have not only the gift of your extraordinary editing but also of your extraordinary friendship. Your energy is so much a part of this book. Thank you for your patience, support, love, and guidance. I am so grateful to have been on this journey with you again.

Linda Osvald—Mom, you are my everything. The first person I want to tell any news to, and my source of unending, unconditional love and support. I love you more than I could ever capture in words. Through every stage of my life you have helped me grow and lifted me up, both inspiring me by example and telling me I could do and achieve anything. All I am—all I have become—is because of your love and the light of who you are. Not a day goes by when I don't realize how blessed and lucky I am to be your daughter.

John Osvald—Dad, thank you for all the love and continuing messages. I know it is beautiful where you are.

Marianna Entrup—For all the ways you have helped and given of yourself. Thank you for always being there and being such an important part of our family.

Ann Wood—Honored to have such a strong and classy lady as my aunt!

Christine Osvald-Mruz—my wonderful sister: Thank you for being such a pivotal and important part of my life. You are so incredible, so thoughtful, and always such a good friend. Having you for a sister is a great gift.

John William Osvald—my amazing brother: Your sense of humor and engagement in life are both uplifting and inspiring. Thank you for being a person I can confide in and turn to—and for always finding a way to spark joy in all situations.

Garrett—All the beauty that has come into my life is tied to the light of you. Thank you for being a man of character, strength, and integrity. Thank you for showing up for me time and again, in any and all ways. Sharing this journey though life with you—of parenthood and everything in between—and all it has brought is my heart's greatest treasure.

Ashley—Watching you grow and own your energy is a privilege. I look forward to seeing all the extraordinary things you will discover and create in this world. You are a force like no other.

Hayden—my little Bubba: Your wit and insight are impressive and powerful. But your loving heart is your greatest treasure. May the light of it continue to lead you in all you do and bring to this world.

Juliet—my bottled sunshine and light bringer: You bring joy and kindness wherever you go. May you always have the love you give reflected back to you. You shine so brightly.

To my friends (you know who you are)—Thank you for being such an incredible blessing in my life, for showing up for me in all ways, and for bringing the laughter.

To Whitney Frick—Thank you for stepping in in such a light-filled, enthusiastic way to help guide this book home. I am grateful for the gift of you.

To my team at Penguin Random House—thank you for all your energy and light. This book would not be here without the combined efforts of Sally Marvin, Karen Fink, Rose Fox, Mengfei Chen, Jessica Bonet, Greg Mollica, and Evan Camfield—and of course Julie Grau and Whitney Frick.

To everyone who contributed to the stories in this book, some mentioned by name in the chapters, some names changed for privacy, some here on earth, some on the other side—It has been an honor to share in this journey together. Love is ever-binding and stronger than anything—even death. The stories you shared have proved this.

And to my Team of Light—I trust in your guidance and love, always.

PHOTO © NOA GRIFFEL

LAURA LYNNE JACKSON is a teacher, speaker, and psychic medium. She currently serves as a Windbridge Certified Research Medium with the Windbridge Research Center and is also a certified medium with the Forever Family Foundation. She is the author of *The Light Between Us*, a *New York Times* bestseller. She lives on Long Island with her husband and their three children.

lauralynnejackson.com
Twitter: @lauralynjackson
Instagram: @lauralynnejackson
Find Laura Lynne Jackson on Facebook.

The Dial Press, an imprint of Random House,
publishes books driven by the heart.

Follow us on Instagram:
@THEDIALPRESS

Discover other Dial Press books and
sign up for our e-newsletter:

thedialpress.com